I0795928

IMAGES
of America

OREGON
ILLINOIS

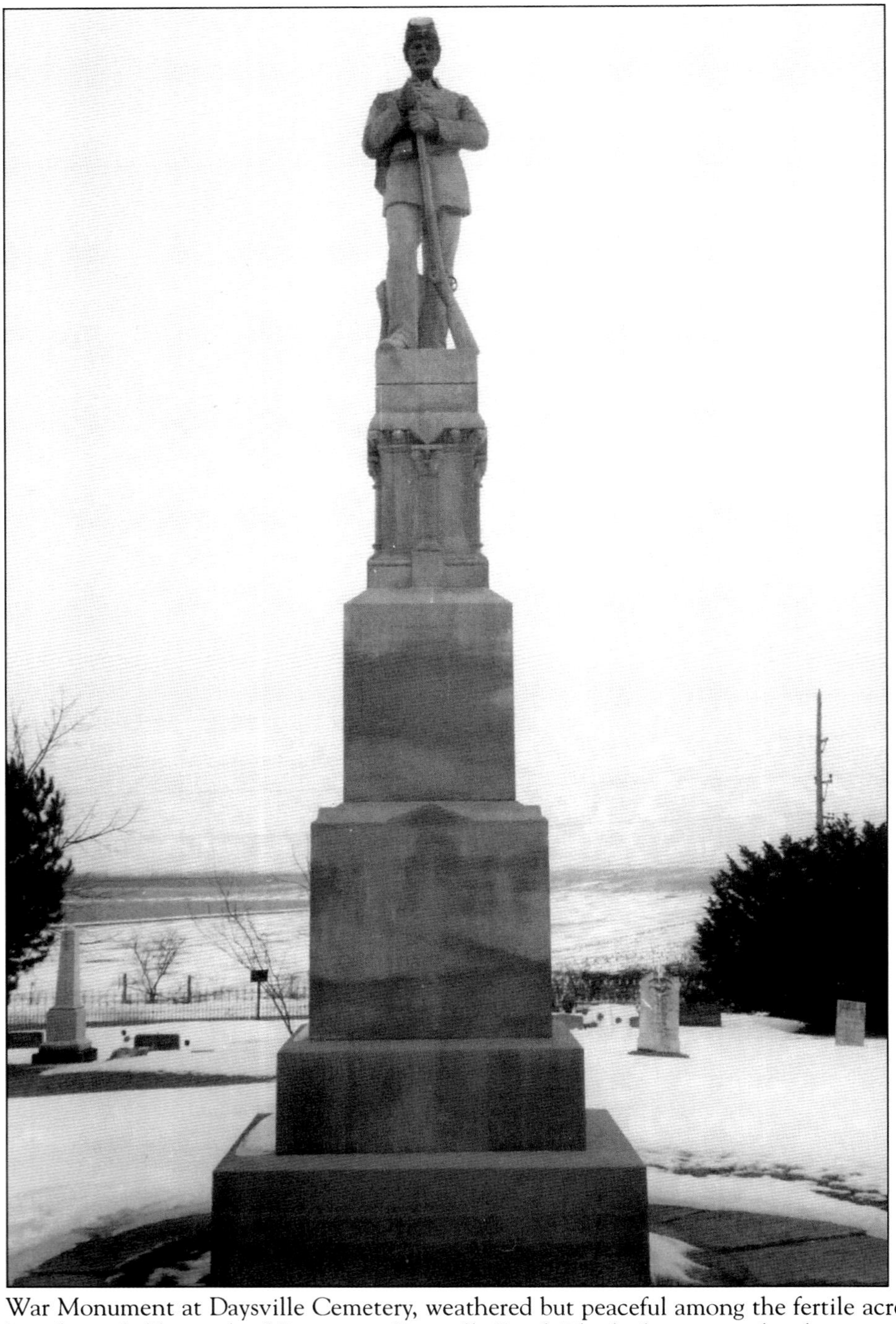

The War Monument at Daysville Cemetery, weathered but peaceful among the fertile acres of woods and cornfields, south of Oregon on Daysville Road. The little graveyard gathers veterans from the War of 1812, the Civil War, the Spanish-American War, WW II, and the Korean War. Its first occupant, Daniel Day (d. 1838) from New England, served two years during the Revolutionary War. Many of Oregon's dead lay here. For many years, Governor Frank Lowden and his family decorated the gravestones on Memorial Day.

IMAGES
of America

OREGON
ILLINOIS

Keith Call

ARCADIA
PUBLISHING

ISBN 978-0-7385-3416-9

Published by Arcadia Publishing
Charleston, South Carolina

Printed in the United States of America

Library of Congress Catalog Card Number: 2005923946

For all general information contact Arcadia Publishing at:
Telephone 843-853-2070
Fax 843-853-0044
E-mail sales@arcadiapublishing.com
For customer service and orders:
Toll-Free 1-888-313-2665

Visit us on the Internet at www.arcadiapublishing.com

To Ruby Call, Who Made Sure

CONTENTS

ACKNOWLEDGMENTS

A crisp salute to the following: Hilary Storm, for suggesting a fateful trip to Autumn on Parade; Linda Call, my spectacularly competent sister-in-law; Lynne Kilker, who tossed me a line in choppy waters; Jan Hartman, Ryan Anderson, and Linda H. Strong, royal keepers of the castle; Meg Bushnell and the Arts Alliance of Ogle County; Paul Behan and the Ogle County Historical Society; Beth McCormick of the Oregon Public Library (librarians are the secret masters of the world!); Vada Wood and Lois Cline, helpful far above the call; Dale Hoppe, fabulous storyteller and encourager; Earleene Hinton of the *Oregon Republican Reporter*; and Ann Marie Lonsdale, my unceasingly supportive editor. Finally, sincere thanks to my Wheaton College colleagues, David Osielski and Jeff Beaird, and my brilliant boss, David Malone, for technical assistance; and Bob Rees, without whose contributions this book would simply not exist.

FOREWORD

My family has its origins in Mt. Morris, five miles from Oregon, with my ancestry in the region going back to my great-grandparents. My father went to Chicago to seek his fortune, returning to Mt. Morris in 1949 to resettle his family and start a law practice. Oregon was a typical small town, not different from others. I was 14 and made friends easily, settling into a lifetime of fond memories about the city. Now most of the old-timers are gone. At the time of my retirement, I became active in initiating the restoration of the Oregon CB&Q railroad depot. With volunteers, donations and help from the city, we were able to replace the failed roof and stop further deterioration. The depot is an ongoing project that will move as fast as funding is acquired. It was because of my efforts with the depot that I was called to serve as the Commissioner of Public Works—timely because of the interest in preserving historic Oregon, maintaining its small town flavor for future generations. This book will generate interest in our past, and it is appreciated.

Bob Rees

INTRODUCTION

When itinerant merchant John Phelps first entered the Rock River valley (called Sinnissippi, or "rocky waters," by the Indians) in 1829, he harbored no intention of staying. Phelps, who'd fought the British at New Orleans and carried an embedded bullet as a souvenir, ventured south from the Galena lead mines, befriending Native Americans and savoring the land. Like all frontiersmen, he was smitten by wanderlust.

However, the beauty of the bluffs shouldering the river intrigued him. Consequently, in the summer of 1833 he hired a French guide, Stephen St. Cyr, a clerk employed with a fur company in the Rocky Mountains. They set adrift, noting the valley's potential resources. With the permanent dispossession of the Indians in 1832, the region was wide open and relatively safe for exploration.

Presently, they came upon a tent situated near the bank, erected by none other than Phelps' old friend, Colonel William S. Hamilton, son of founding father Alexander Hamilton, killed by Aaron Burr in the infamous 1804 duel. Hamilton, a government land surveyor, supplied Phelps with bread, bacon, and sound advice. Informing Phelps that he knew of a location about three miles west "that could not be surpassed in point of beauty . . . embracing all the advantages that were necessary to make a comfortable and convenient home," Hamilton handed him a note with specific directions for finding the spot.

Phelps required no further persuasion, recalling decades later, ". . . these beautiful undulating and rich prairies left an impression on my memory that no time could erase." He remained long enough to raise a crop before departing to fetch his family, returning permanently in 1835. Soon, others joined the clan, sawing lumber, dividing lots, and raising livestock. Eventually a blacksmith set up shop, then a tavern, a post office, and a church were established. In time, he and his brothers built a sawmill on Pine Creek, cutting trees for roofing, doors, and flooring; they also constructed a ferry, essential to the development of the burgeoning settlement.

As additional pioneers trudged westward, traders were soon paddling down the shallow Sinnissippi, navigable for steamboats but not deep-bellied barges. Mail arrived every Saturday from Buffalo Grove (now called Polo), delivered on the Galena and Dixon route. By 1847 Oregon's population had reached 225. In 1869, the Illinois General Assembly of the State of Illinois officially recognized Oregon City, called Florence in its early days. The first election was held on March 21, 1870, with one of its earliest residents, James Gale, elected as mayor.

As it grew, the tough little town nurtured strong men and women. In the "War of the Rebellion," 160 men were enlisted; 10 died of wounds and one, John Kelley, died imprisoned at the unspeakably horrible Andersonville Prison Camp in Georgia, a martyr for the Union. There was Edward B. Spalding of Company E, 52nd Illinois Infantry, the only Congressional Medal of Honor recipient to emerge from Ogle County during the Civil War. Years later, other brave young men toured Germany, Korea, and Vietnam. Some returned, many didn't. With the rest of the bruised country, Oregon buried its dead, raised its crops, and moved on.

Unlike the Hudson or the Mississippi, the Rock River valley does not quite resonate in the national mythic memory. The river, originating in the Horicon Marsh of Central Wisconsin, snaking south into Illinois and surrendering at last to Old Man at Rock Island, Illinois, cuts a decidedly thinner groove through American history than its compatriot waterways.

But every so often the Rock wends its way into the wider, noisier vistas of pop culture. For instance, Terry Brooks, bestselling fantasist originally from Sterling, Illinois, now living in the Pacific Northwest and Hawaii, sets his *Word & Void* trilogy in the Sinnissippi valley. Brooks expresses his own thoughts through the reflections of a character:

> She . . . recalled anew how Sinnissippi Park had appeared to her that first time . . . a vast, sprawling, mysterious world of secrets waiting to be discovered and adventures begging to be lived . . . She took it all in for a moment, embracing it with her senses, reclaiming it for herself as she did each time. . . . She felt that the park—that through her peculiar and endemic familiarity with its myriad creatures, its secretive places, its changeless look and feel, and its oddly compelling solitude, it was hers. She felt this way whenever she stepped into the park, as if she were fulfilling a purpose in her life, as if she knew that here, of all places in the world, she belonged.

Journalist Peggy Noonan also recognizes the valley's enduring enchantment through the vicissitudes of time, distance, and illness. In her memoir, *When Character Was King: A Story of Ronald Reagan*, Noonan relates the President's treasured early years in Dixon:

> . . . He became a lifeguard. Fifteen and then twenty dollars a week, good money, and in seven years he saved seventy-seven lives at Lowell Park on the Rock River. (It was the last job he remembered having when he was old and sick.)

The Rock's heritage, however local, is secure.

Now villages, estates, industry, and state parks nestle along its banks like bright beads on a string, with Oregon its anchor gem, settled snugly amid a clot of sandstone hills. Oregon (population 4100), 90 miles west of Chicago, eight miles north of Dixon and 20 miles south of Rockford, is the administrative seat for Ogle County.

As is true for many others who grew up in Northern Illinois, I cherish a basketful of Oregonian memories, but one in particular shines. As child or adult, whenever crossing the bridge on Highway 64 entering town, I'd never miss an opportunity to cast a glance upriver at the massive concrete statue called Blackhawk, as though checking to see if someone might've stolen him while I was away.

But there he stands, as tall as the trees, The Eternal Indian. Researching Oregon and its neighboring communities, I thoroughly comprehend his vigilance, and the affectionate regard apparent in those massive features so carefully fashioned by his creator, Lorado Taft, for the quiet hills and fields flanking the river below.

Now when I peer at Blackhawk, I am not looking at him, but with him.

One

SUMPTUOUS SOLITUDES

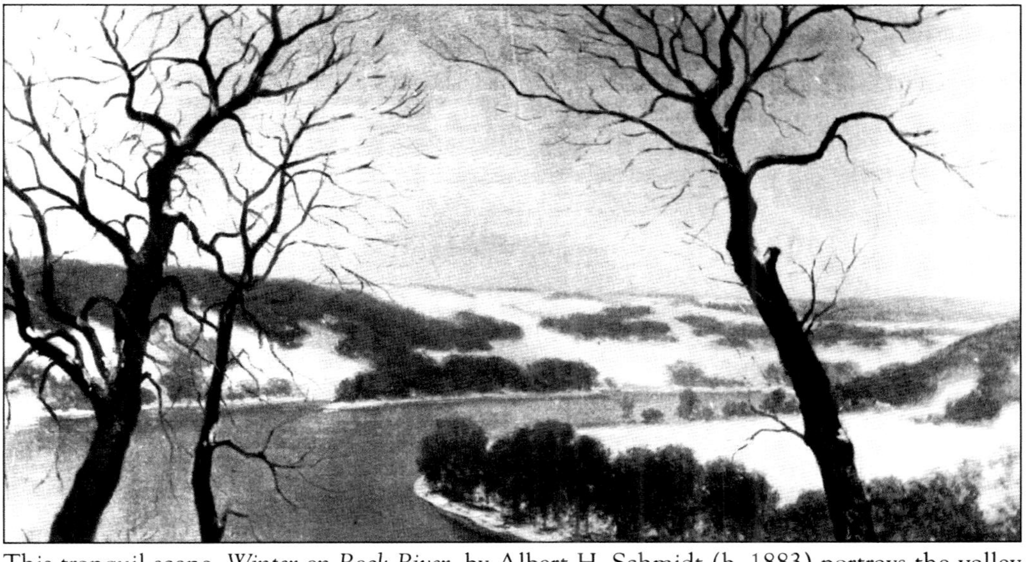

This tranquil scene, *Winter on Rock River*, by Albert H. Schmidt (b. 1883) portrays the valley after an early spring snow. The land is open and undeveloped, much as Oregon's earliest visitors encountered it a few decades earlier. At various times, the Spanish, French, and British all owned this region of North America. In 1778, Col. George Rogers Clark wrested a huge portion of the territory from British control, and the United States government held these tracts until 1842 when it sold parcels to squatters. Initially, Eastern pioneers accustomed to woodlands balked at the prospect of tilling the vast Illinois prairies, covered with six-foot grass. They reasoned that if the soil couldn't support trees, it couldn't support crops, either. But slowly the farmers experimented with growing crops, first near the river, then farther out. The land proved productive. Later, with the arrival of John Deere's self-scouring plow and Chester Nash's cultivator, all prejudice vanished.

Schmidt, probably a student of Eagle's Nest colonist Charles Francis Browne, was acquainted with a local family who maintained close relations with the colony. Born in Chicago, he studied at both the Art Institute and the Julian Academy in Paris. The painting was exhibited in Chicago Artists 22nd Annual Exhibition in 1918. It is displayed at the Oregon Public Library. (Courtesy Arts Alliance of Ogle County.)

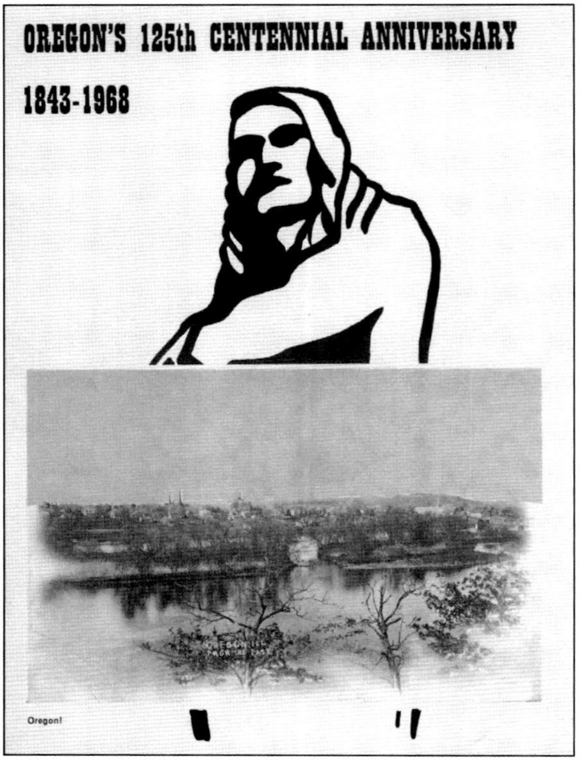

The city's first "official" history, *Oregon's 125th Centennial Anniversary: 1843–1968*, edited by Armin G. Weng, dates its founding from the year wherein the name changed from Florence to Oregon City. It was functioning as a village as early as 1835. This fine book offers invaluable interviews and rare photos; and is introduced by then-mayor Harry F. Wade, president of Oregon's 125th Anniversary Celebration.

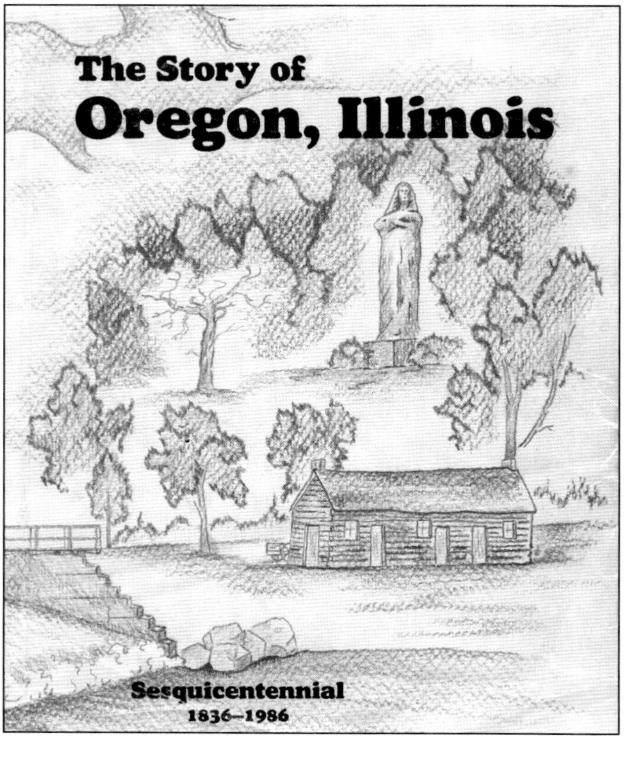

The Story of Oregon, 1836–1986, with cover art by Jon Spoor, is a superb, comprehensive limited edition hardcover edited by Charles W. Mongan, Lynne Kilker, Viola Meyers, and Anne Jones. Dedicated to historian and long-time resident Charles W. Mongan (1906–1988) who died shortly before its release, the book presents hundreds of priceless photographs and innumerable anecdotes relating to the city's rich history.

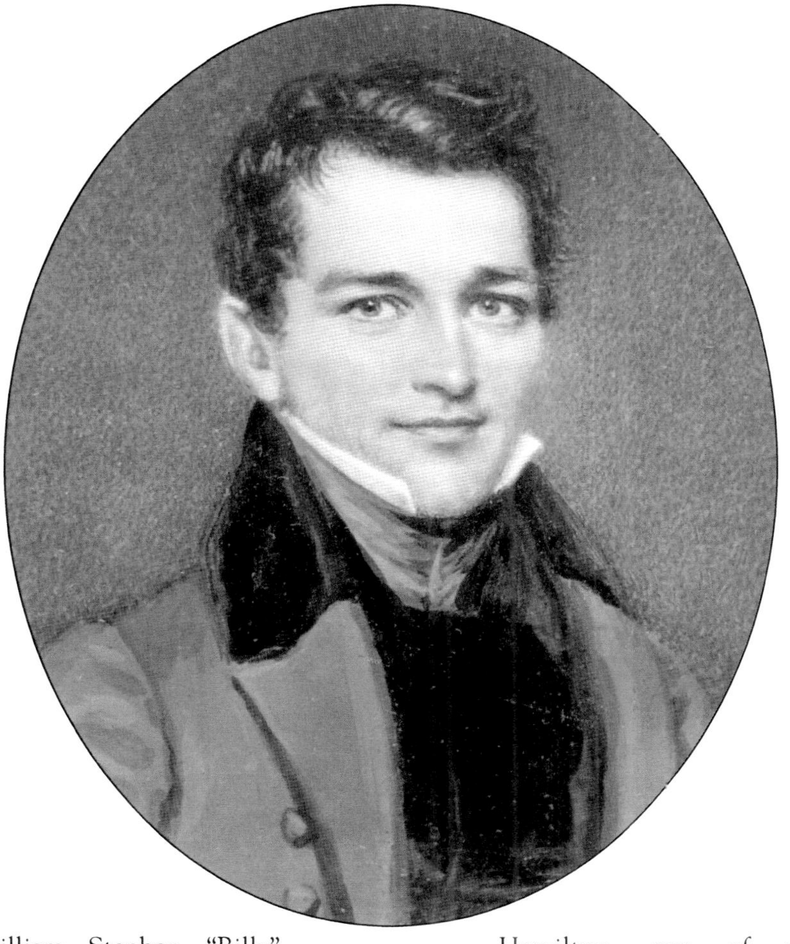

When William Stephen "Billy" Hamilton, son of statesman Alexander Hamilton, was born in 1797, his father wrote to George Washington: "It seems Mrs. Hamilton has lately added another boy to our stock." After his father was mortally wounded by Aaron Burr in 1804, he and his siblings were lined up before his deathbed; during the funeral, Billy sat next to Founding Father Gouverneur Morris, who delivered the eulogy. Billy studied law at West Point before mysteriously resigning in 1817. Soon he ventured to St. Louis, Missouri, accepting an appointment under William Rector, Surveyor General for Arkansas, Illinois, and Missouri. From there to Illinois, where Hamilton charted the original city of Peoria, naming several streets after Revolutionary War heroes. Colonel Billy Hamilton was surveying land in Northern Illinois for the U.S. government when John Phelps entered the Rock River valley in 1833; Hamilton lived in a cabin near the lead mines in Galena, Illinois, where he hoped to establish a thriving commercial hub called "Wiota." Sadly, his plans crumbled when the Pecatonica River flooded, destroying the settlement's few houses. A lifelong bachelor, he spoke fluent French, read widely, and was elected to the Illinois General Assembly in 1824. In the mid 1840s he also served as a member of Wisconsin's Territorial Legislature. During his tenure in Wisconsin, his mother, the widow Hamilton, visited him at age 80. In 1849 he heard rumors of plenteous gold out west and quite willingly surrendered to the rush, heading straightway for California. He sifted gold and pursued other interests before succumbing to cholera in 1850. His headstone reads: *In size and features, in talent and character, he much resembled his illustrious father*. (Courtesy of the Wisconsin Historical Society, WHi-3458.)

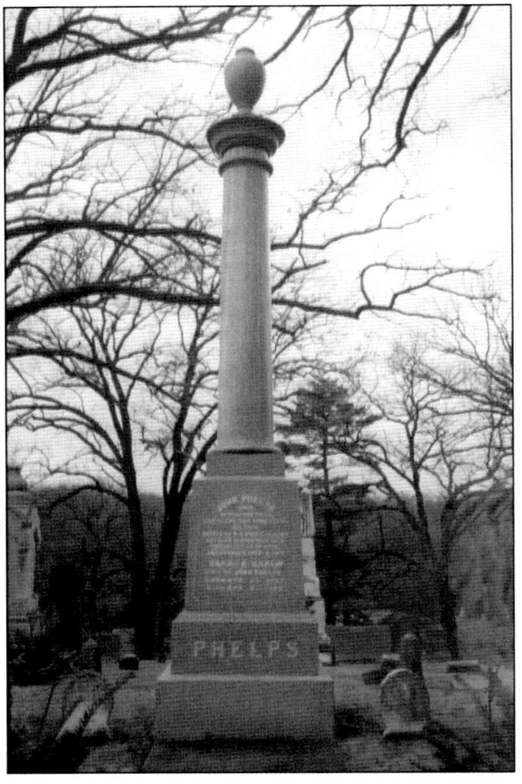

The gravestone of John Phelps (1796–1874), Oregon's founder, commands Riverview Cemetery. Born in Bedford County, Virginia, he married Sarah Rogan Carlin in 1816. An entrepreneur, Phelps temporarily left his family at home while he worked the lead mines in Galena. After some meandering, he finally settled in the Sinnissippi valley, hoping to secure a point between Galena and Chicago, seeking legislation to secure the route. In 1841, Phelps partnered with Wesley Johnston, establishing a mercantile business. Sarah died in 1879.

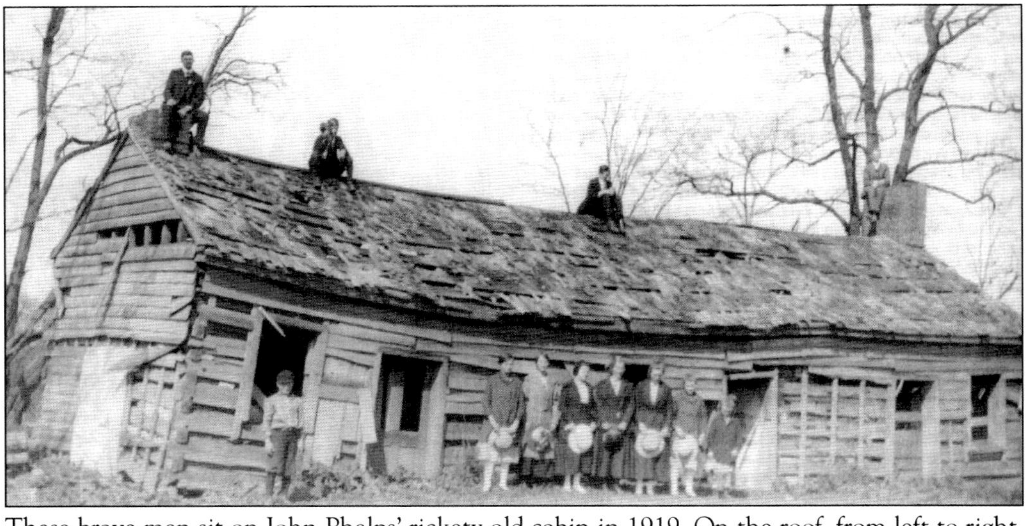

These brave men sit on John Phelps' rickety old cabin in 1919. On the roof, from left to right, are Harold Roos, John Roos, Adolph Roos, and Peter Roos; In front are Andrew Buhs, Helen Buhs, Fredricka Roos, Grace Roos, Grace Buhs, Jennie Buhs, and Martha Buhs. As their fortunes increased, the Phelps family abode in considerably finer digs. Timber and stone pulled from these ruins were used to build the VFW fireplace.

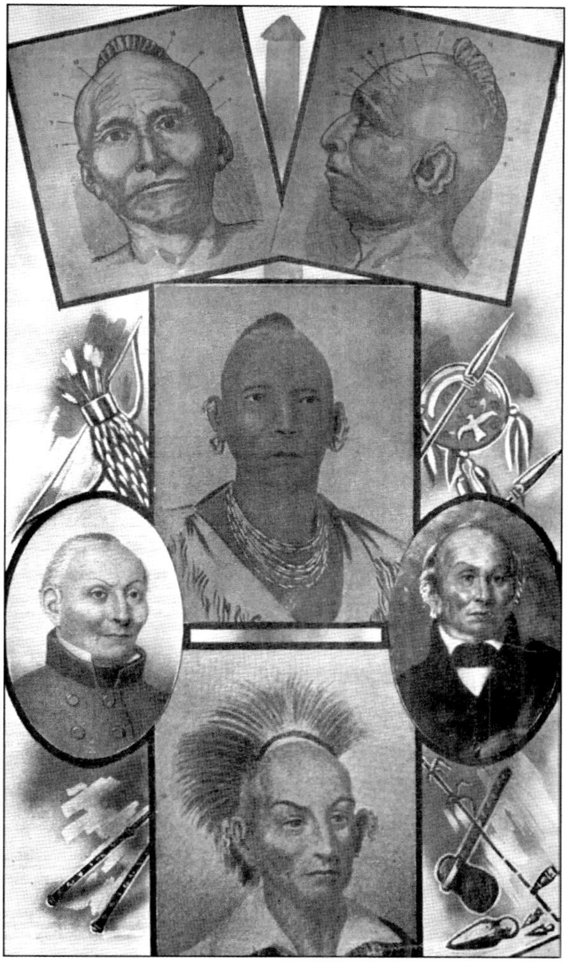

Blackhawk of the Sauk was born in 1767 near the confluence of the Mississippi and Rock rivers. As a result of a poorly-negotiated 1804 treaty, the Sauk and Fox agreed to abandon all territory east of the Mississippi. Soon white pioneers and lead miners were confidently pushing westward. Resisting their expansion, Blackhawk and his followers sided with the British in the War of 1812, terrorizing American settlements. In the years following, as the Fox and Sauk receded to Iowa, Blackhawk stoutly refused displacement, proclaiming that his people had been duped. In *Blackhawk, An Autobiography*, he laments, "Why did the Great Spirit ever send the whites to this island, to drive us from our homes, and introduce among us poisonous liquors, disease and death? They should have remained on the island where the Great Spirit first placed them." He returned from Iowa with hundreds of resolute braves and their families, opening violently against the Illinois militia (including Abraham Lincoln, Zachary Taylor, and Jefferson Davis) positioned to resist the uprising. Routed north, Blackhawk was captured by the Winnebago and handed over to the whites. He was then whisked to Washington where he met President Andrew Jackson. Many in the East viewed Blackhawk as a romantic hero. In 1833, he was allowed to return to Iowa to live, greatly revered, on a reservation until his death in 1838. Later his body was shamelessly exhumed and displayed in a museum, which burned to the ground in 1855. The last line of his autobiography is a poignant prayer: "May the Great Spirit keep our people and the whites always at peace. . . ." The Sinnissippi valley at Oregon was beloved to the great Sauk general.

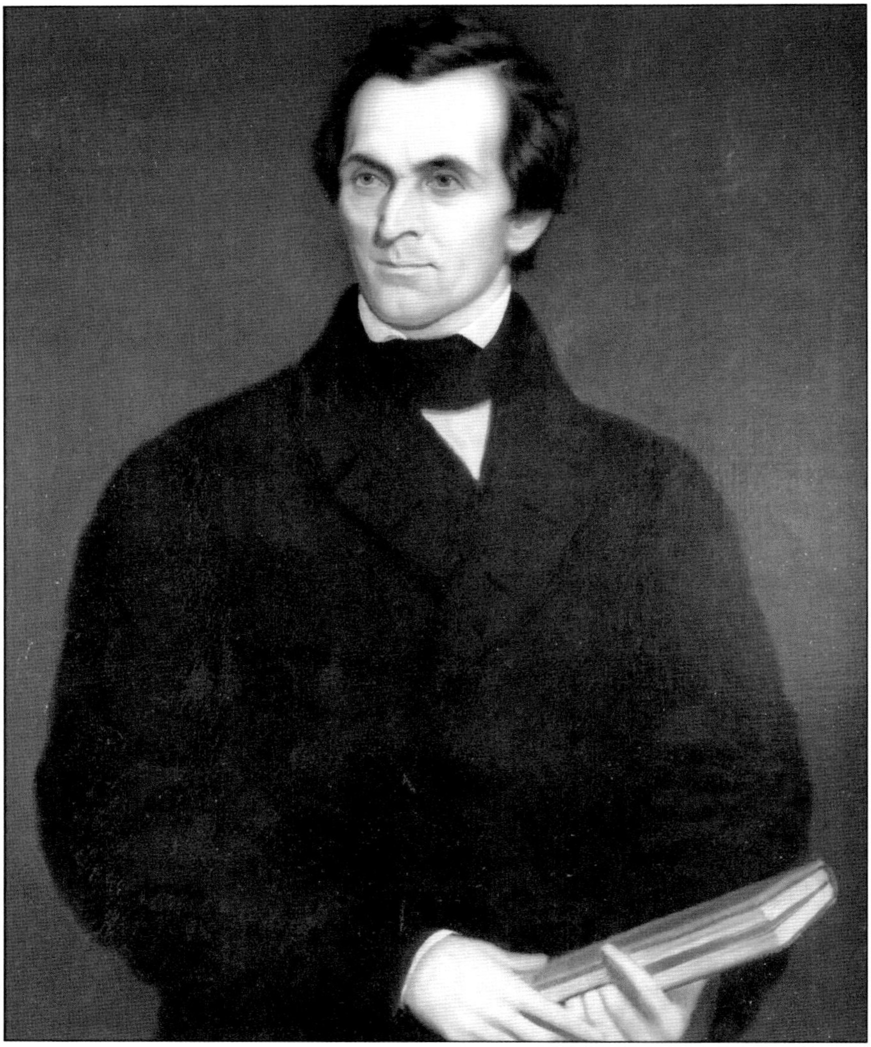

The Honorable Thomas Ford, friend of founder John Phelps, resided for two years in a log cabin west of Oregon, and there housed his family while performing legal duties. Ford, judge to the Ninth Judicial Circuit, was holding court at the old Ogle County Courthouse in 1842 when news arrived announcing his nomination as governor. Unfortunately, his voice failed as he read his inaugural speech and another finished it for him. A piano played at the event is now displayed at the Ogle County Historical Society in Oregon. A man of deep integrity, Ford rescued his state from catastrophic debt, struck hard against prairie pirates and, most controversially, commanded forceful opposition against Joseph Smith and the Mormon agitation in Nauvoo, Illinois, which resulted in the deaths of Joseph and his brother, Hyrum. Completing his term, Ford published the perceptive *History of Illinois* while practicing law in Peoria, Illinois. "The governor wrote compactly, forcibly and precisely," observes Robert P. Howard in *Mostly Good and Competent Men*, an assessment of Illinois governors. "Even if he wrote with cynicism, his book has been recognized as a superior analysis of American politics." What he lacked in looks and charisma was amply compensated in wisdom and honesty; he is considered one of Illinois's great governors. Ford died of tuberculosis in 1850, one month after his wife died of cancer. He is buried in Peoria. (Courtesy of the Illinois State Historical Society.)

James V. Gale, *c.* 1865, was one of Oregon's first residents and its first mayor. Born in Concord, New Hampshire, Gale attended West Point for one year before moving west. An enterprising and courageous man, he was Oregon's first Justice of the Peace, was elected State Representative in 1863 and directed the Chicago and Iowa Railroad in 1870.

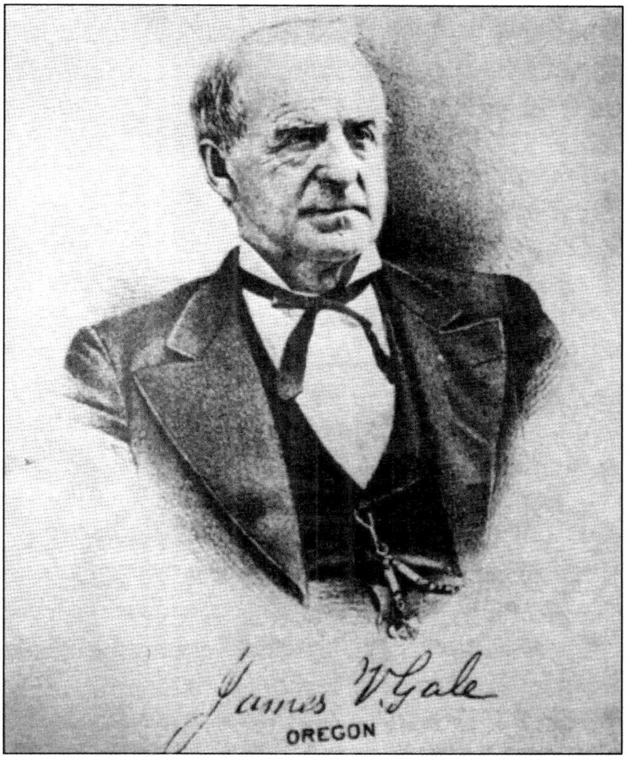

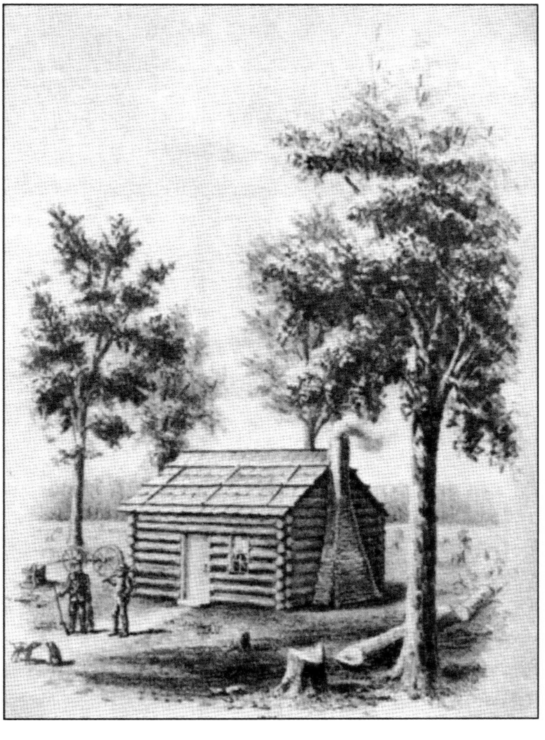

James Gale's cabin was completed in 1835 and stood near the site of Oregon grade school on Madison Street. Gale farmed until 1838, before opening a mercantile business, then a saw mill.

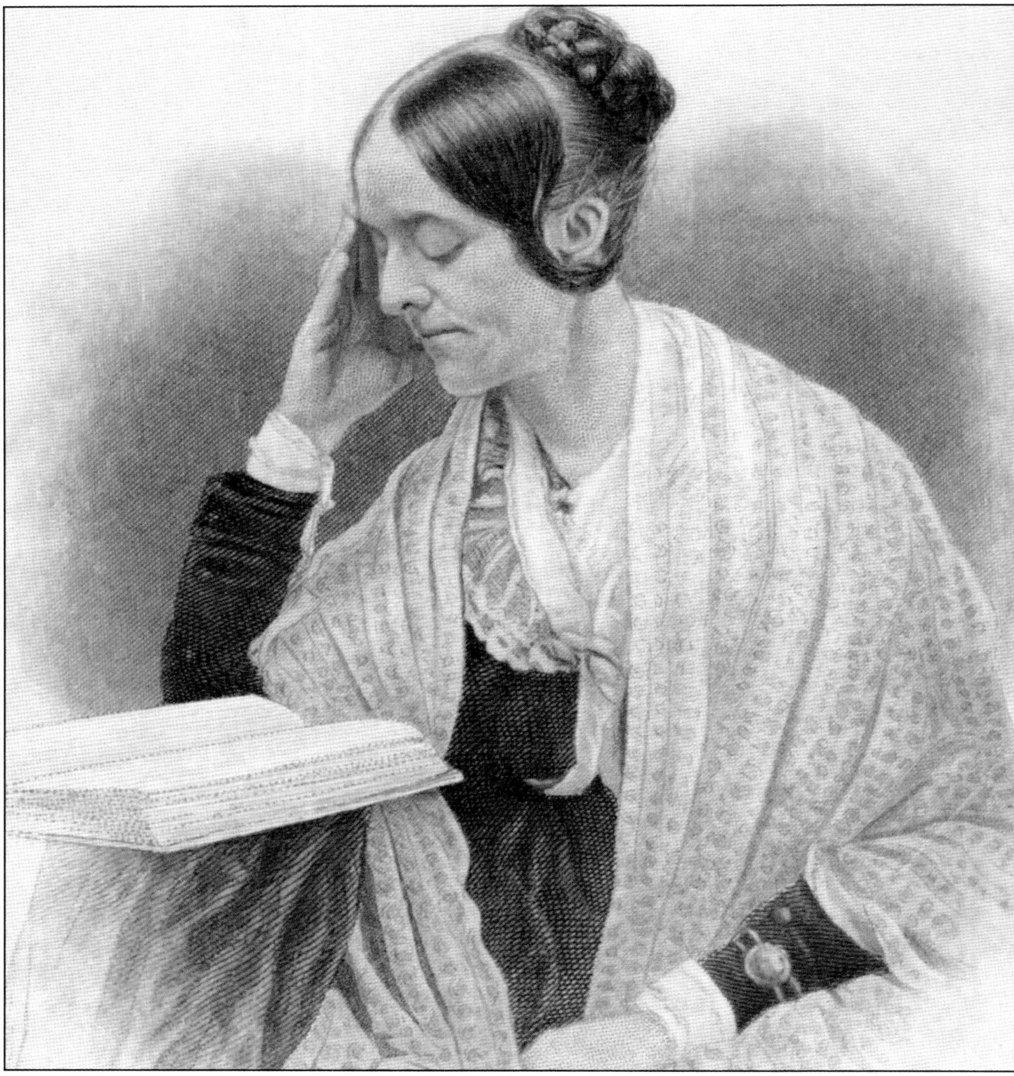

Boston transcendentalist Margaret Fuller (Countess D'Ossoli), author, editor, and associate to Ralph Waldo Emerson, earnestly desired a journey to the West, so enchanted was she with its fantastic tales. In 1843, she accompanied William, Margaret, and Sarah Clarke by boat from Buffalo to Chicago, then by lumber wagon from Chicago to Dixon, crossing at Dixon's Ferry, lodging for a few days at the home of businessman Alexander Charters. From Dixon they rode to Oregon where her uncle, William Fuller, a Harvard-trained lawyer, practiced. Tracing the Blackhawk Trail, Fuller remarked, ". . . that an Indian brave accustomed to ramble in such paths might be mistaken for Apollo." Visiting various settlers, Fuller resented their fine amenities brought from the uppity East, such as pianos. She preferred guitars. "Bring to the West what the West requires," she reasoned. "You cannot climb an Indian mound in satin shoes." On the 4th of July, Fuller happily participated in the festivities, joining Oregon as it celebrated with ice cream, fireworks, and drums. At her farewell party she read a poem, "Farewell to Rock River Valley." *Farewell, yet soft and sumptuous solitudes! / Ye fairy distances / Ye lordly woods. . .* In 1845 Margaret Fuller married an Italian revolutionary, the Marquis D'Ossoli. Returning from Europe in 1850 with her husband and daughter, their ship wrecked near the port at New York City and all perished.

Fuller relished watching the eagle's swoop into their nests, held aloft in this weathered cedar. A tablet memorializing her visit was inserted in a casement surrounding the spring, stating: *Ganymede's Spring named by Margaret Fuller (Countess D'Ossoli) who named this bluff Eagle's Nest and, beneath the cedars on its crest, wrote "Ganymede to His Eagle" July 4, 1843.* The tablet, damaged by vandalism, has been removed and is now displayed at the NIU Taft Campus. (Courtesy of the *Oregon Republican-Reporter.*)

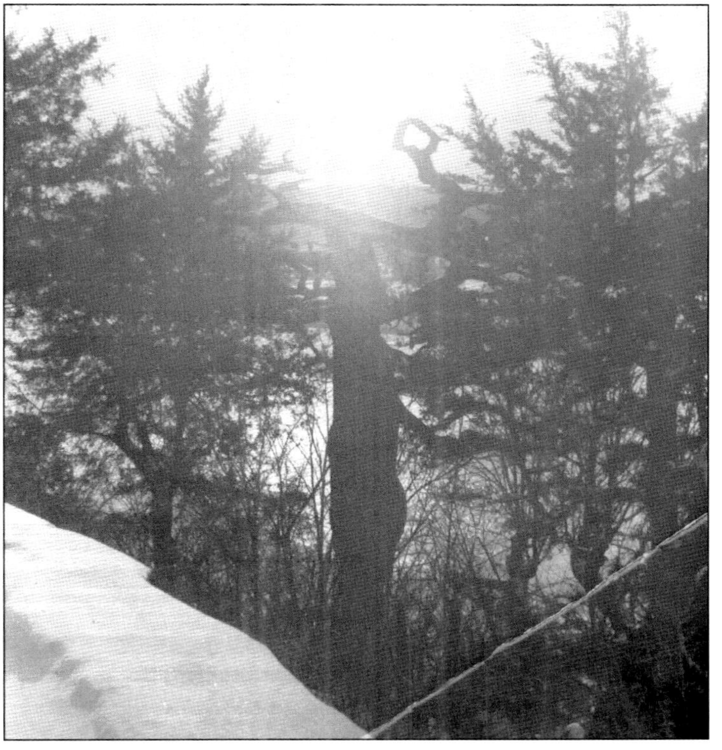

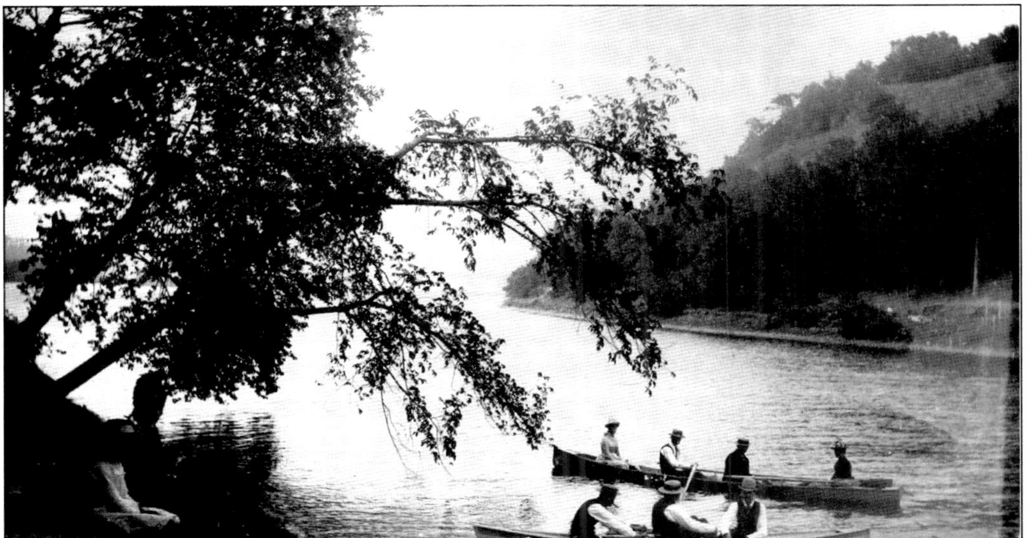

Margaret Fuller Island in 1880, the year it was christened in her honor by Col. B.F. Sheets. Commendatory letters by Oliver Wendell Holmes and Bronson Alcott were sent and read at the event. Fuller's hosts ferried her from their cabin on the river, showing the marks of tomahawks cut into trees by Indians dispossessed a few years earlier. For decades it was customary for picnickers to fill a bucket of water at Ganymede Spring before rowing to the island for the afternoon. (Courtesy of the *Oregon Republican-Reporter.*)

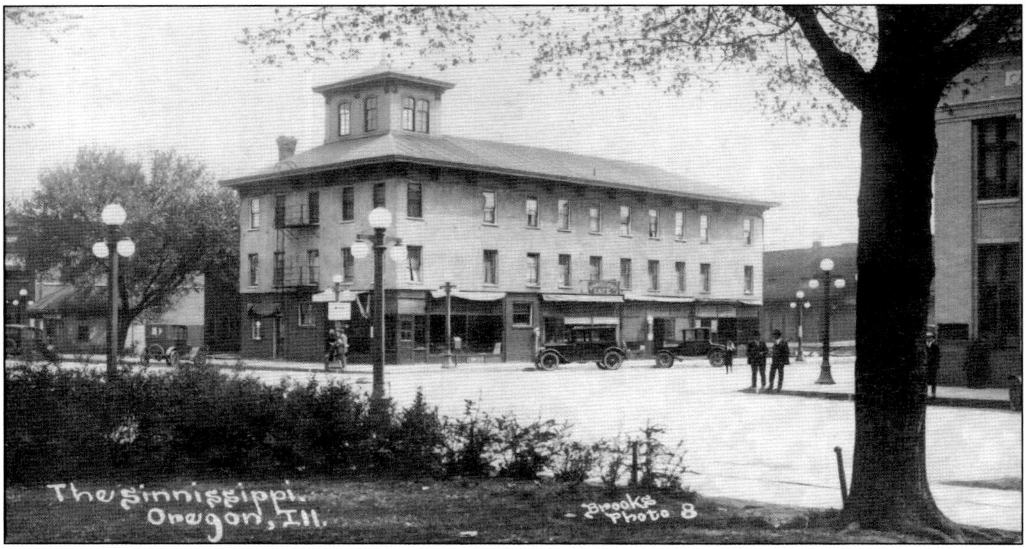

The Sinnissippi House hotel, built in 1847. When Oregon's depot opened in the early 1870s, the House's tower served as a lookout for the train and stagecoaches. The rooms were heated with stoves rather than a boiler, which accounts for the several chimneys. In 1914 steel underpinnings were installed to reinforce the foundation, allowing additional businesses on its first floor. At various times the House contained a café, flower shop, barber shop, and an appliance store. (Courtesy of the Ogle County Historical Society.)

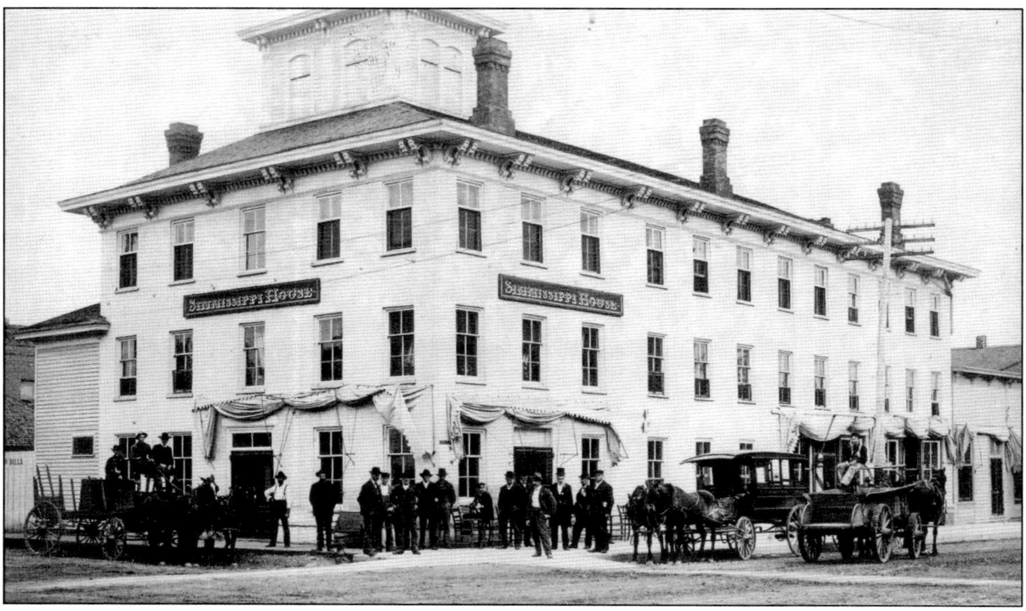

An Oregon landmark for 125 years, the trusty old House survived the decades but not the judge's gavel; deemed unsafe and condemned by the fire marshal, attempts to preserve it reached the Illinois Supreme Court, who overturned the case. It was razed in 1971. The corner property has since been utilized as a gas station and real estate office. (Courtesy of the Ogle County Historical Society.)

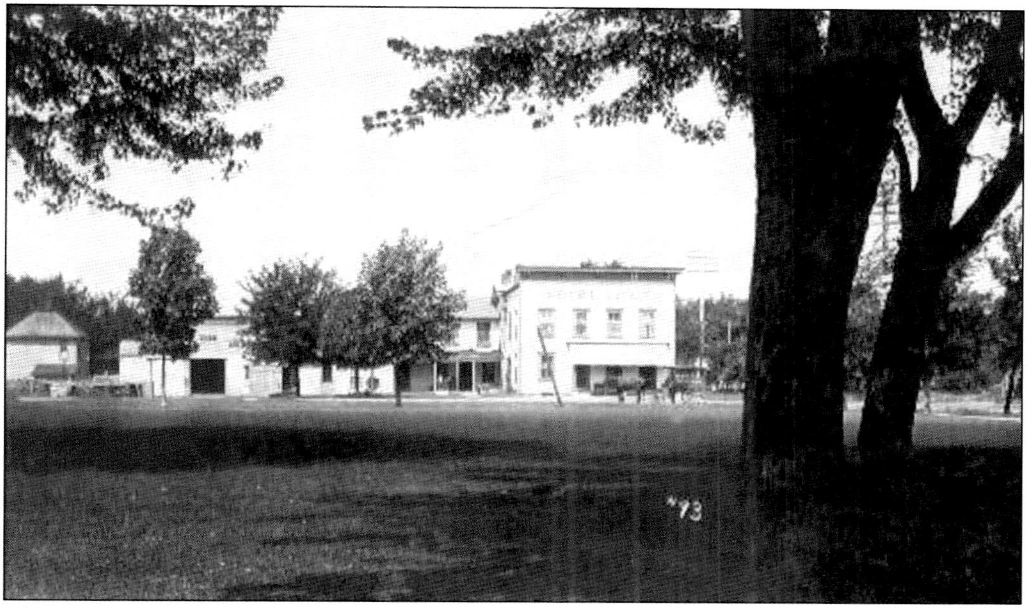

The Spoor Hotel at 5th and Washington, owned by Austin and Anna Spoor, c. 1890, was razed to allow room for a service station. Before the Spoors purchased it, the inn was called The American House. The Harry Spoor Livery was located a few doors south. (Courtesy of the *Oregon Republican-Reporter.*)

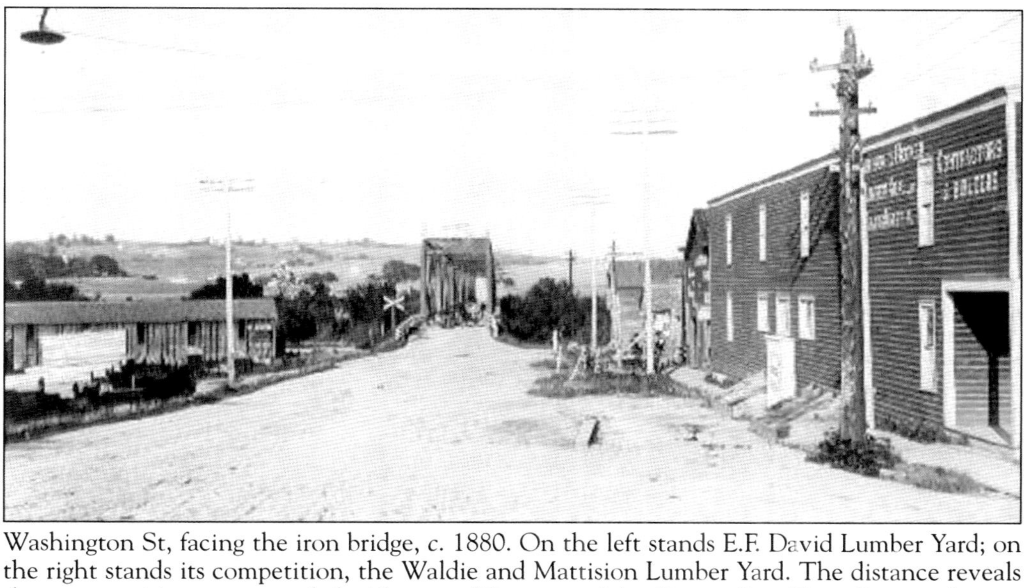

Washington St, facing the iron bridge, *c.* 1880. On the left stands E.F. David Lumber Yard; on the right stands its competition, the Waldie and Mattision Lumber Yard. The distance reveals the open prairies, now crowded with trees. (Courtesy of the *Oregon Republican-Reporter.*)

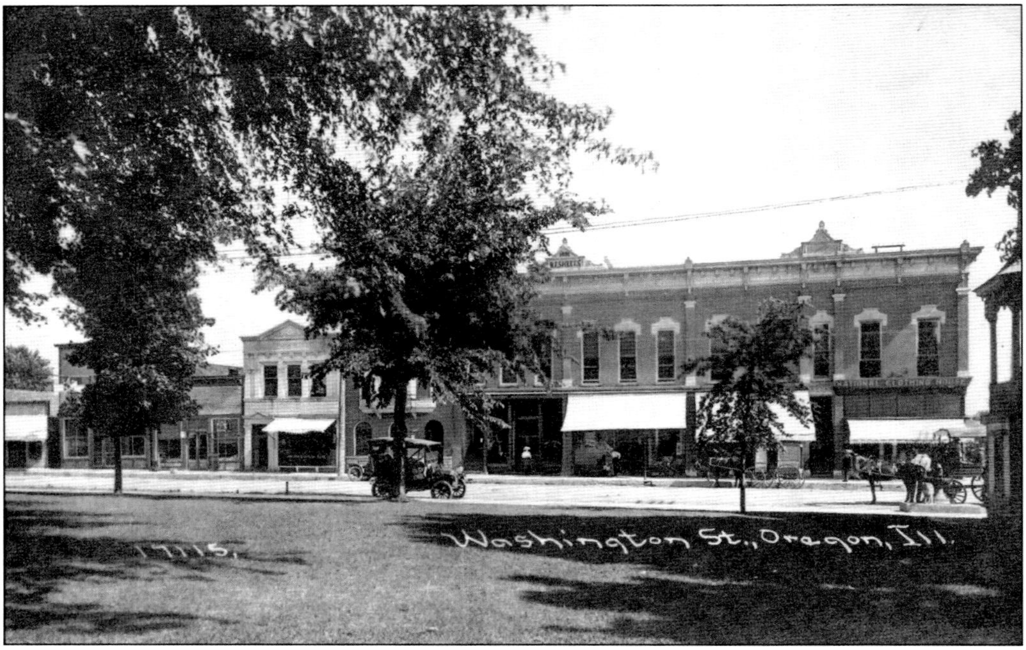

The shop at the corner of Washington Street is the National Clothing House, *c.* 1890. To the far right is glimpsed a section of the bandstand, Oregon's social center. The ground level contained the police station, its upper level functioned as a platform for Sousa bands and orators, including one poor fellow who publicly apologized for rude remarks tendered after President McKinley's assassination. Later, it was moved to the fairgrounds and used as offices. (Courtesy of the *Oregon Republican-Reporter*.)

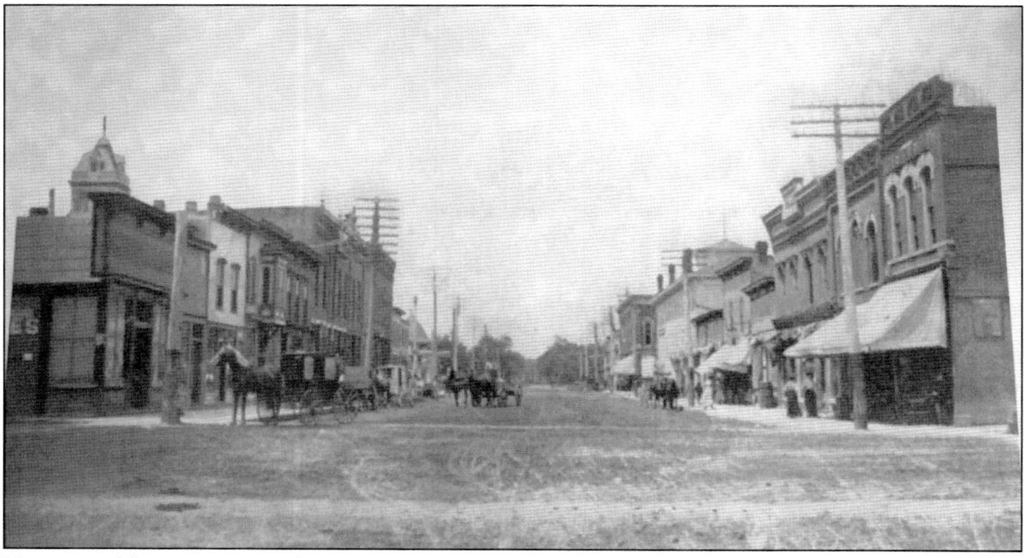

Horses and buggies on Washington Street, no bricks yet, just plentiful dirt. Carriage wheels cut deeply into the soil. After a heavy rain, travel was nearly impossible in the thick, oozing mud. This image is *c.* 1870.

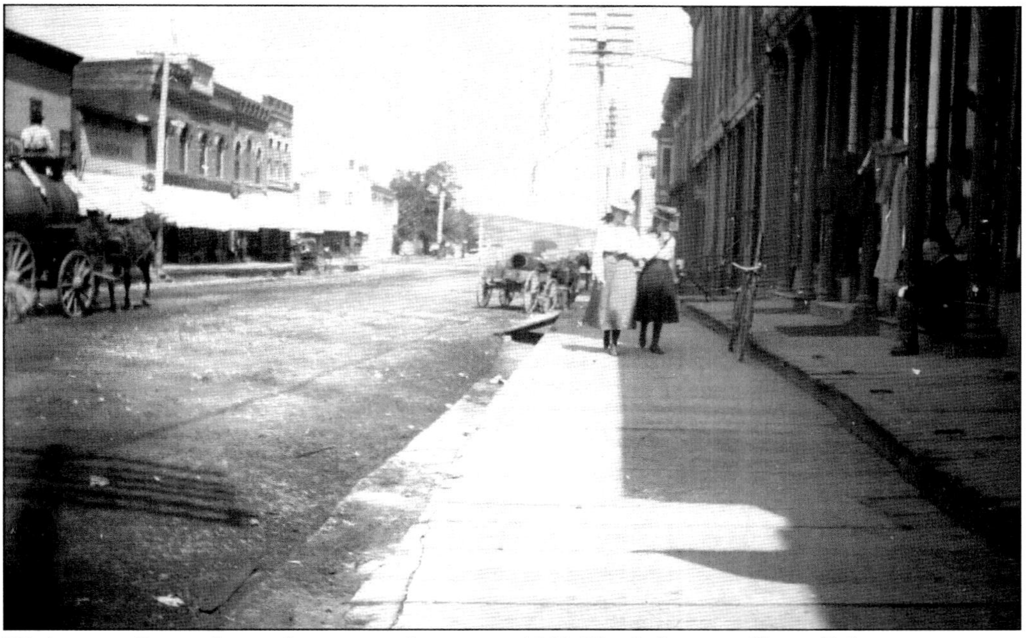

Washington Street, facing the river to the west, c. 1880. Two ladies casually stroll the main avenue, alongside horses and carriages and bicycles. (Courtesy of the *Oregon Republican-Reporter*.)

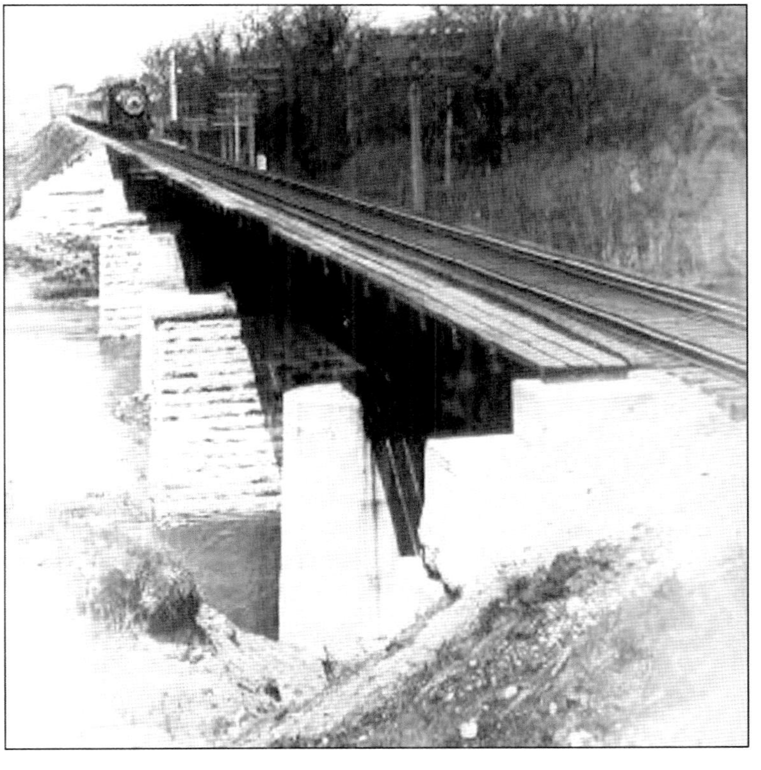

A train barrels over one of the first bridges in Oregon. (Courtesy of Bob Rees.)

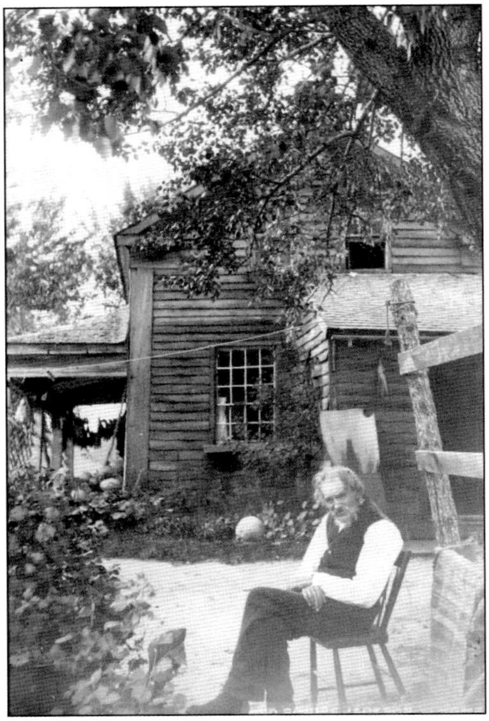

Old Squire Jackson sits comfortably on his porch, c. 1880. His weathered demeanor perfectly characterizes the tough frontiersman and farmers who settled and sustained the Sinnissippi valley in the 19th century. The location of his house is unknown. (Courtesy of the *Oregon Republican-Reporter*.)

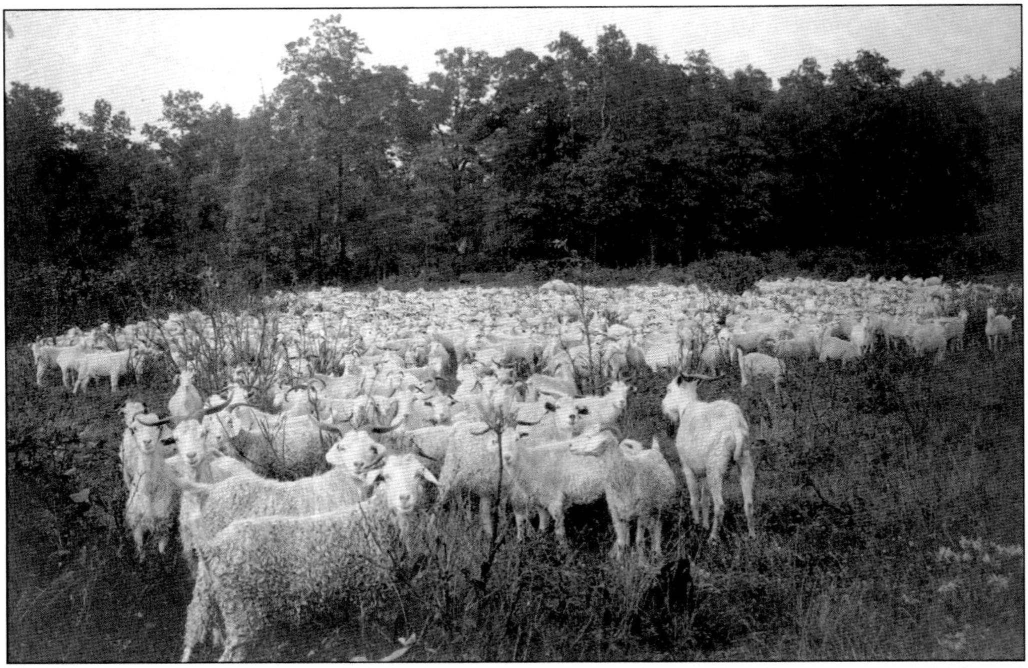

Sheep graze contentedly outside Oregon. The region's open acreage and nutritious soil allowed for prosperous farmland and ranches. With great anticipation farmers looked forward to the annual Ogle County Fair, a tremendous opportunity to display livestock, tractors, corn, beans, and other wares. (Courtesy of the *Oregon Republican-Reporter*.)

The drive to Ganymede Spring was a wide dirt path running along the Rock River. The road remains, ending at the spring's ruined casement where a marble tablet commemorating Margaret Fuller's visit was displayed for decades before removal due to vandalism. Lowden State Park and the Taft Field Campus occupy the property on the bluff above. (Courtesy of the *Oregon Republican-Reporter*.)

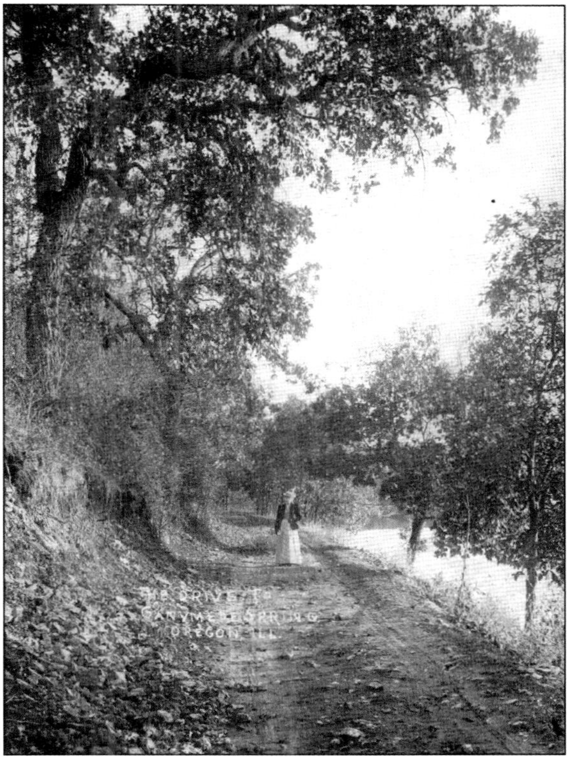

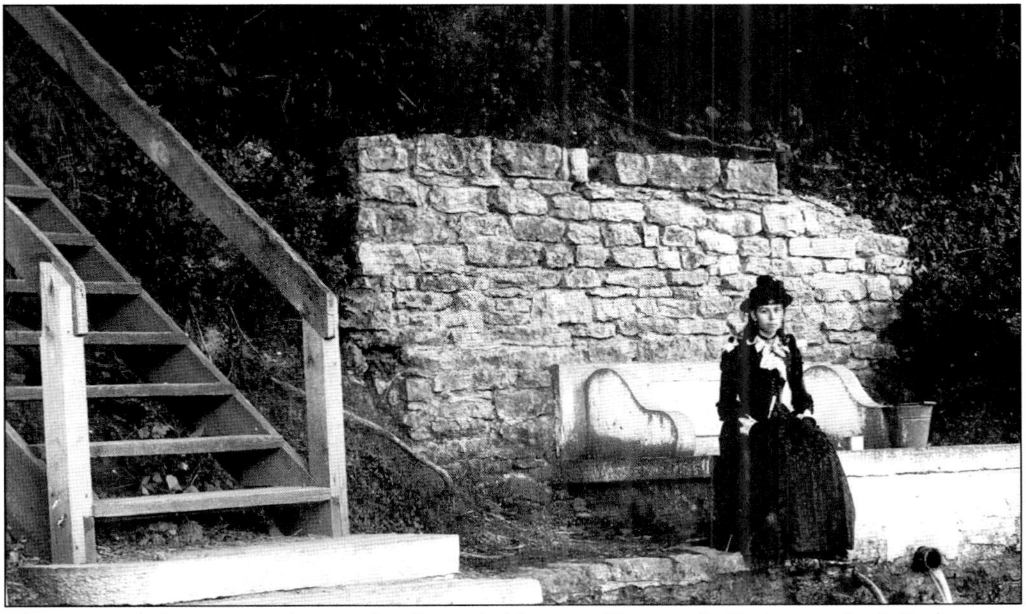

This young lady rests on the riverbank, probably near Ganymede Spring or the Mix home, a much-used watering hole for early Native American travelers and thirsty animals. The steps ascend to the bluff where a road leads to town. This image is c. 1890. (Courtesy of the *Oregon Republican-Reporter*.)

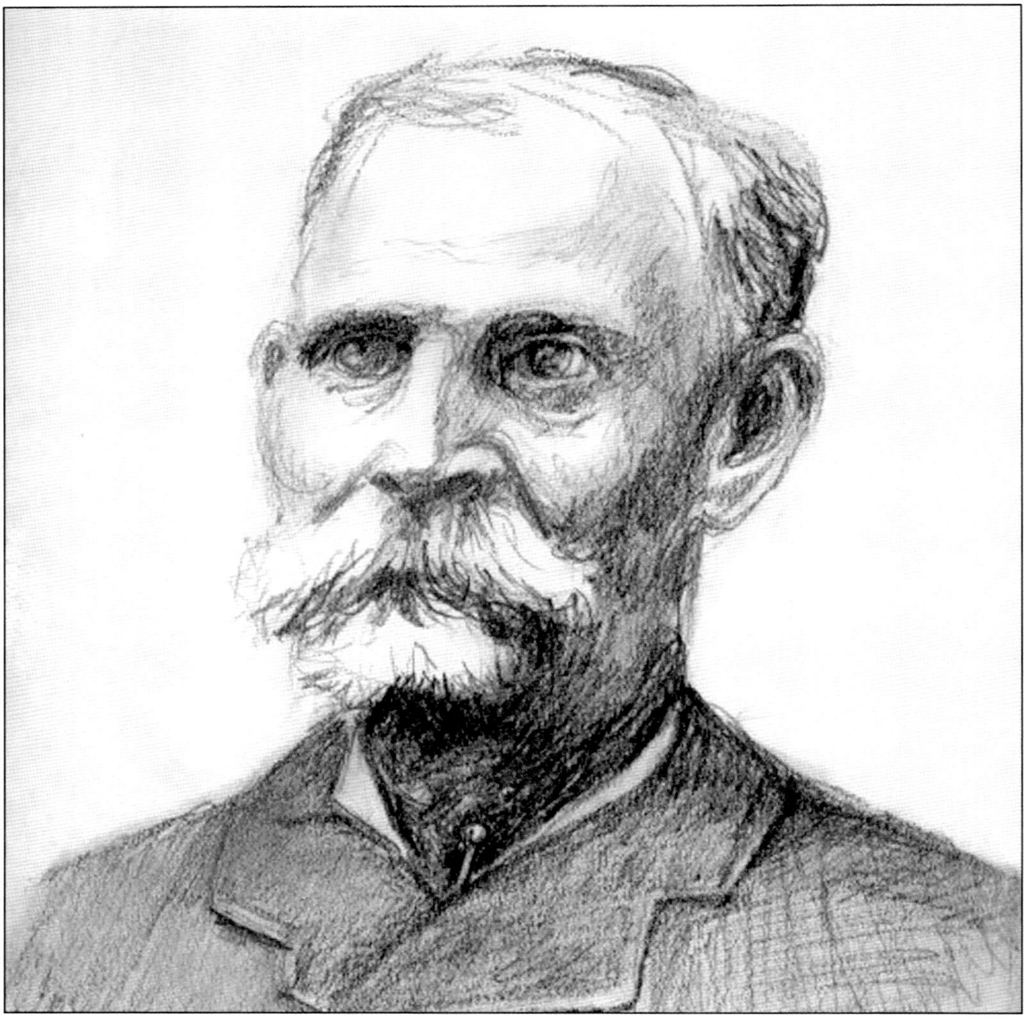

Charles E. Boles, known as "Black Bart," borrowed his infamous nickname from a dimestore thriller. Supposedly, shortly after the Civil War and following his discharge from the 116th Illinois Infantry, he resided briefly in Oregon (one account places him at New Oregon, Iowa), staying long enough to abandon his wife and two daughters before trekking solo to Montana and California, embarking on a successful career robbing Wells Fargo stagecoaches. Crafty, cautious, and polite, he injured no one, leaving only snippets of bad verse as his signature. For example: *I've labored long and hard for bread / For honor and for riches / But on my corns too long you've tred, / You fine-haired sons of b——es*. During holdups, he ingeniously propped sticks behind rocks, cheating the appearance of additional firepower. If a guard attempted to stop him, Bart would yell to the rocks, "If he makes a move, give him a volley, boys." After much dogged sleuthing, the law finally caught up with him, and Bart was sentenced to eight years in San Quentin. Upon release, asked if he offered further poetry, he responded, "Young man, didn't you hear me say I will commit no more crimes?" When he ceased corresponding in 1888, his wife assumed he was dead. The "Boulevardier Bandit" was never seen again. Biographer George Hoeper posits that Bart resumed his old ways and botched a robbery in Nevada. He was consequently shot dead and lay in an unmarked grave somewhere in the desert. (Courtesy of artist Annie M. Trimble.)

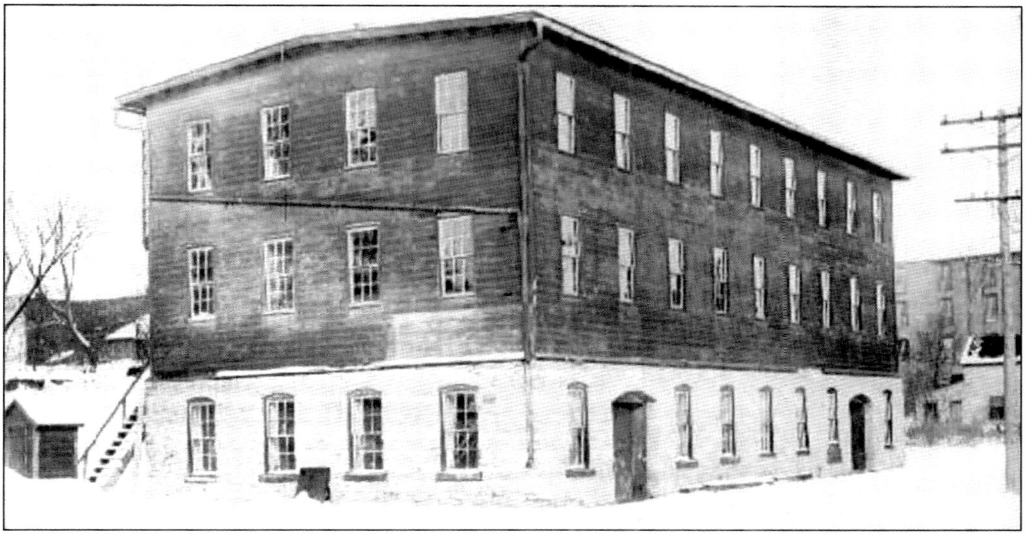

Chester Nash, contemporary of John Deere and father of schoolteacher Ruby Nash, used this building at 202–204 North 2nd St. for manufacturing his patented cultivator, which opposed weeds that prevented corn growth. In its early days, the cultivator was constructed from wood. Nash discontinued the plows and later concentrated on planing tools. A model of the cultivator is displayed at the Ogle County Historical Society. (Courtesy of Bob Rees.)

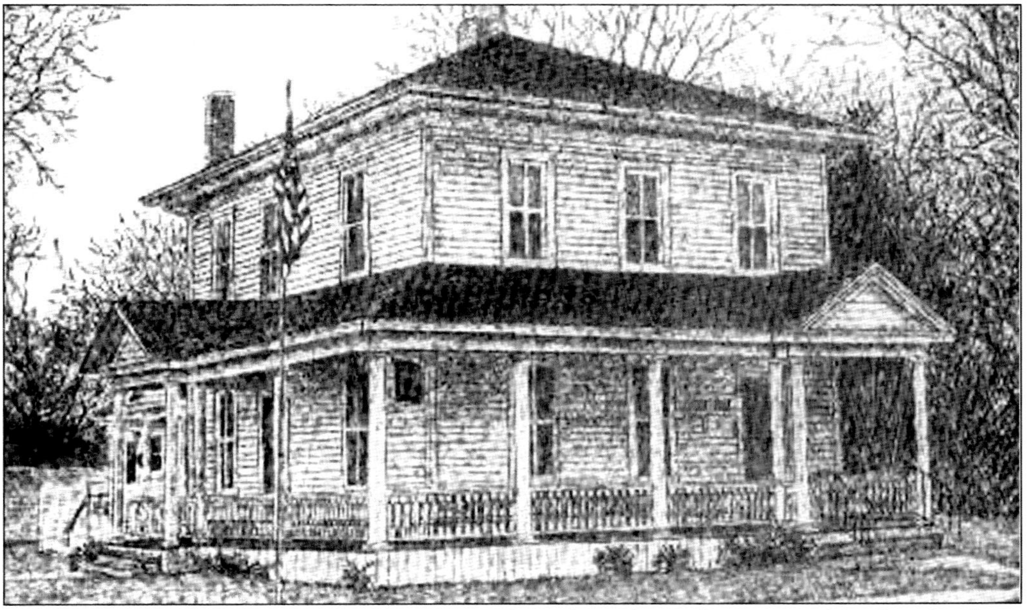

The Chester Nash home at the corner of 6th and Madison, later owned by his daughter, Ruby Nash, now serves as the Ogle County Historical Society, established in 1962. The homestead is furnished not only with charming period décor, but also many items pertinent to the history of Ogle County, including rare photos, posters, books, postcards, WW II medals, uniforms, and records. The society's unofficial archivist, the incomparable Vada Wood, has documented much of this material. (Courtesy of the Ogle County Historical Society.)

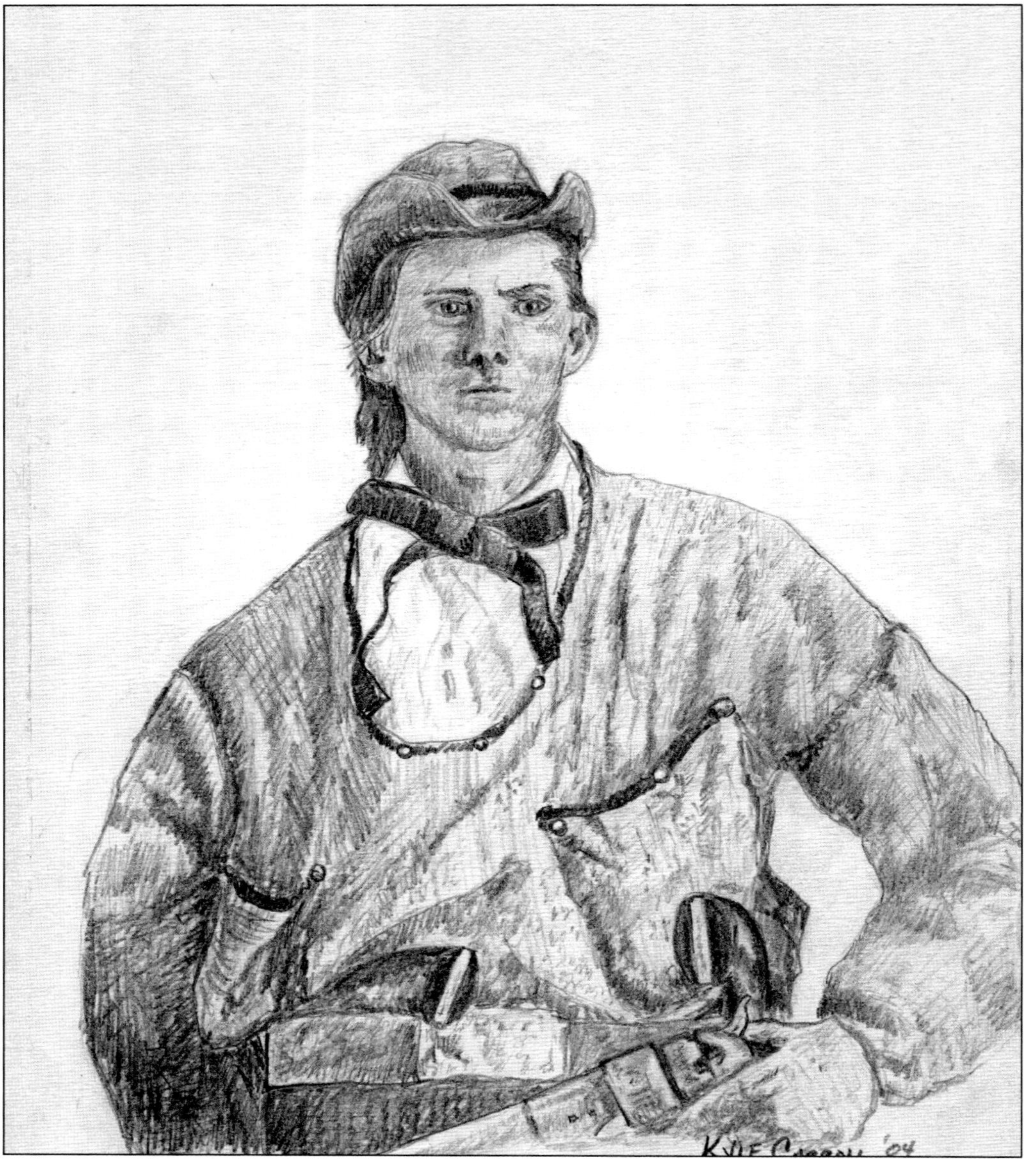

In 1876, Jesse James with brother Frank, the Younger Boys, Clell Miller, Charlie Pitts, Bill Chadwell, and several other outlaws visited the Ogle County Fair in Oregon to enjoy a bit of horse racing. According to eyewitness recollections, they were nattily-groomed, well-armed, and rode expensive horses. Though fair organizers feared that James and his cronies might relieve them of their hard-earned proceeds, the men had stopped in Oregon only as a brief diversion as they headed north to Northfield, Minnesota, to pursue their more serious ambitions in bank-robbing, an undertaking which they had been successfully executing since 1865. In Northfield, the gang's reflexes were dulled due to drinking and consequently the job was bungled, resulting in several deaths and injuries. The Northfield incident marked an irrevocable blow to James's reputation as a folk hero. After years of dodging the authorities, he was killed in 1882 at his home in St. Joseph, Missouri, surprised by a bullet to the head while housecleaning. (Courtesy of artist Kyle Carroll.)

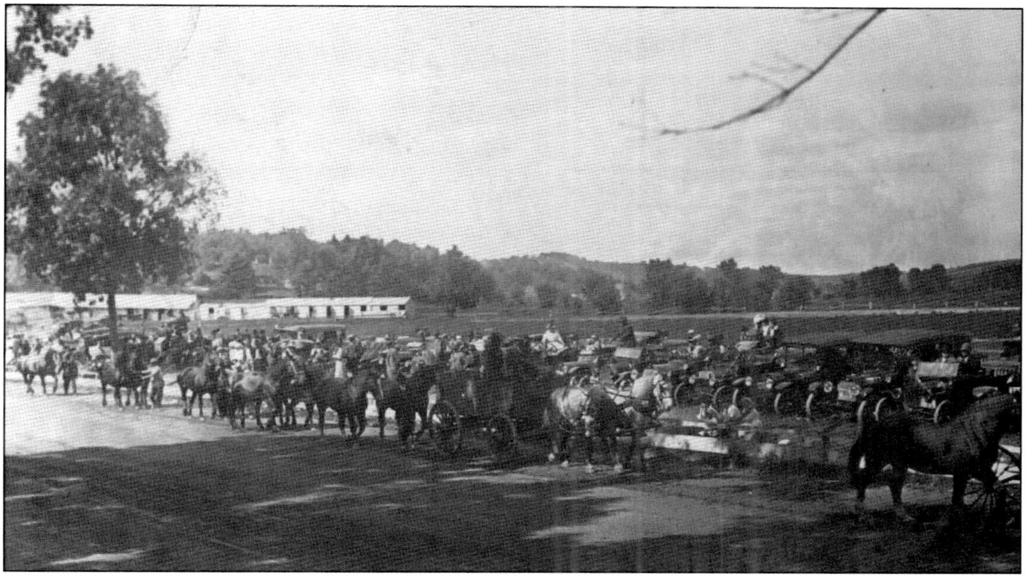

The Ogle County Fair on Route 2, north of Oregon. Between the 1880s and 1986, one yearly public wedding was performed, with the county donating a marriage license and local merchants donating $250. The last couple wedded worked for the carnival. In addition to its romantic appeal, the fair presented annual opportunity for ranchers to display bulls, hogs, sheep, and horses. (Courtesy of the *Oregon Republican-Reporter.*)

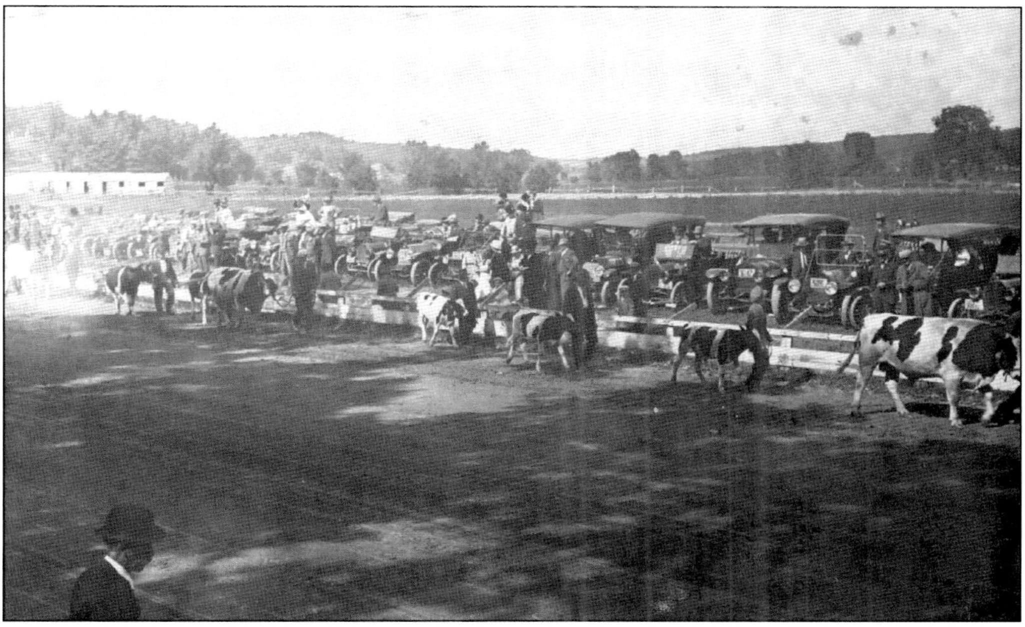

Citation, the mare owned by Judge Cartwright and trained by Dick McMahon at Springvale Farm north of Oregon, set a record in Columbus, Ohio, finishing at 2:01 for the mile. When Citation returned home, she was greeted at the train station by a band, bedecked in roses, and led downtown for further celebration. (Courtesy of the *Oregon Republican-Reporter.*)

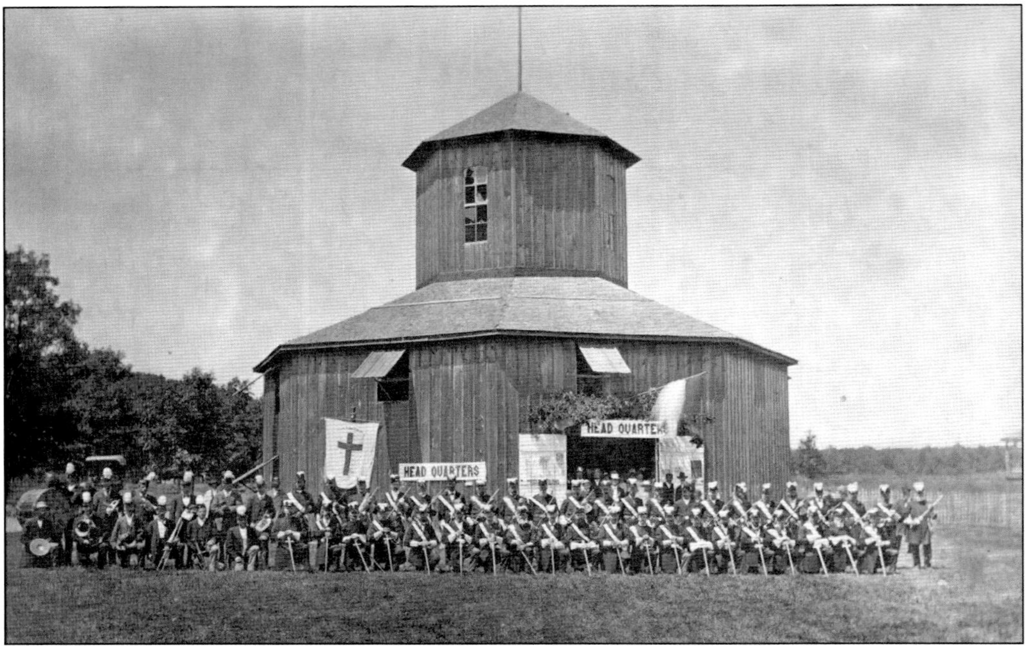

The Knights of Columbus are gathered about an old round barn at the Ogle County Fair, perhaps recruiting. Years later the Knights' offices were located in the more comfortable confines of the Oregon Coliseum. (Courtesy of the *Oregon Republican-Reporter*.)

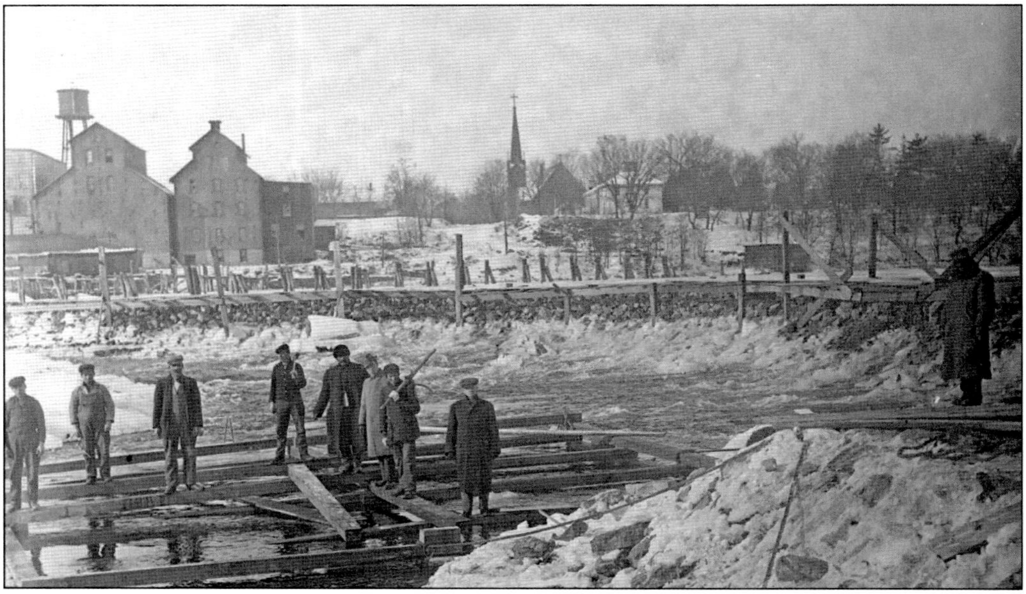

These men construct a wooden crib to be weighted with rocks quarried from the Lime Kiln. The crib was sunk and an apron was then placed over the frame. One man holds a hook used for carrying railroad ties. The buildings on the shoreline are the Oat Mill, Stan Jones's house, St. Mary's spire (pre-lightning), and the Conference Building of the Church of God. This image is c. 1880. (Courtesy of the *Oregon Republican-Reporter*.)

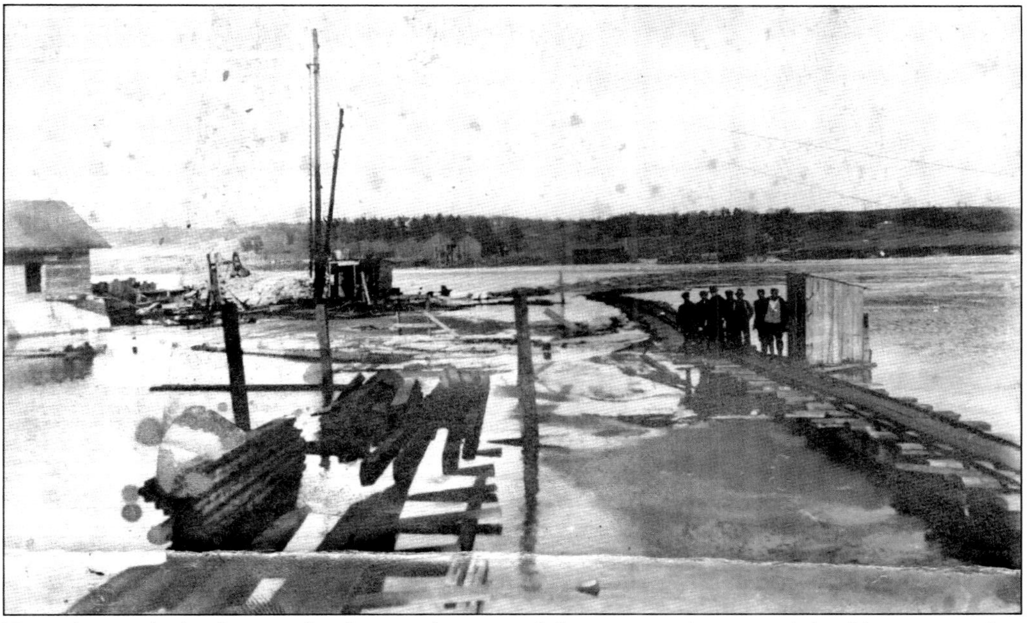

Note the tracks leading to the dam worksite, used for transporting materials. Also present is a small wooden shed, possibly an outhouse, *c.* 1880. Partial funding for the dam was provided by the Mix family. (Courtesy of the *Oregon Republican-Reporter*.)

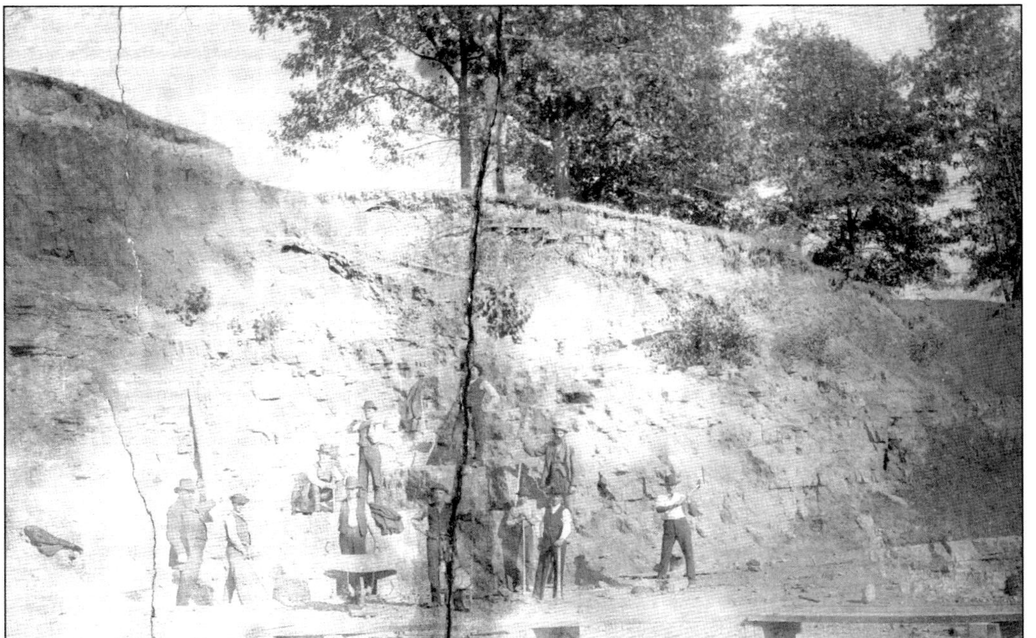

Workmen pause for an 1891 photo at the Lime Kiln atop Liberty Hill. The kiln ceased operating in the 1910s, and now lay in ruins on private property. Stones quarried from this pit were used for the 1892 courthouse foundation. (Courtesy of the *Oregon Republican-Reporter*.)

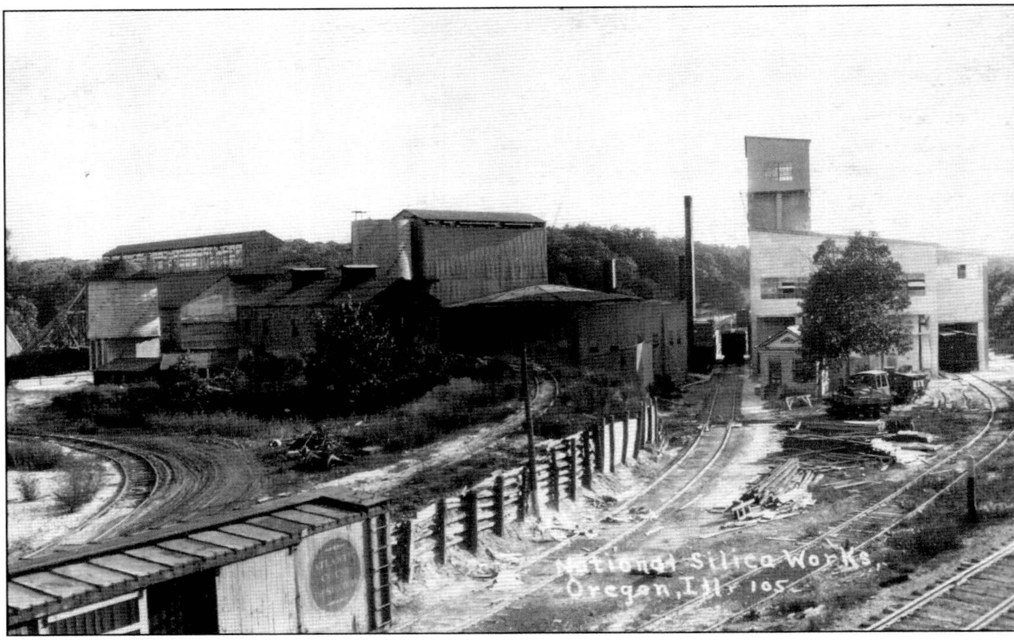

The National Silica Company, c. 1890, south of Oregon, generated millions of tons of flint and sand. Though no longer producing flint, the plant continues to process the silica used as an essential ingredient for ceramics, tiling, soaps, insulators, cosmetics, and many other products. (Courtesy of the *Oregon Republican-Reporter*.)

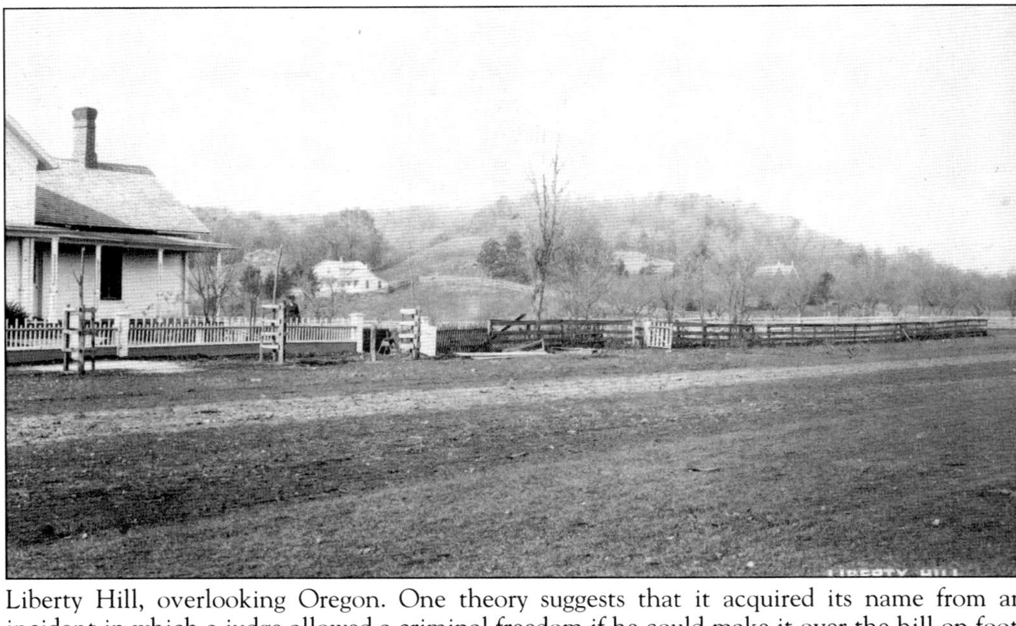

Liberty Hill, overlooking Oregon. One theory suggests that it acquired its name from an incident in which a judge allowed a criminal freedom if he could make it over the hill on foot. Evidently the outlaw succeeded. (Courtesy of the *Oregon Republican-Reporter*.)

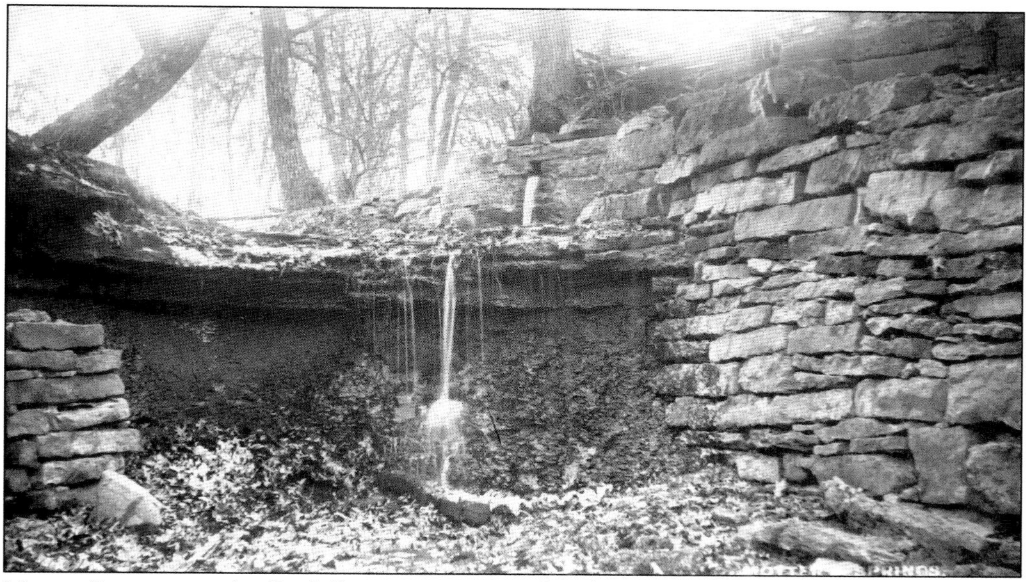

Motter Spring near the Rock River, c. 1890, enclosed with flat stone slabs. (Courtesy of the *Oregon Republican-Reporter.*)

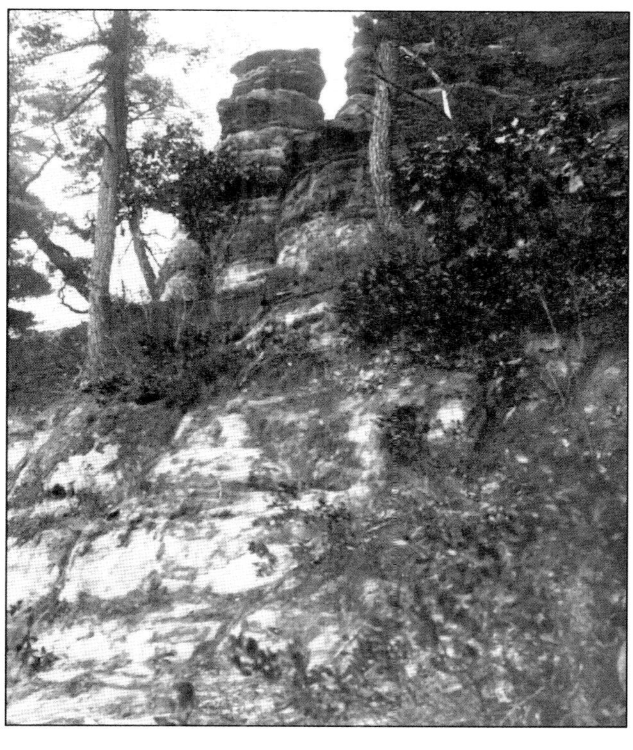

Blackhawk's pulpit, the sandstone outcropping at which the Indian chief supposedly gathered his people. Erosion from wind and water create often fantastic shapes in the stone, with accompanying legends . . . or at least finely spun embellishments of confirmed facts. (Courtesy of the *Oregon Republican-Reporter.*)

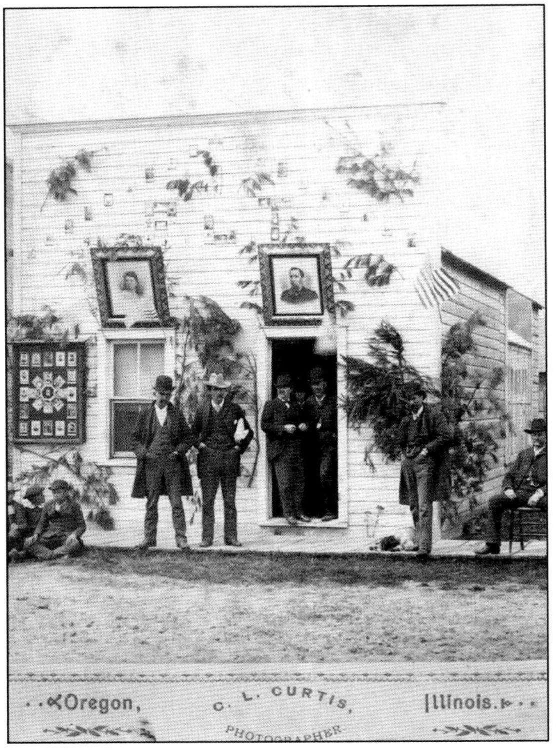

The Charles L. Curtis Photography Studio, 114 North 3rd Street, located south of the Geiken building. Examples of Curtis's handiwork adorn the outside walls. A sailing ship was etched on the front door's frosted glass pane. (Courtesy of the *Oregon Republican-Reporter*.)

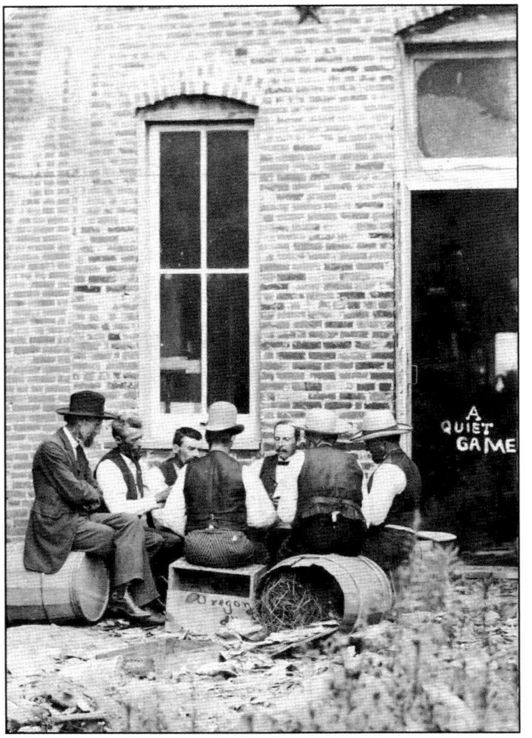

Hardy gents deal their hands, *c.* 1890, behind a shop on Washington St. The photo is entitled *A Quiet Game*, and might function quite satisfactorily as an illustration for a short story by Mark Twain or Bret Harte. The fellow with his back to the camera sits on a crate labeled "Oregon." (Courtesy of the *Oregon Republican-Reporter*.)

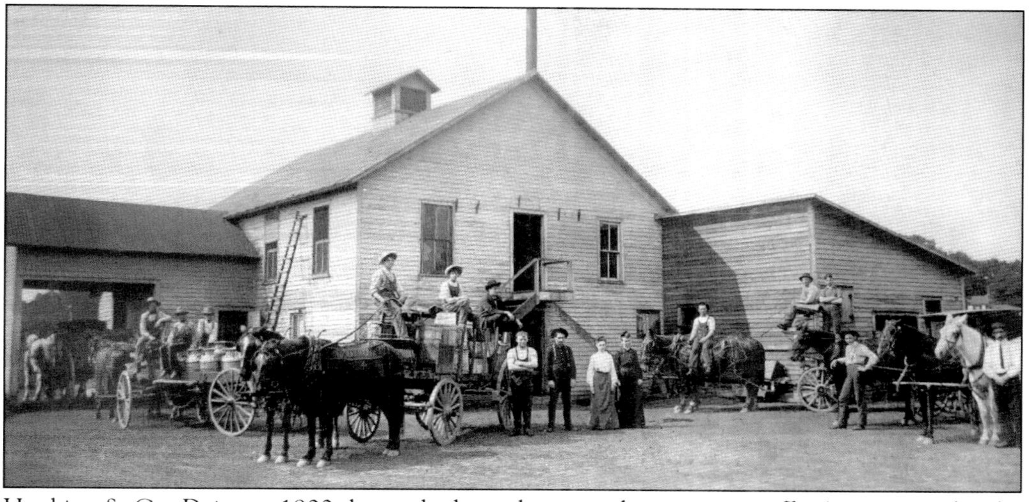

Hopkins & Co. Dairy, c. 1900, located where the city administrative office's now stand. Like the Oat Mill, the creamery derived its business from the proliferation of regional farms. The arrival of the modern Pacific Coast Condensed Milk Company marked a speedy end to the Creamery. (Courtesy of Bob Rees.)

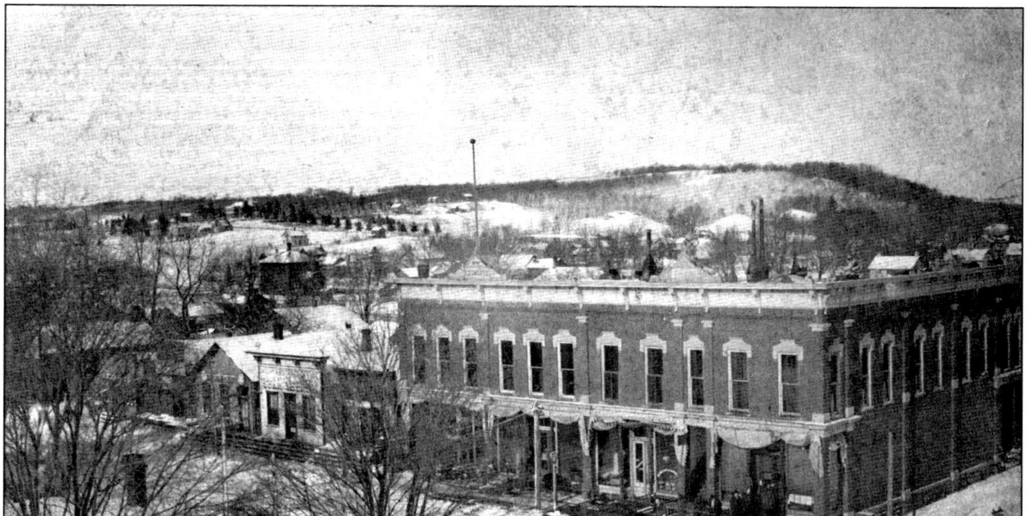

Looking northwest from Union Hall (Opera House) at the Jacobs Block, shortly after a snowfall. Shop awnings are rolled up, and hitching posts positioned in front. Liberty Hill rises gently in the distance. This photograph is c. 1890s. (Courtesy of the *Oregon Republican-Reporter*.)

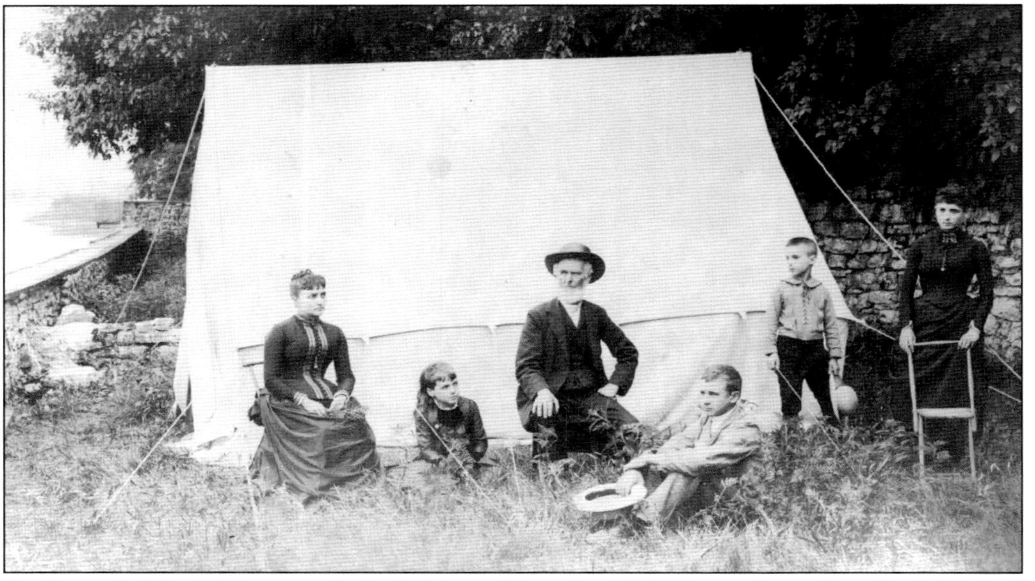

Dr. Henry A. Mix, M.D., sits with the "Chicago Camp," c. 1890. Mix graduated from Rush Medical College in 1864, serving as Assistant Surgeon under General Sherman during the "War of the Rebellion," and later as Surgeon of the Sixty-fourth Illinois Volunteer Infantry. He was considered one of the finest physicians of his day. (Courtesy of the *Oregon Republican-Reporter*.)

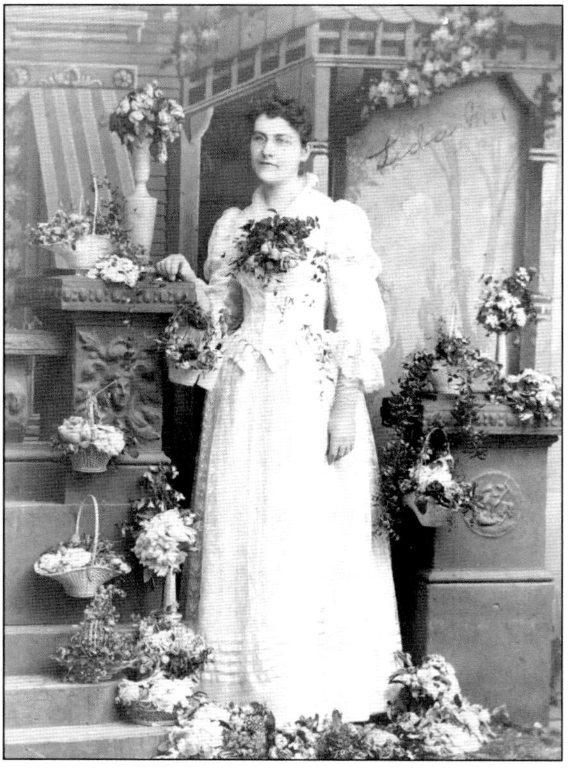

Mrs. Mix attends to her roses. The Mix family were among the oldest and most respected in Oregon, contributing to many philanthropic causes. (Courtesy of the *Oregon Republican-Reporter*.)

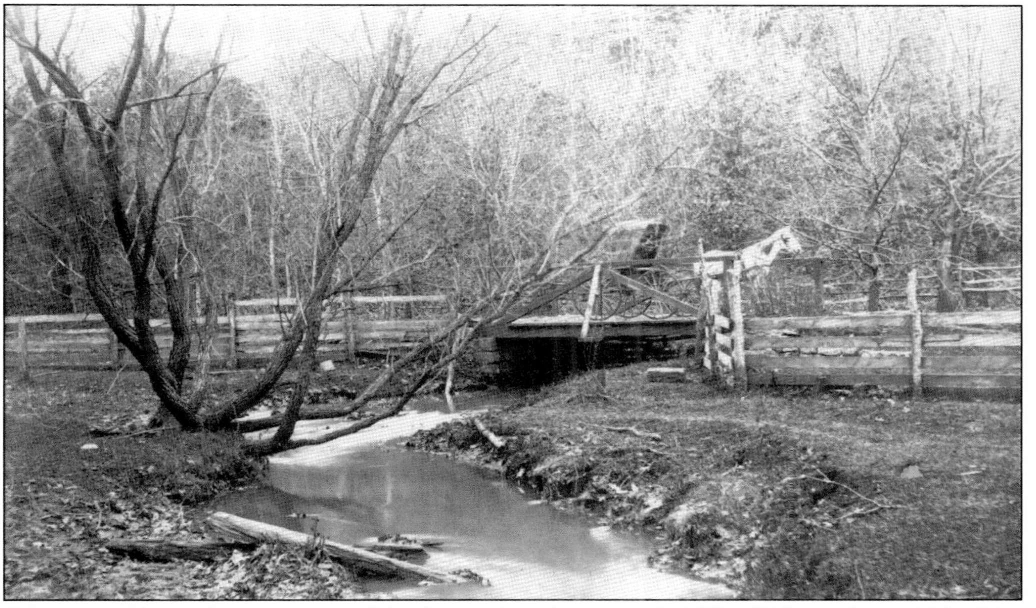

A horse and buggy linger at a small bridge in this photo entitled "On Old Mix Farm." The Mix homestead lay on the Rock River on the northern tip of Oregon. There the renowned Dr. Mix maintained an office, seeing his many patients, also performing autopsies. The property has since been developed. This photograph is *c.* 1900.

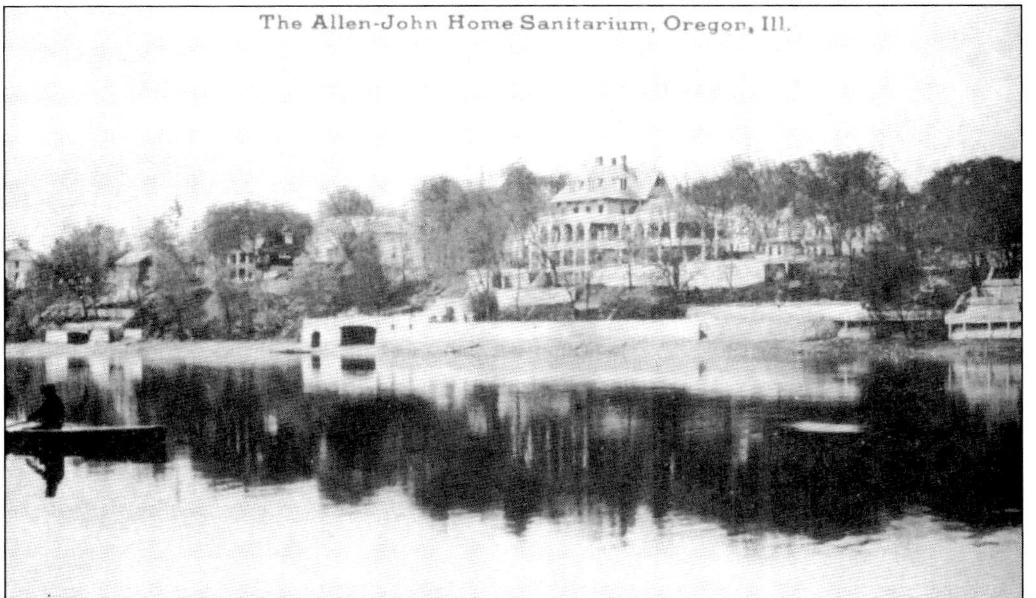

After the Mixes departed, the homestead, built in 1874, became the Allen-John Sanitarium, a facility for patients from Chicago or Rockford recovering from hospital sojourns or other illnesses, such as tuberculosis. The grand mansion has been demolished and the property is now occupied by apartments. (Courtesy of the Ogle County Historical Society.)

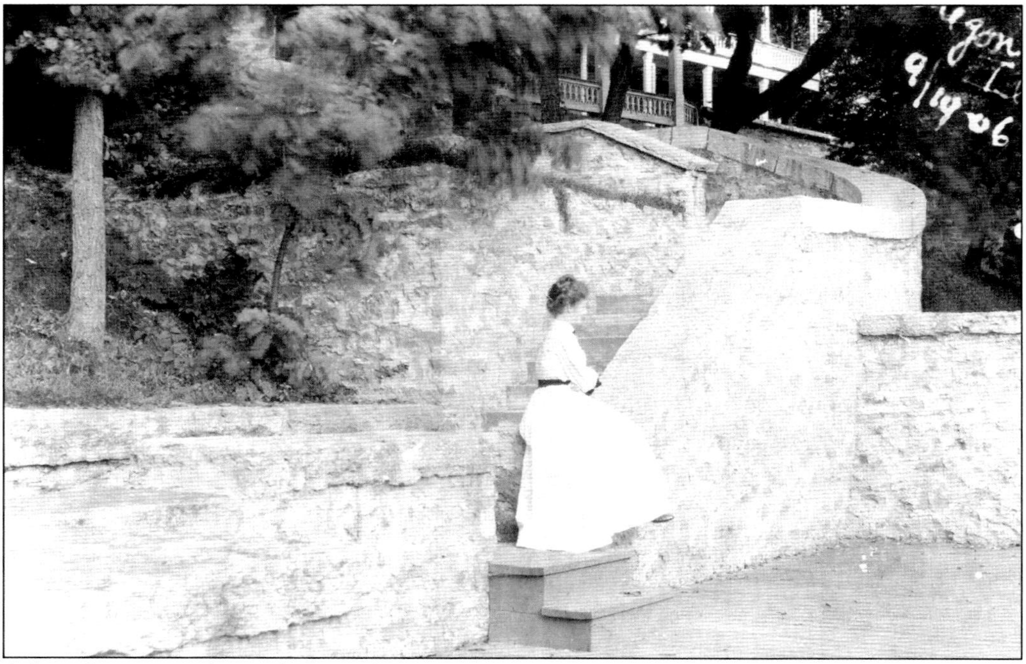

A broad staircase descends from the Mix house to a stone dock on the Rock River. Here the Mixes frequently convened. The mansion and dock are gone, but a few overturned stones remain on the riverbank. (Courtesy Ogle County Historical Society.)

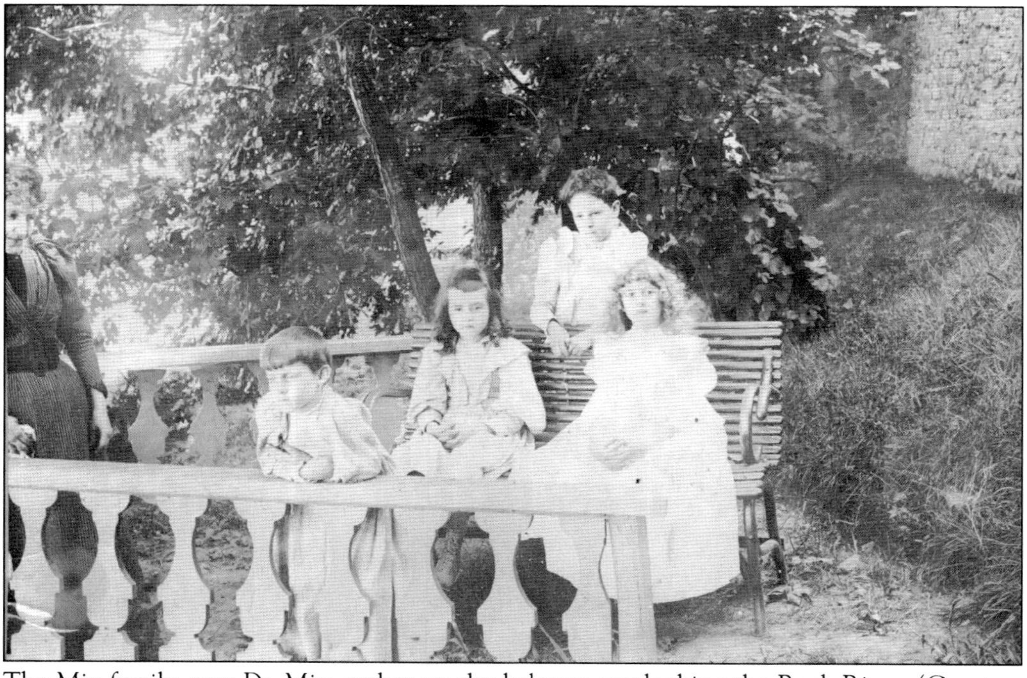

The Mix family, sans Dr. Mix, gather on the balcony overlooking the Rock River. (Courtesy Ogle Co. *Republican-Reporter*.)

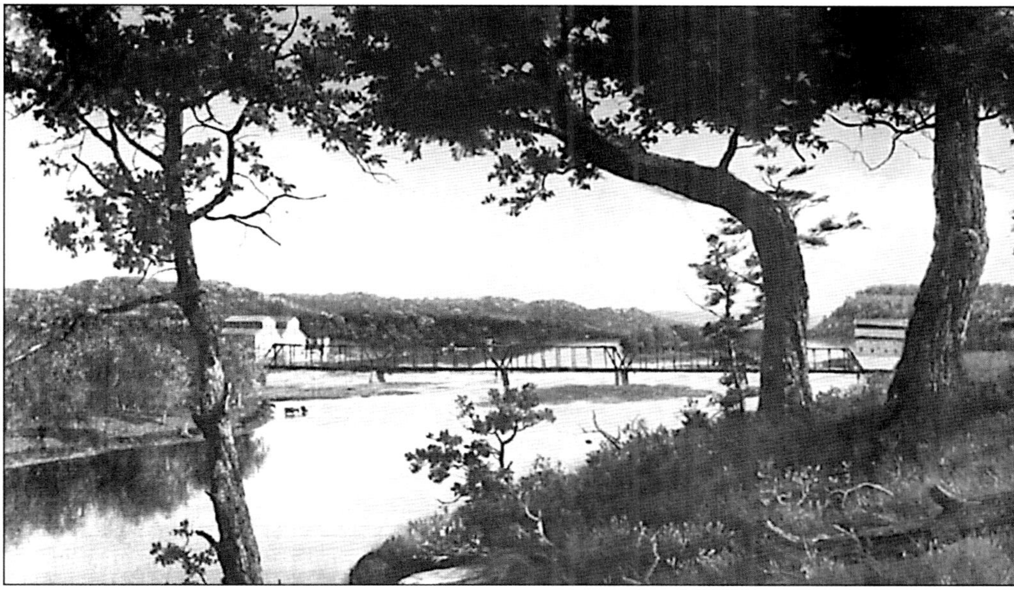

This painting by Henry Howard Bagg (1853–1928), *The Old Bridge (at Oregon)*, shows the Douglass, Stewart and Forrest Oat Mill on the Western bank. The mill provided steady employment, utilizing the fertile farmland surrounding the region. Two cows are seen drinking at the river. The painting is displayed at the Oregon Public Library. (Courtesy of the Arts Alliance of Ogle County.)

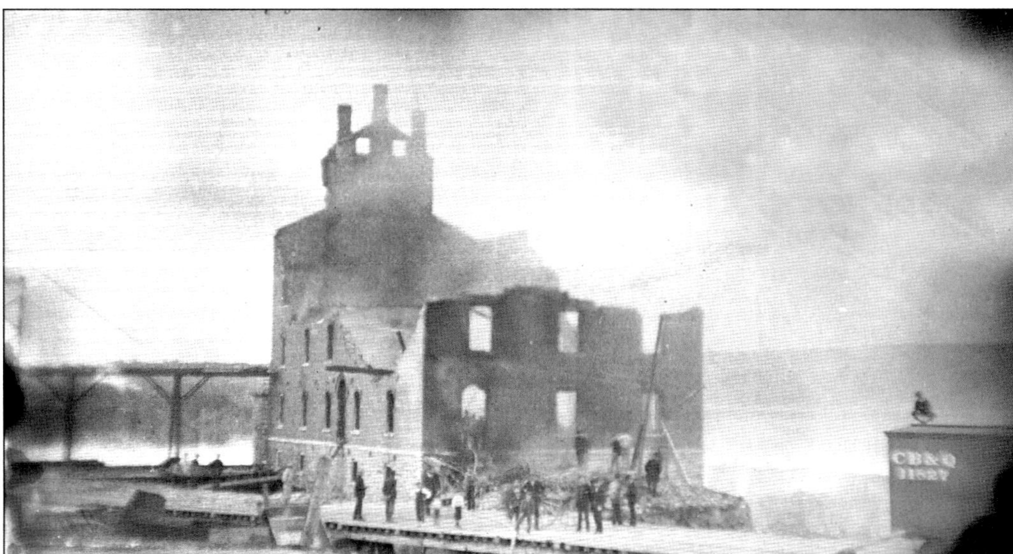

The oat meal mill burns in 1883, the second fire in five years. Firemen were clled all the way from Rochelle, transported to Oregon by train. After the fire entered the second ventilator, "all the hose companies west of Chicago could not have stopped the conflagration then," explained the newspaper. Company foreman Frank Munger dodged a collapsing brink wall, "just in time to save his bacon," the same story reported. (Courtesy *Oregon Republican-Reporter*.)

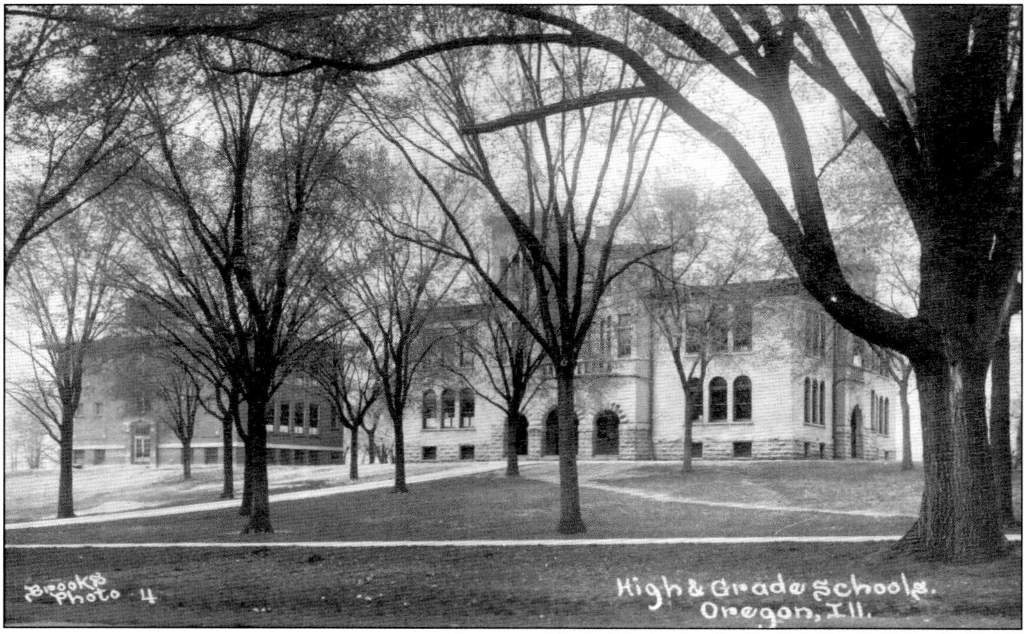

The Oregon School, built in 1896, later named Madison School. Later yet it was re-named Nash Elementary School in honor of Miss Ruby Nash, beloved teacher of first grade who never missed a day. (Courtesy of the Ogle County Historical Society)

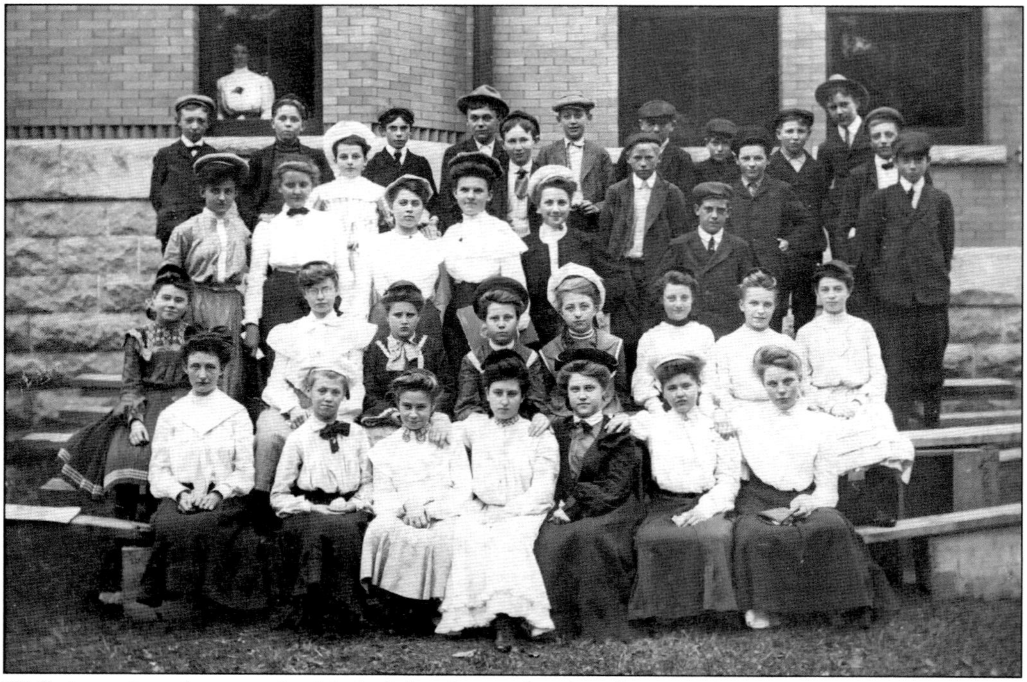

Well-dressed students at the Nash School pose for the photographer on a dangerously sagging plank. The boys are gathered into one group, the girls in another. Note the woman in the window, who may be the teacher. This image is c. 1880. (Courtesy of the *Oregon Republican-Reporter*.)

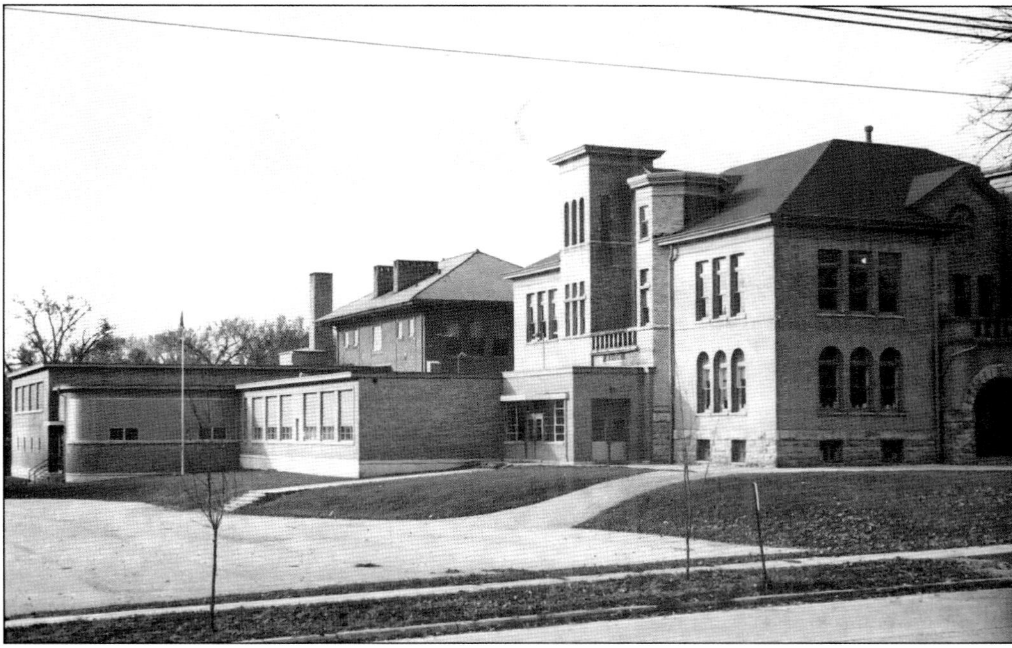

This photo shows Nash School without the cupolas. The original 1896 structure was demolished in 1986, allowing space for expansion and modernization. (Courtesy of the Ogle County Historical Society.)

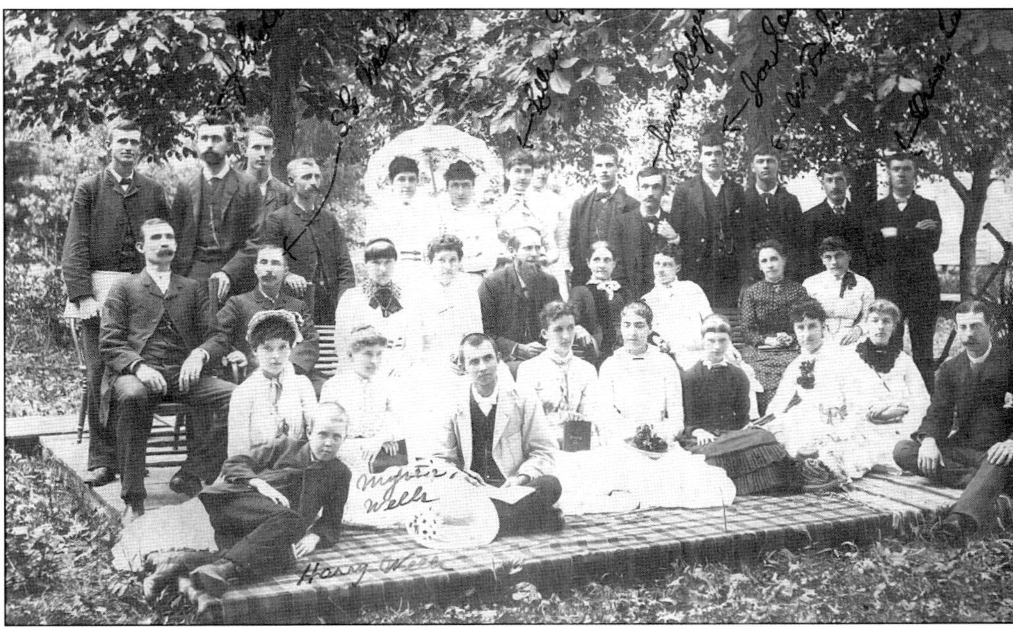

These unidentified men and women attend a teachers' training camp. For generations Oregon has hosted a variety of educational training programs, whether through Northern Illinois University's Taft Field Campus or the availability of other local retreat and camp grounds. This image is c. 1890. (Courtesy of the *Oregon Republican-Reporter*.)

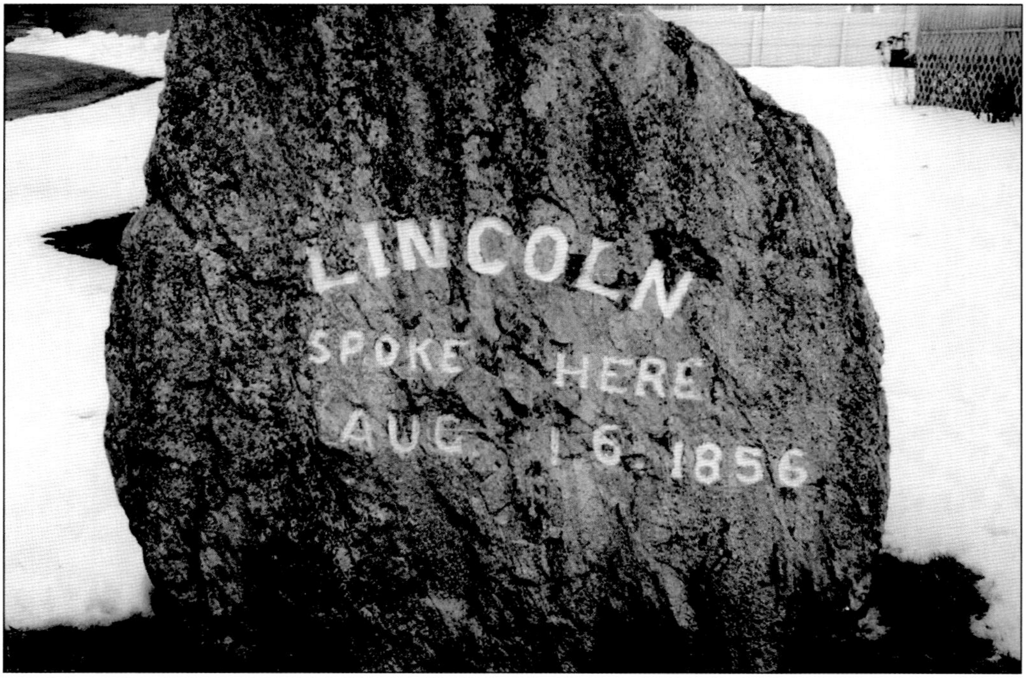

The rock marks the spot where Lincoln debated "Long John" Wentworth, the future mayor of Chicago, who was, at the time, much better known than Lincoln. A wooden platform erected for the lauded event collapsed during a local minister's benediction. Thomas Ferguson, who'd attended the debate, recalled in 1909: ". . . Wentworth turned to Lincoln and said, 'Abe, if you and I had been on that platform with our great load of sin, there would have been little wonder if it went down.'"

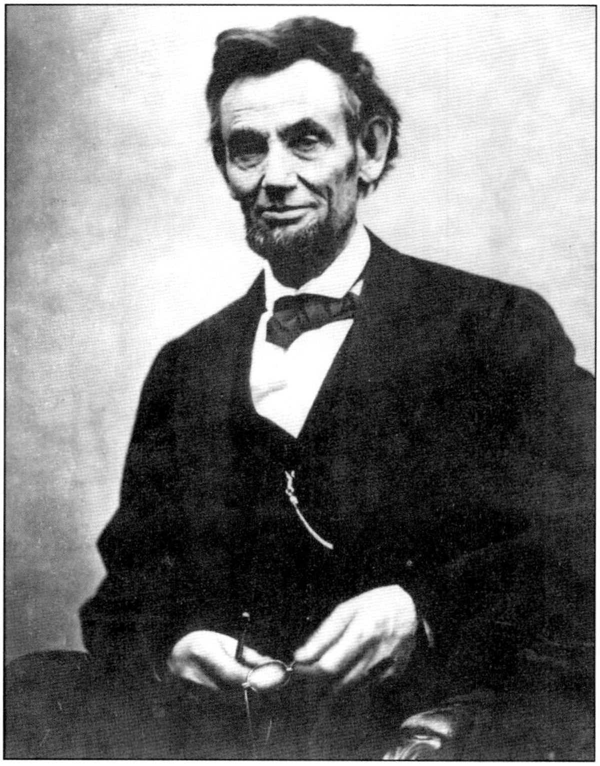

As Lincoln prepared to speak, a plum tree branch irritated his head, so he produced a knife and expertly snipped it. Not surprisingly, eyewitness accounts testify that the lanky logsplitter from Springfield far outshone his opponent and "held his audience spellbound for an hour." Lincoln spent at least two nights in Oregon, a fact proudly touted by the inn at which he supposedly slumbered.

Jonathan Blanchard poses with Mary, his wife. Blanchard, leather-lunged abolitionist and determined educator, served as the first president of Knox College in Galesburg before serving as the first president of Wheaton College, Billy Graham's *alma mater*. Commenting on Blanchard, Carl Sandburg wrote: "He was a lion, a bear, a buffalo, and in the realm of human behavior rated himself half horse and half alligator." (Courtesy of Wheaton College Archives and Special Collections.)

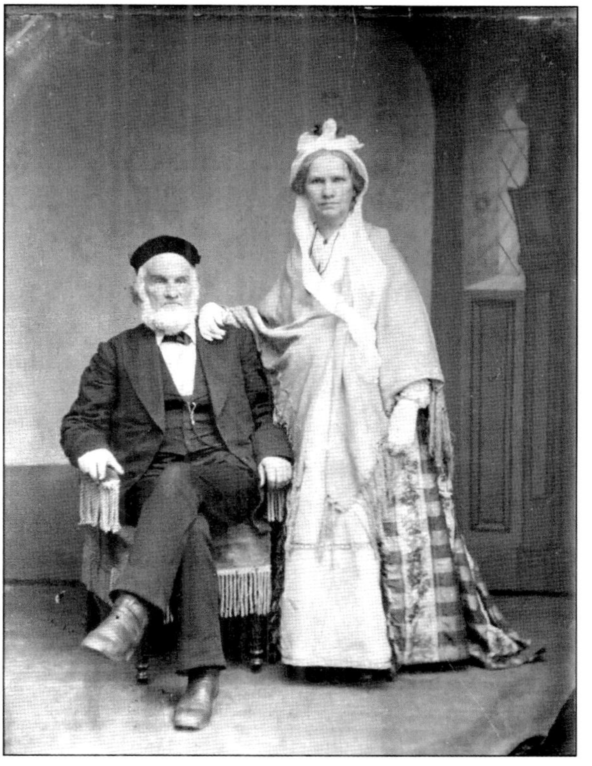

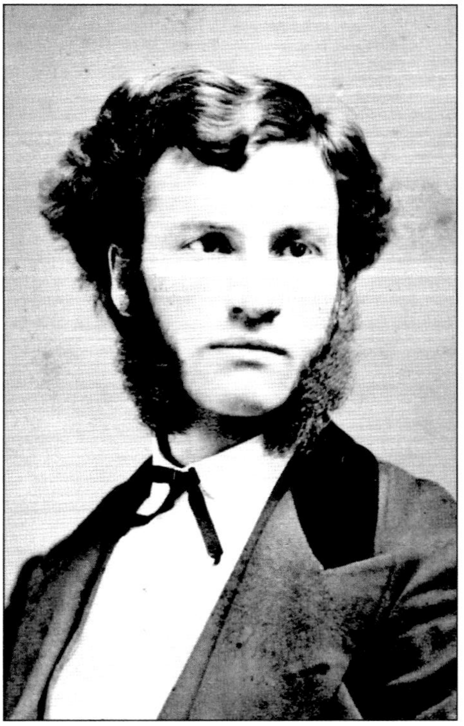

Charles, Jonathan and Mary's son, tilled the fields around Byron, north of Oregon, living with his sister and brother-in-law as he and other family awaited completion of the Blanchard house in Wheaton, Illinois After his father's death, Charles assumed the presidency of Wheaton College, lectured, and authored books. A bold, flexible leader, Blanchard remained deeply loyal to the Christian liberal arts and classical studies program. (Courtesy of Wheaton College Archives and Special Collections.)

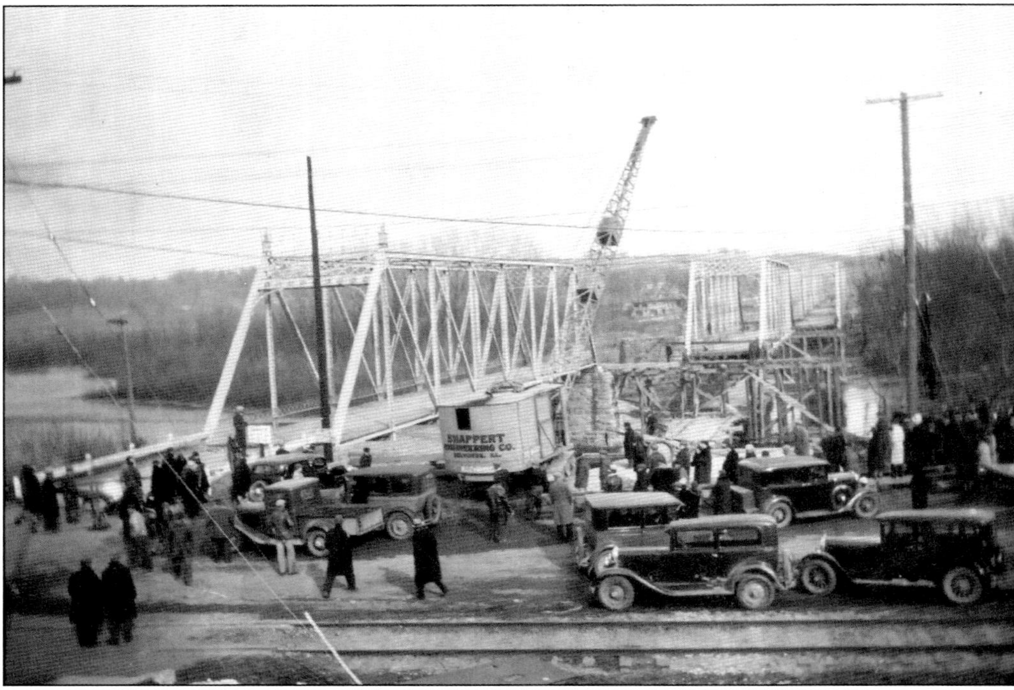

This iron bridge represents the assortment spanning the Rock River in Oregon at various times, including wooden and steel. In the 1920s, pontoons allowed temporary crossing for citizens and supplies while the actual bridge was constructed. (Courtesy of the *Oregon Republican-Reporter*.)

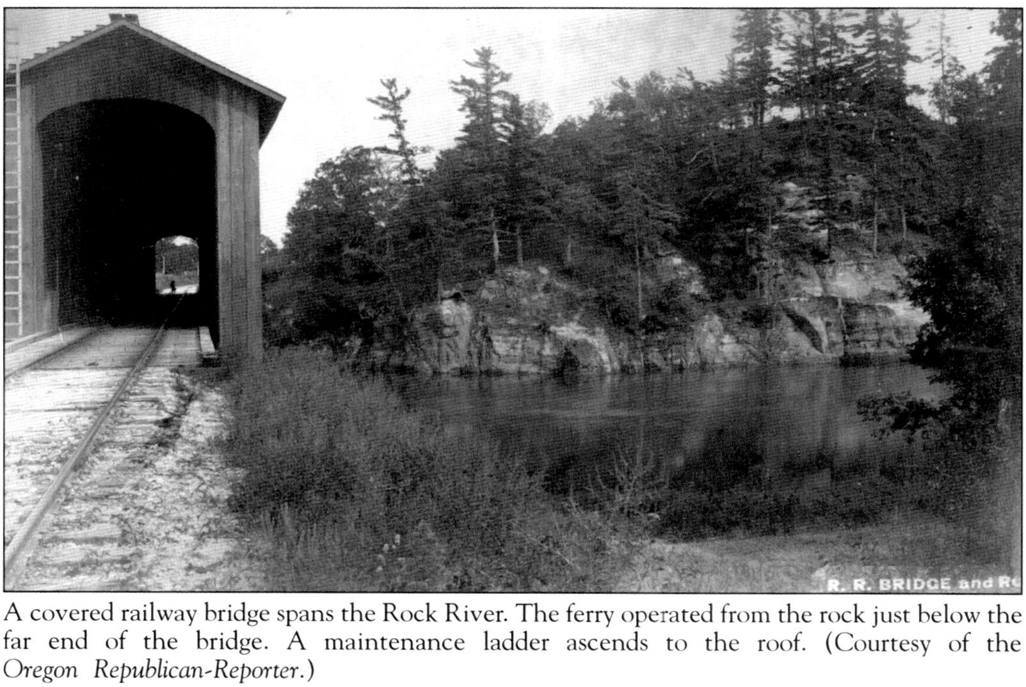

A covered railway bridge spans the Rock River. The ferry operated from the rock just below the far end of the bridge. A maintenance ladder ascends to the roof. (Courtesy of the *Oregon Republican-Reporter*.)

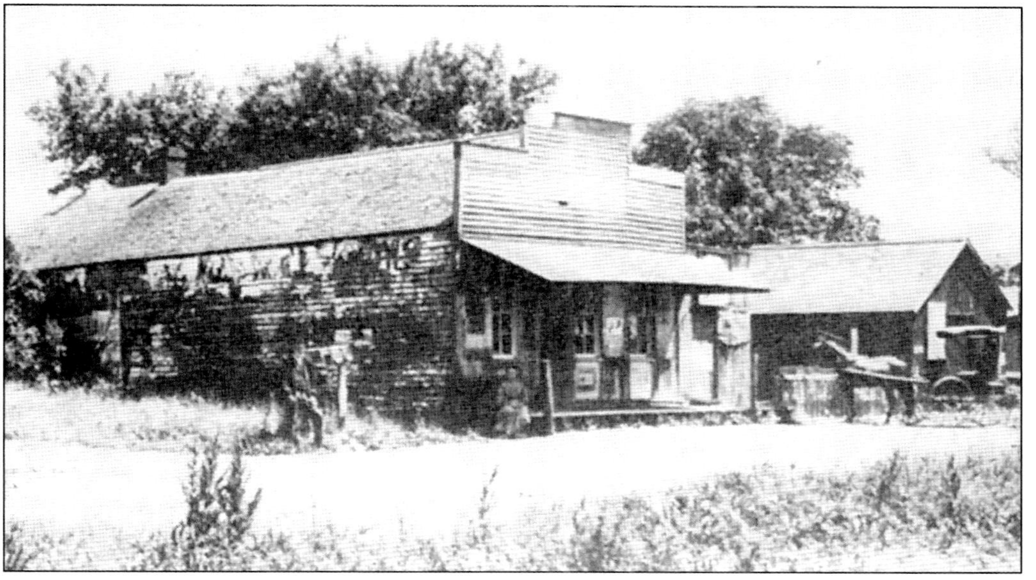

A supply store in Daysville, c. 1890, a small village edging Frank O. Lowden's Sinnissippi Farm. Like nearby Chana and Grand Detour, Daysville did not fare as well as Oregon, lacking its transportational and recreational benefits. (Courtesy of Bob Rees.)

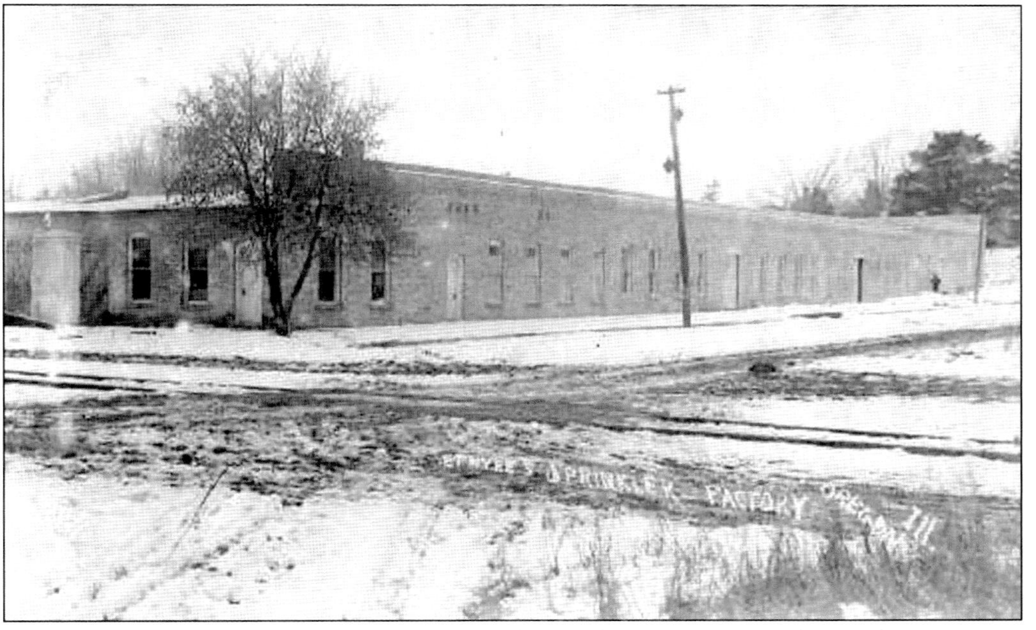

E.D. Etnyre, Inc., founded in 1895 by Edward Daniel Etnyre to manufacture hog-waterers. Throughout the years, Etnyre has expanded to produce tanks and water-sprinklers, "horseless carriages" (very briefly), sprinkling wagons, and asphalt distributors, and many other road maintenance products used throughout the U.S. In WWII, Etnyre built equipment for the military, and was presented with an Army and Navy "E" Award in 1944. (Courtesy of the Ogle County Historical Society.)

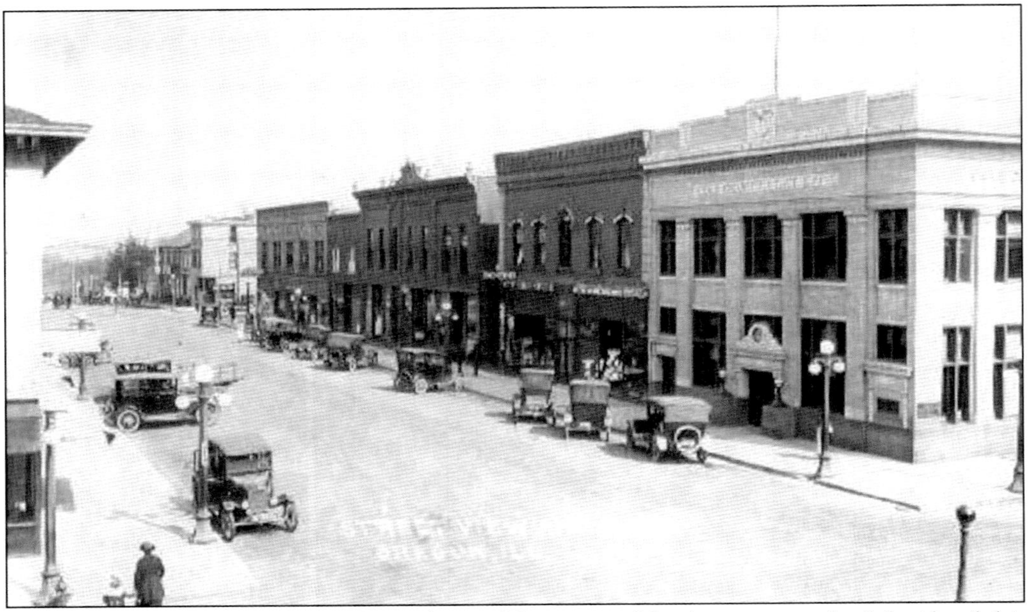

Corner of Washington and Fourth. A sliver of Sinnissippi Hotel is seen on the left side of this c. 1915 photo. The gray stone building on the right, the Ogle County National Bank, was recently reprieved from an Illinois Department of Transportation (IDOT) proposal to either demolish or dramatically alter its exterior to accommodate a roundabout for long trucks experiencing difficulty in turning at this tight intersection. (Courtesy of the *Oregon Republican-Reporter*.)

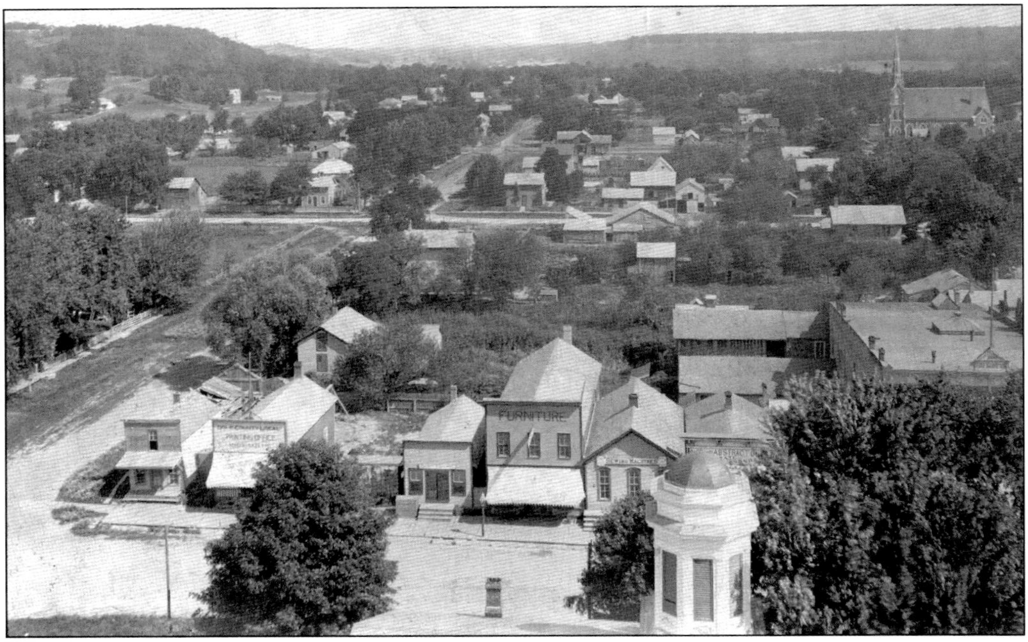

Looking northwest from the courthouse, c. 1895, at Washington Street and beyond. St. Mary's Catholic Church is seen to the right, still sporting the high spire later struck and toppled by lightning. (Courtesy of the *Oregon Republican-Reporter*.)

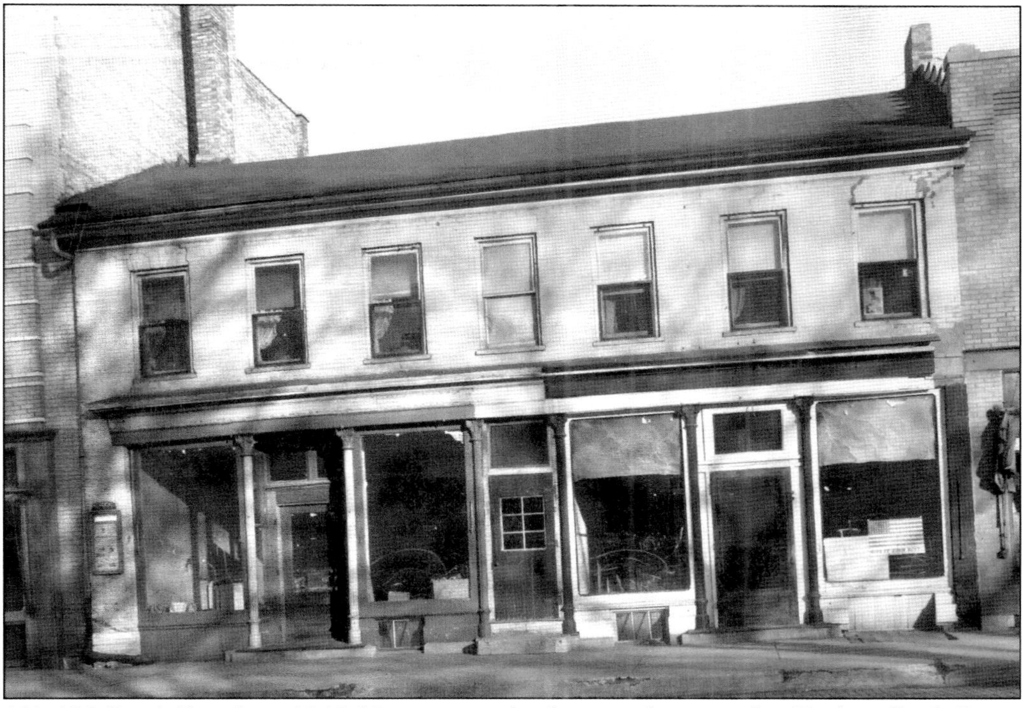

121–123 South Fourth, *c.* 1940. Here empty, this location has served as Fischers Book Store, Clifford and Bryson toymakers, a Piggly Wiggly grocery; Charles Lamb Firestone Store, Oregon Home Appliance, an insurance agency, and, most recently, a restaurant. In 1947, the façade was remodeled with stone facing. Note the cobbled street. (Courtesy of the *Oregon Republican-Reporter*.)

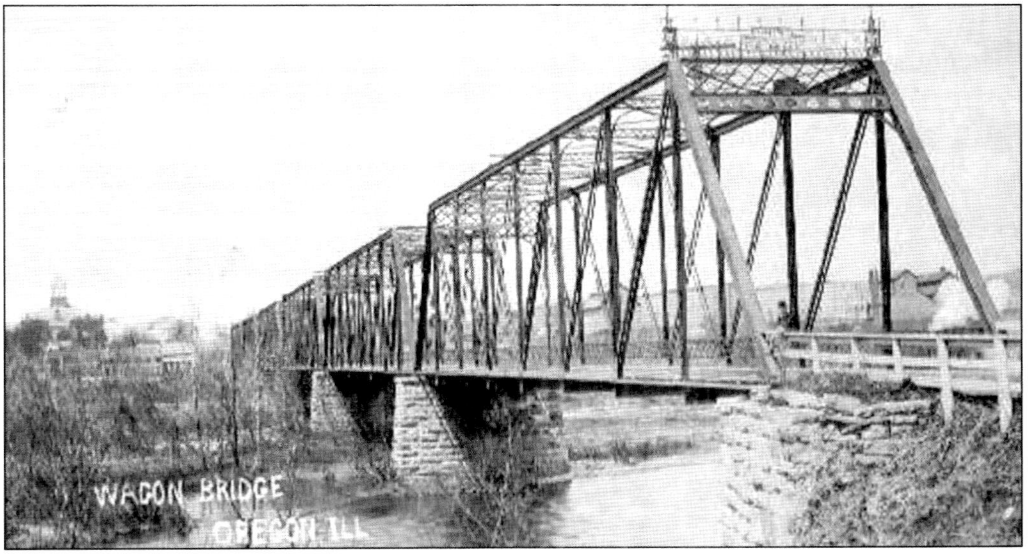

The first wagon bridge over the Rock River. To the left is the courthouse tower. (Courtesy of Bob Rees.)

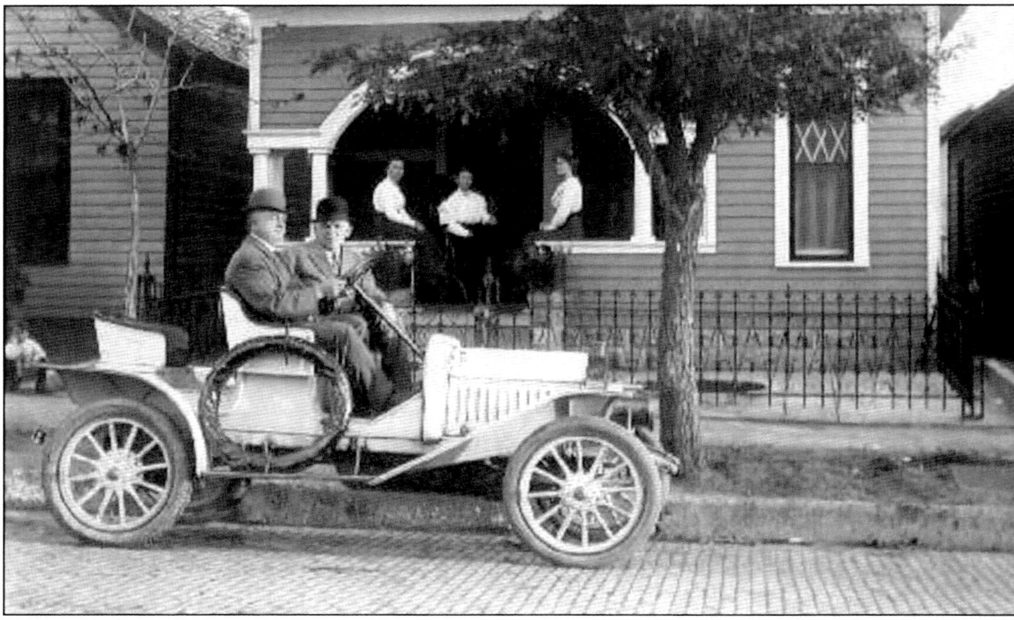

Mill and Elwood Knauss out for a ride, *c.* 1910. (Courtesy of the Ogle County Historical Society.)

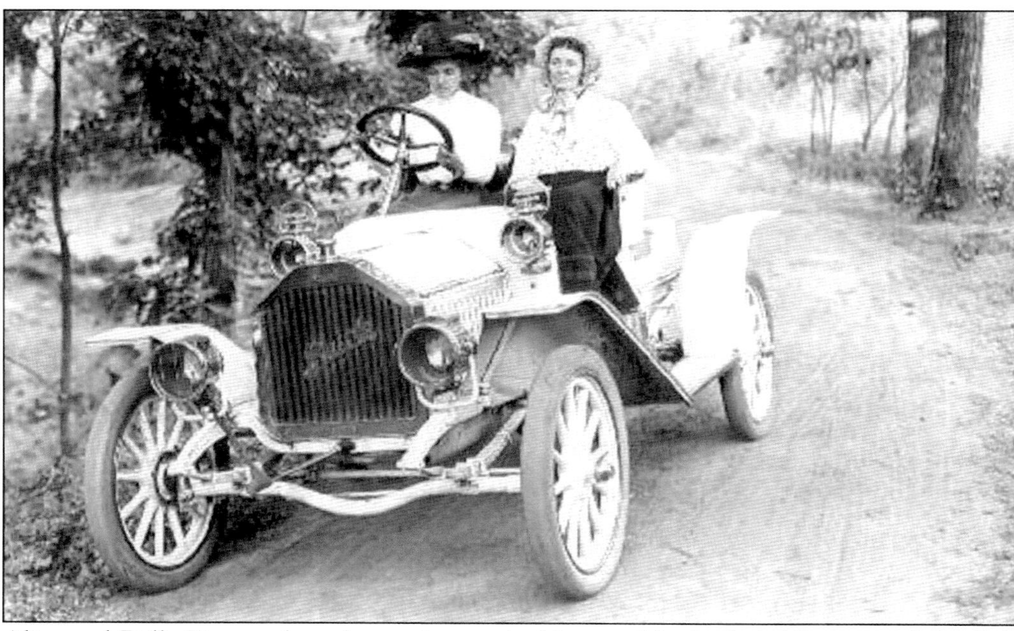

Alice and Della Knauss also take a spin, not looking terribly thrilled. (Courtesy of the Ogle County Historical Society.)

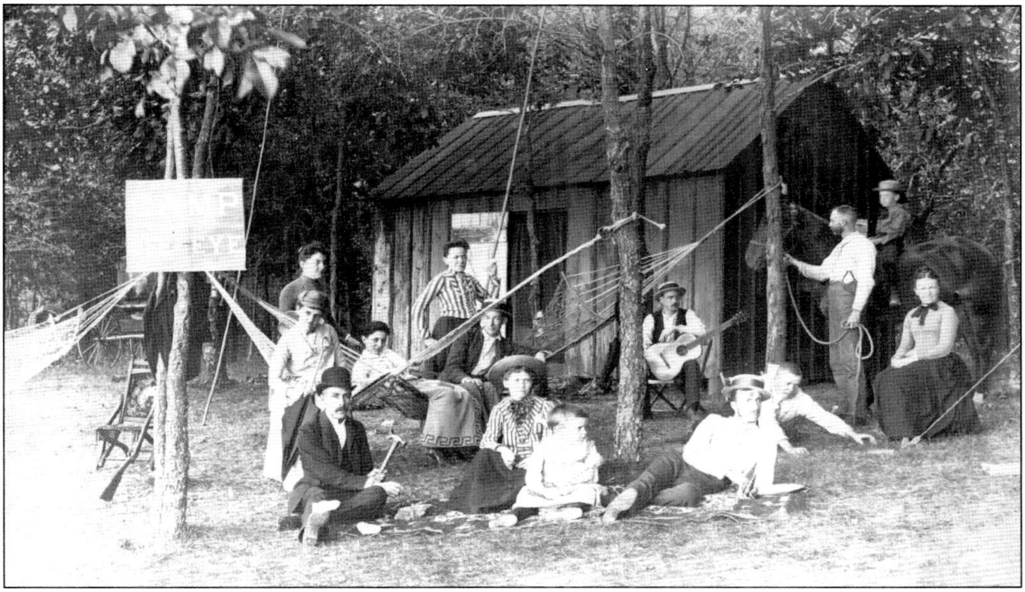

These unidentified folks attend "Camp See & Eye," probably a company picnic for vacationing C & I (Chicago and Iowa Railroad) employees, *c.* 1890. (Courtesy of the *Oregon Republican-Reporter.*)

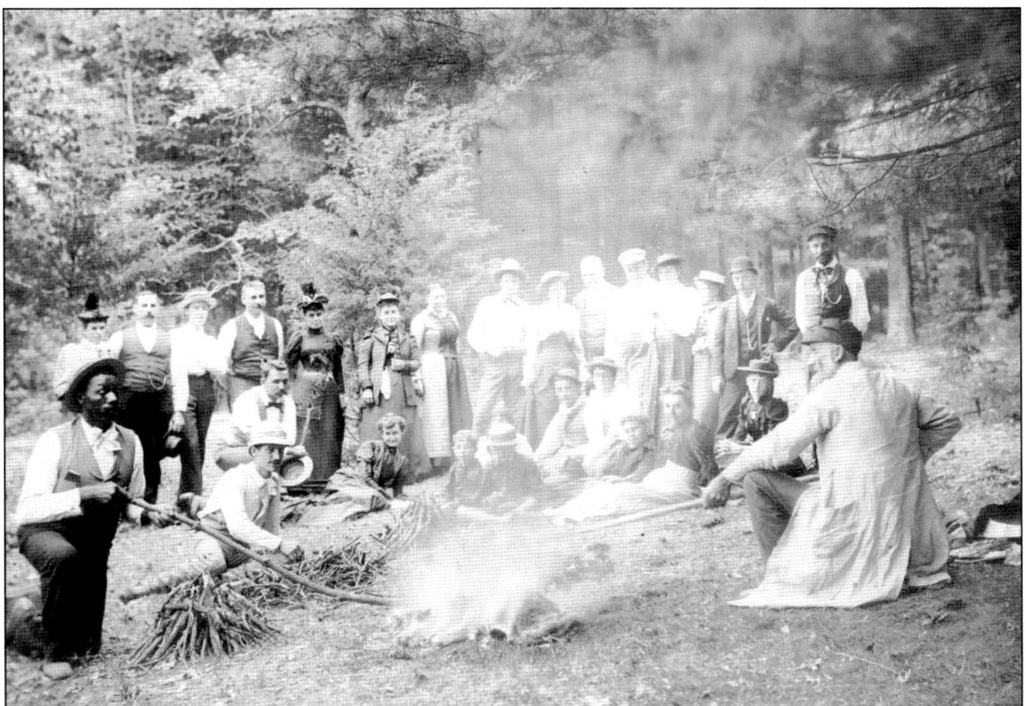

More unidentified campers tending a fire. They represent one camp among countless others using the beautiful land in the Sinnissippi valley. This image is *c.* 1880. (Courtesy of the *Oregon Republican-Reporter.*)

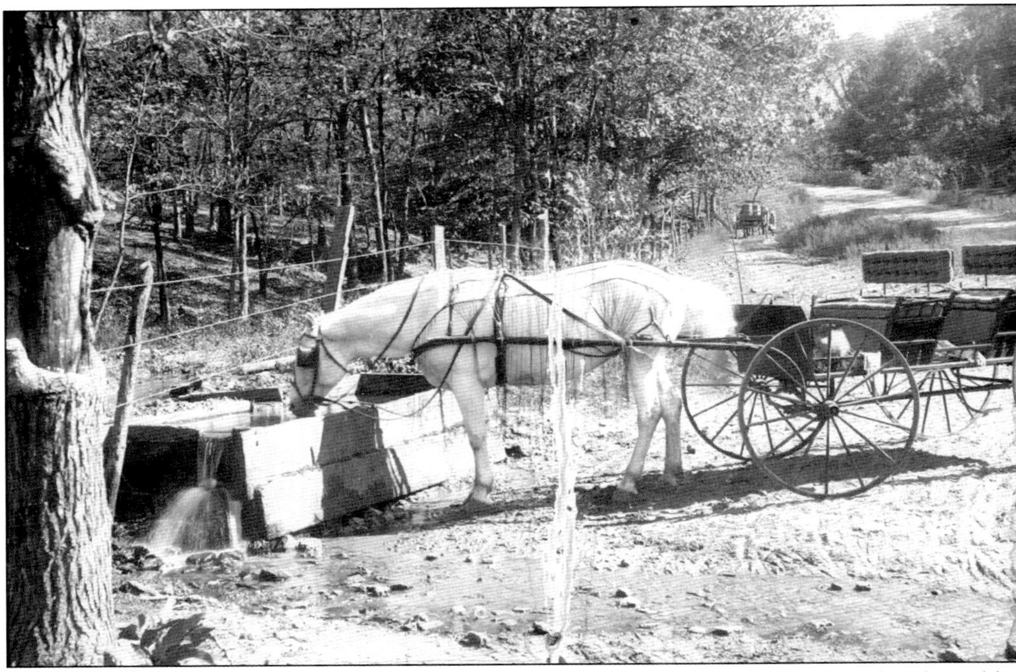

Lawyer J.C. Seyster's magnificent horse drinks from a trough, *c.* 1900. Note the deeply padded seats on the surrey, as close to shock absorbers as the era allowed. (Courtesy of the *Oregon Republican-Reporter.*)

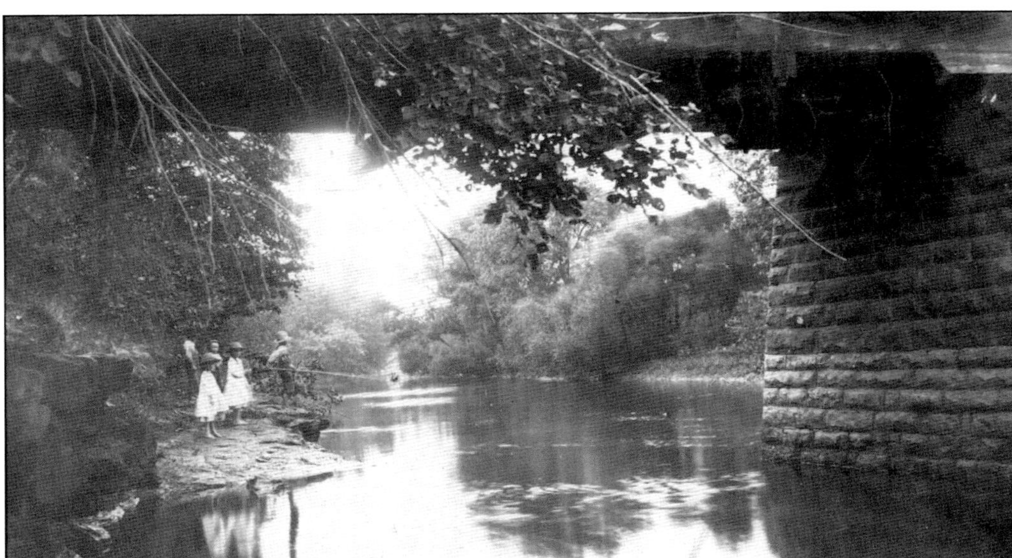

Kyte Creek flows under the stone bridge at Daysville Road, southeast of Oregon. The Kyte is making its way to the Rock River, which subsequently empties into the Mississippi. In this *c.* 1910 photo, visitors enjoy the peace and scenery, and a bit of fishing. (Courtesy of the *Oregon Republican-Reporter.)*

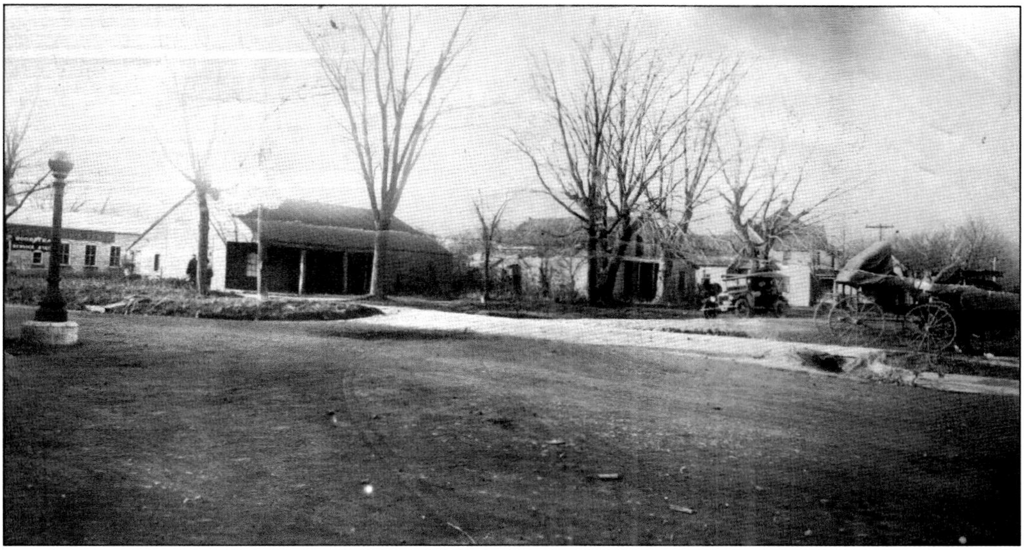

Here stood two frame dwellings, one a rented residence, the other the home of Jonas Seyster, c. 1912. Both buildings were burned to the ground in 1918 when ecstatic Oregonians celebrated the end of WWI and the signing of the Armistice. The new post office was constructed near this sight. (Courtesy of the *Oregon Republican-Reporter*.)

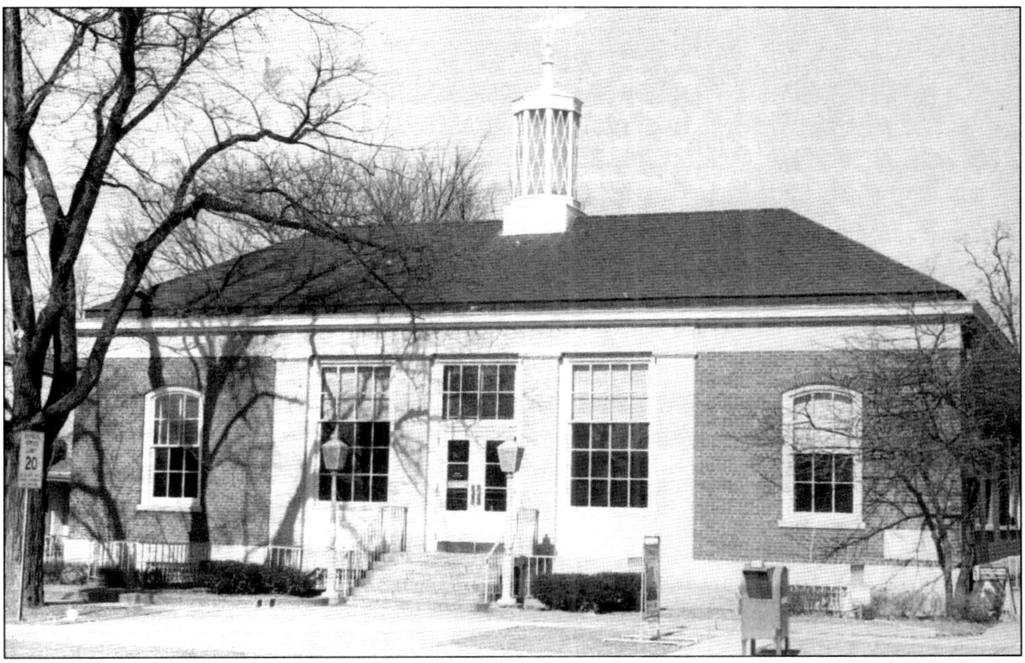

The new post office at the corner of Washington and Fifth, dedicated in November 1939, by Frank H. Ellis, Superintendent of the Division of Post office service bureau of the First Assistant Postmaster General. The assembly of 300 lunched at the Oregon Coliseum before the event. "There is no finer barometer to business and progress," said speaker Ellis, "than the postal receipts of a community." This photograph is c. 1960.

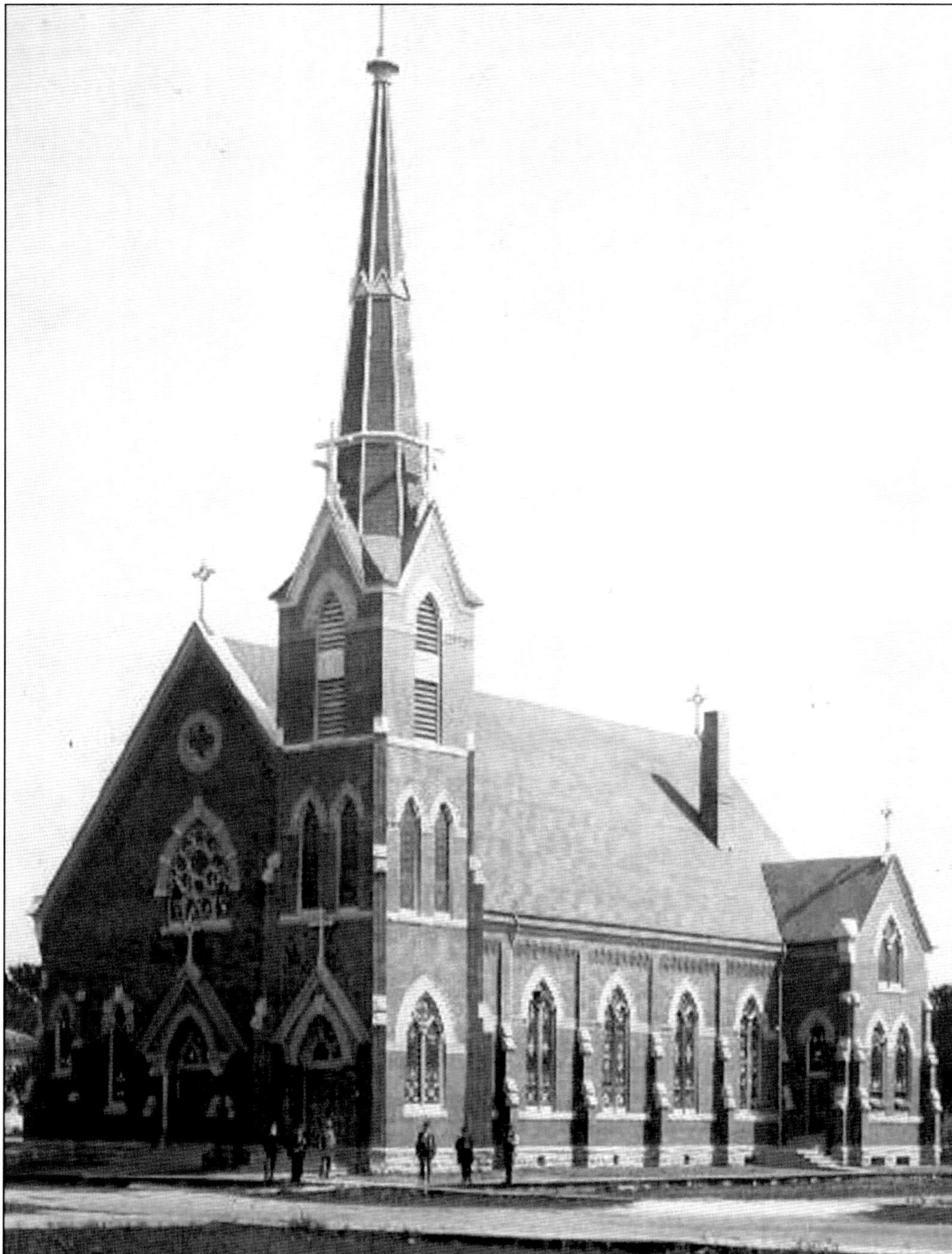

Catholic worship in Oregon began in 1833 when a priest began to visit the valley. In 1862, parishioners raised $1,600 for a small stone church near the river, later purchased by the Church of God. In 1891, Father Toomey raised $17,000 for the St. Mary's, which lost its spire to a bolt of lightning. The truncated tower is now capped a few feet above the roof's apex. (Courtesy of Bob Rees.)

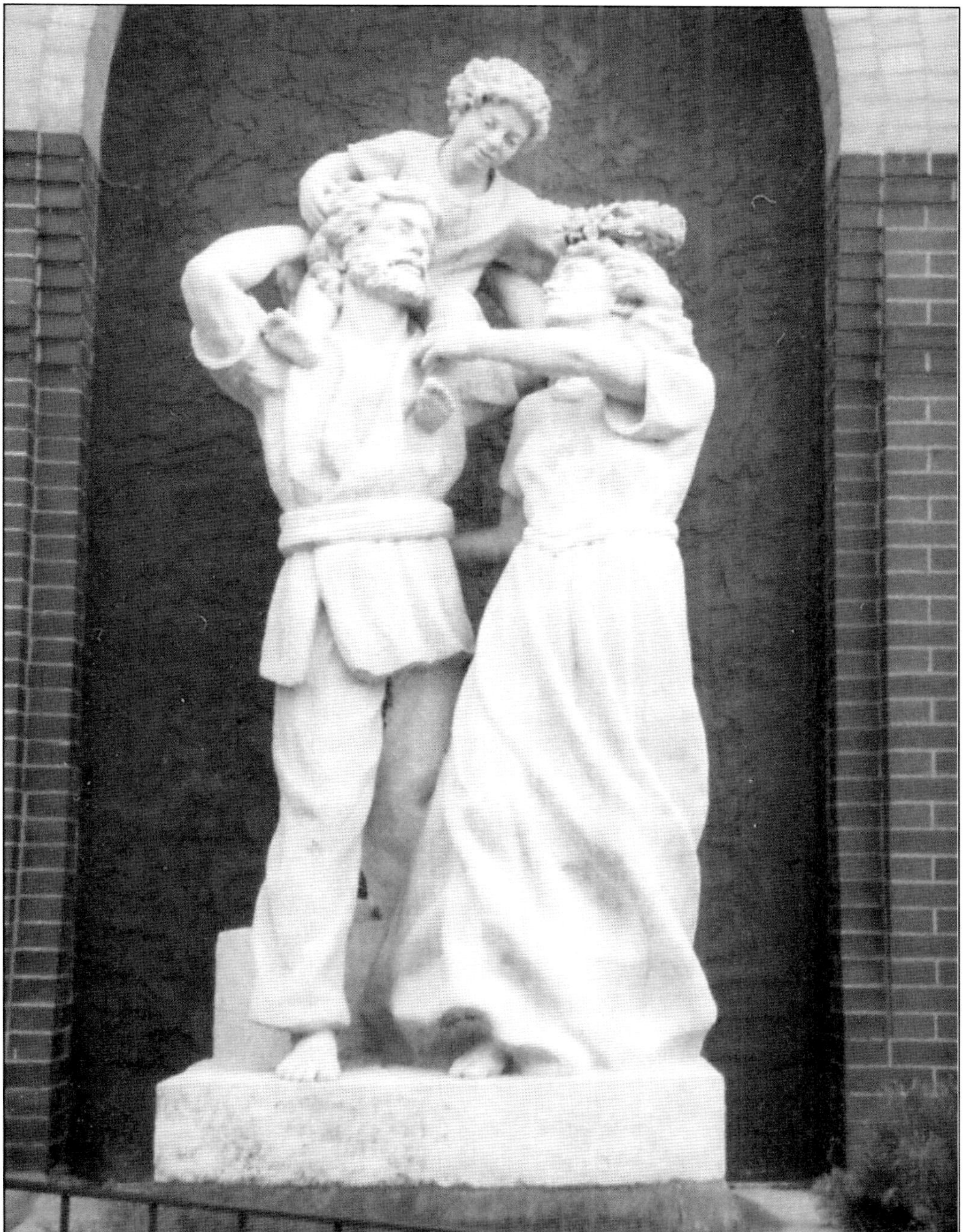

This nine-foot statue depicting the Holy Family stands in front of the Church of St. Mary at the corner of Route 2 and Monroe, and is positioned before a blocked doorway at the base of the steeple tower. The Christ Child places a wreath of lilies on the Blessed Mother's head. It was sculpted by David Seagraves from a 3 1/2 ton block of Indiana limestone, requiring 2 1/2 years to complete. The Holy Family was presented in conjunction with the centennial celebration and renovation of St. Mary's in 1991.

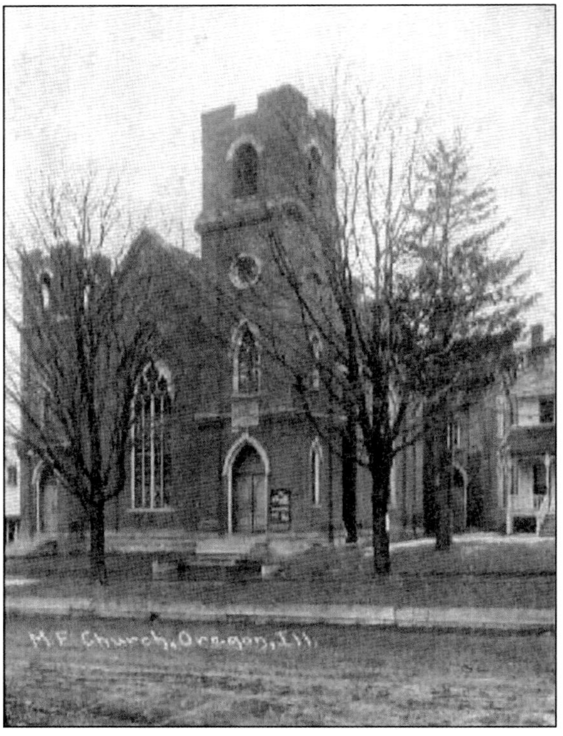

The first Methodist Episcopal Church was located at 200 S. 3rd, pastored by Rev. Henry L. Martin. The second, present structure, c. 1930, was built in 1874 with an annex added in 1952, stands at 200 S. 4th, now called The United Methodist Church. The parsonage on the right was moved when the church was renovated. (Courtesy of the *Oregon Republican-Reporter.*)

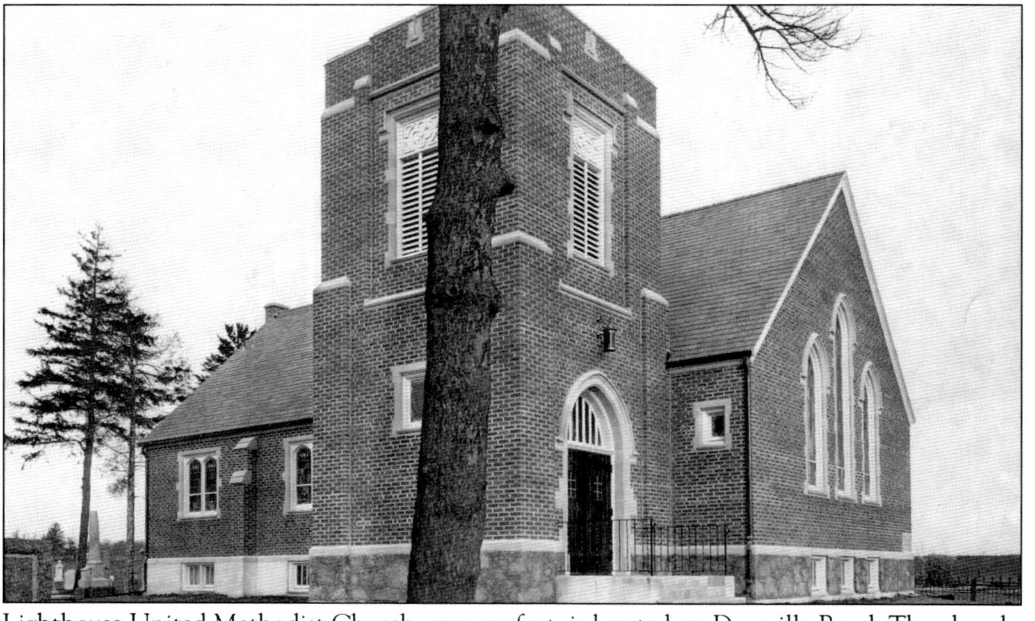

Lighthouse United Methodist Church, gem-perfect, is located on Daysville Road. The church, with its accompanying graveyard, assumes its name from Dr. Roe, a sometime preacher who in the 1830s set a candle in his window to guide lonely prairie schooners as they traversed Ogle County on dark nights. Lighthouse United Methodist remains an active worshipping assembly in the Rock River valley. (Courtesy of the *Oregon Republican-Reporter.*)

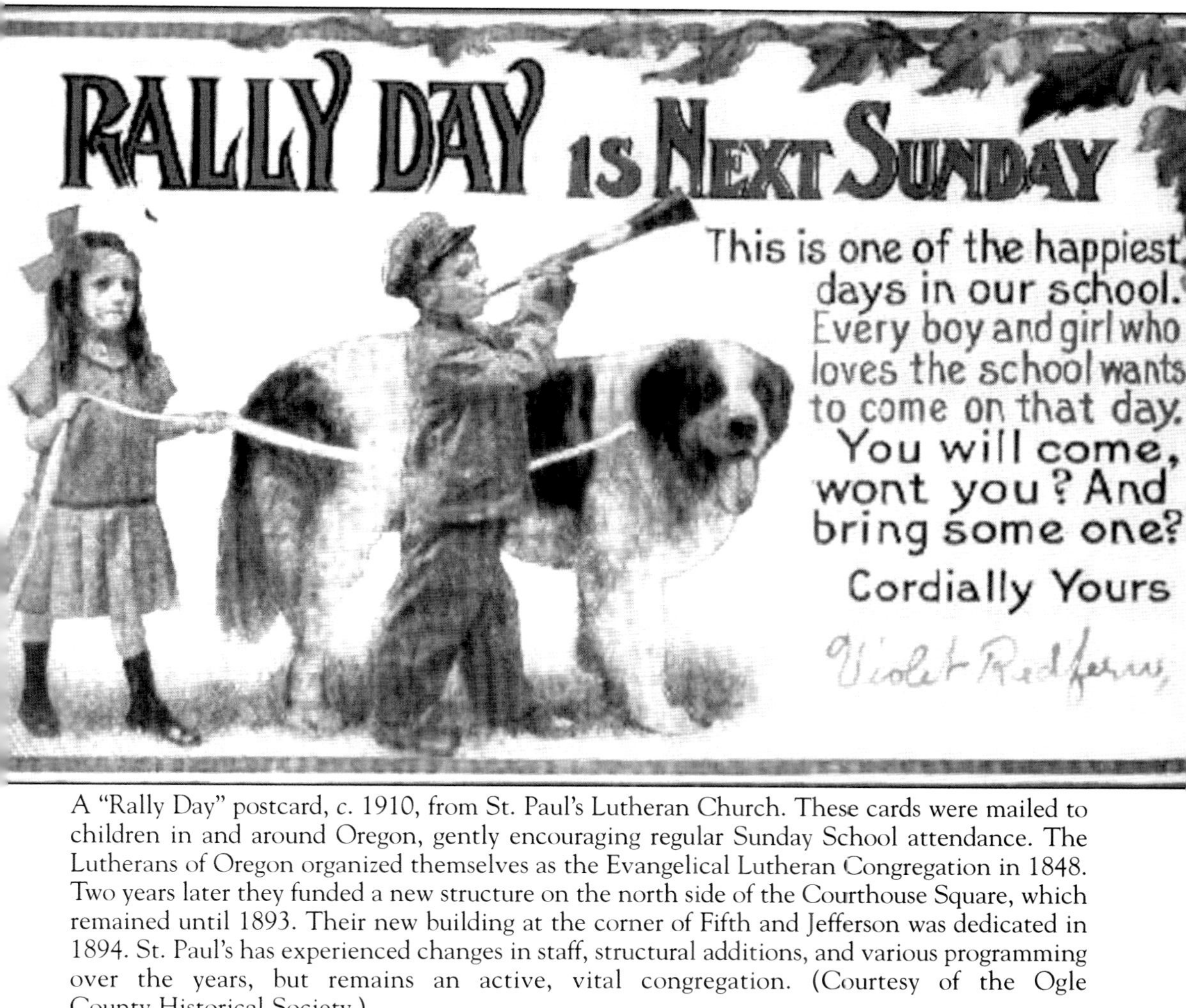

A "Rally Day" postcard, *c.* 1910, from St. Paul's Lutheran Church. These cards were mailed to children in and around Oregon, gently encouraging regular Sunday School attendance. The Lutherans of Oregon organized themselves as the Evangelical Lutheran Congregation in 1848. Two years later they funded a new structure on the north side of the Courthouse Square, which remained until 1893. Their new building at the corner of Fifth and Jefferson was dedicated in 1894. St. Paul's has experienced changes in staff, structural additions, and various programming over the years, but remains an active, vital congregation. (Courtesy of the Ogle County Historical Society.)

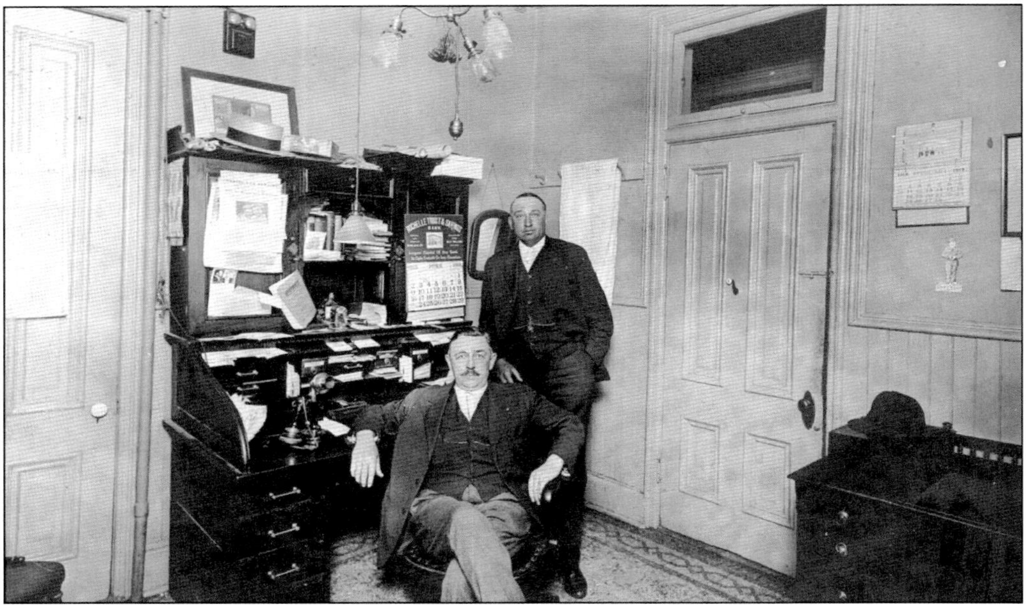

William Mackey (seated), and Deputy George Banning in the jail office, rather elegantly Italianate-styled. The jail, described as "one of the handsomest of its type," stood on the corner where the present courthouse parking lot is located. (Courtesy of the *Oregon Republican-Reporter*.)

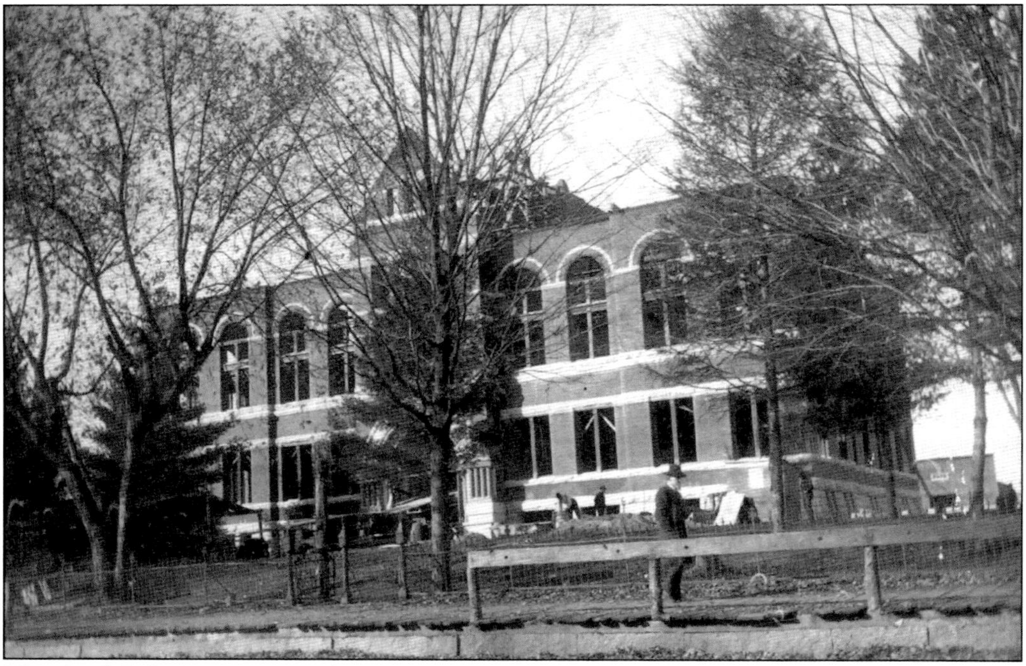

The third Ogle County Courthouse is pictured under construction in 1892. The first building was burned by the Driscoll gang, hoping to destroy incriminating indictments and free a few pals-in-crime. Alas, a clerk had taken the records home for the evening and the gang was unsuccessful. The second courthouse, constructed in 1848 for $3,000, was demolished to create space for the present structure. (Courtesy of the *Oregon Republican-Reporter*.)

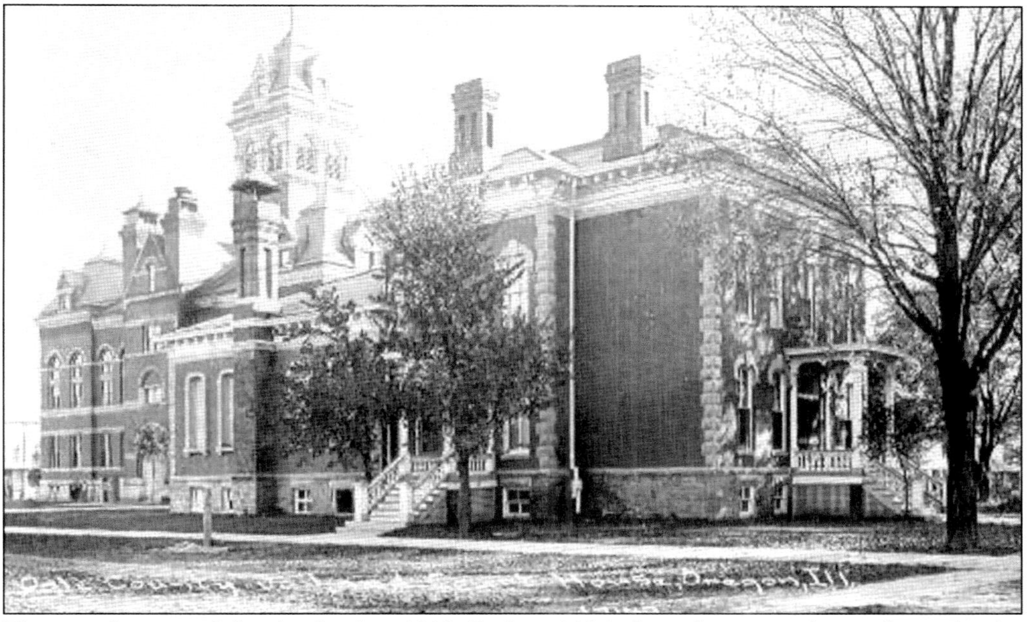

The courthouse and the third jail, c. 1900. Built in 1874, the jail contained a residence for the sheriff and his family on the first and second floors, with a hardwood staircase spiraling to the landing. Males were jailed in cells on the first floor, with females on the second. Each cell contained a window, and prisoners often teased passers-by. The jailhouse cook was often the wife or daughter of the sheriff. (Courtesy of the *Oregon Republican-Reporter*.)

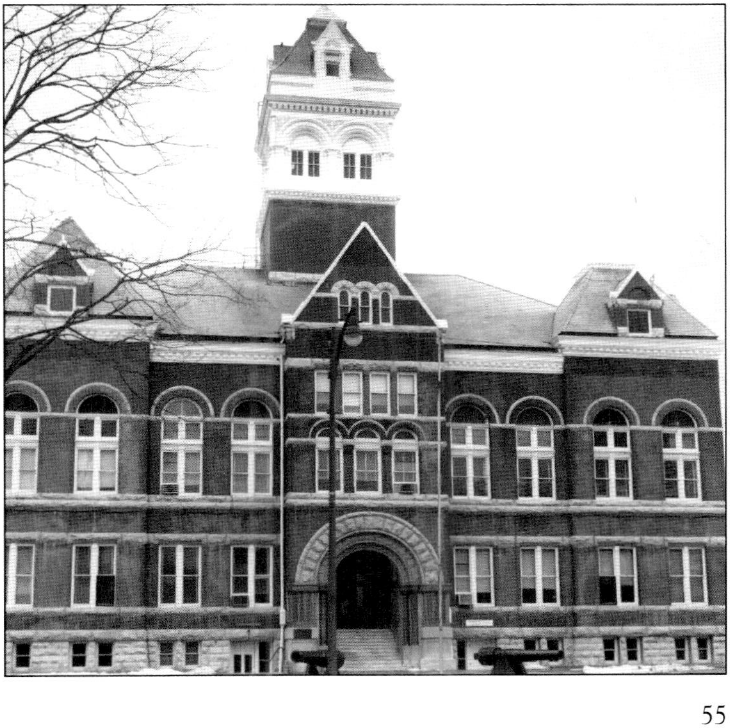

The current Ogle County Courthouse, symmetrical and pristine, c. 1930. In 1981, courthouse offices moved to the Nash Recreation Center while the building, inside and out, was renovated, streamlining it for energy efficiency. It is listed on the National Register of Historic Places. (Courtesy of the Ogle County Historical Society.)

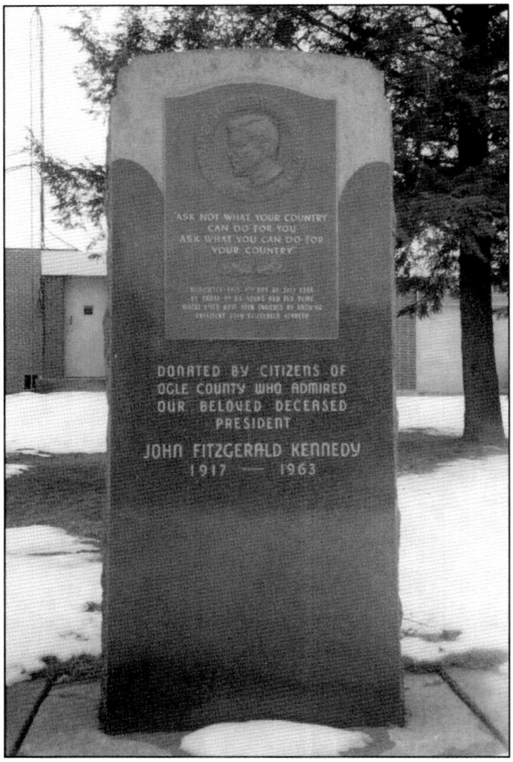

A fine, understated memorial to John F. Kennedy stands on the courthouse lawn, a few yards from Taft's Soldiers' Memorial. The JFK monument was dedicated on July 4, 1966, ". . . by citizens of Ogle County who admired our beloved deceased president." The building in the background is the county jail.

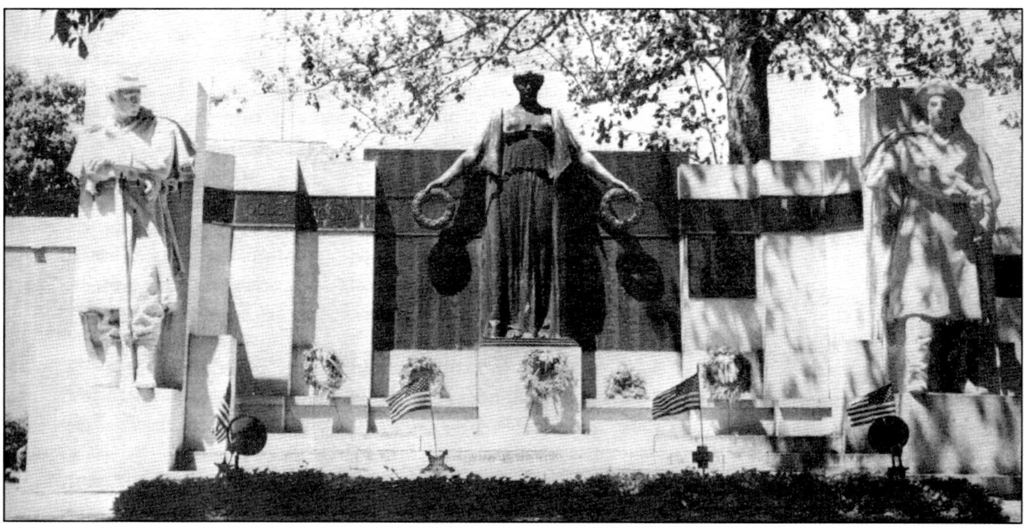

The Soldiers' Monument, located on the courthouse square, was dedicated on July 4, 1916, honoring Ogle County veterans of the Civil War, Spanish-American War, and the War of 1812. Designed by Lorado Taft with assistance from Pond & Pond (who designed the exedra), the sculpture depicts a bronze woman holding two wreaths representing the United States. On either side stands a Union solider, one infantry, the other cavalry. Taft read a brief speech during the ceremony.

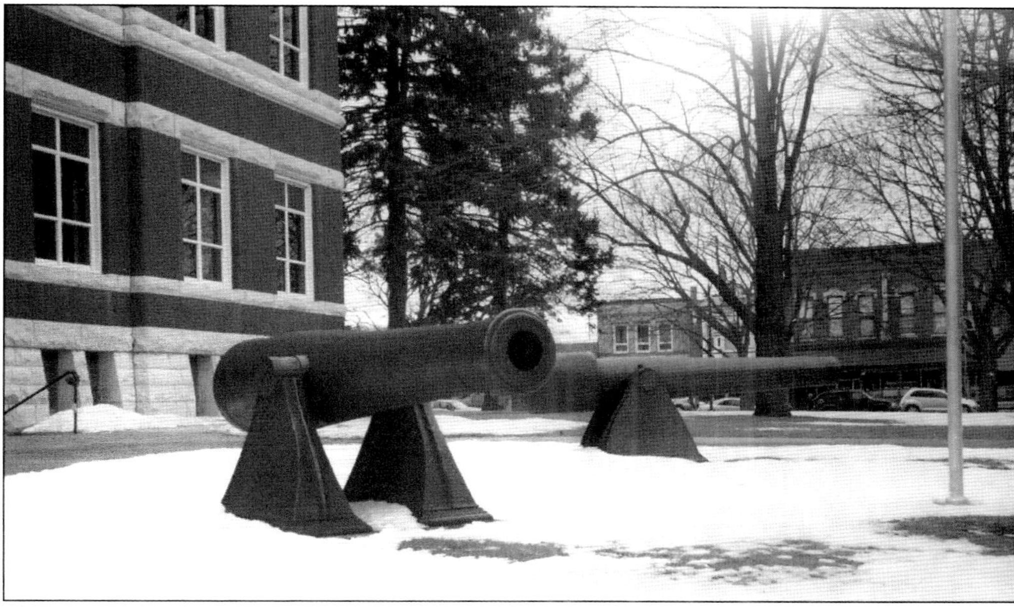

The GAR memorial cannons on courthouse lawn are actually different models, one a Parrott naval rifle, the other a Columbiad. In the early 1900s, members of the raucous Owls Club decided to fire them, stuffing the barrels with bricks and gunpowder. Fortunately, only shop windows were blown out. Former mayor Harry E. Wade, when asked in 1948 if he, a young man when the cannons fired, was involved, answered, "Was I in on it? Well, I'd just as rather not say."

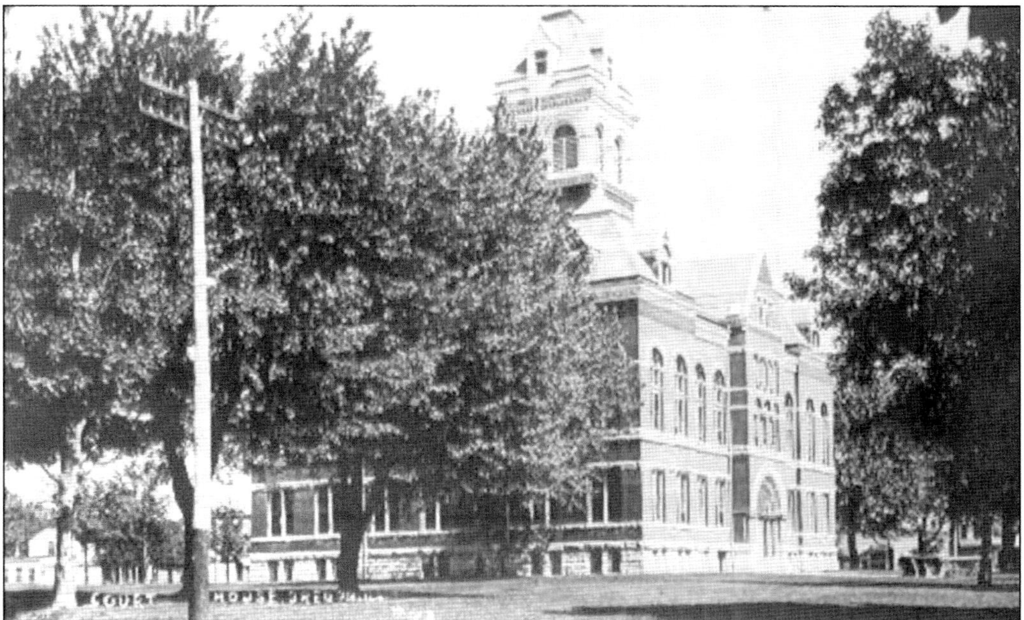

The old jail was razed in 1969, allowing for the construction of the new facility, now located on the open southern lawn seen here. (Courtesy of the *Oregon Republican-Reporter*.)

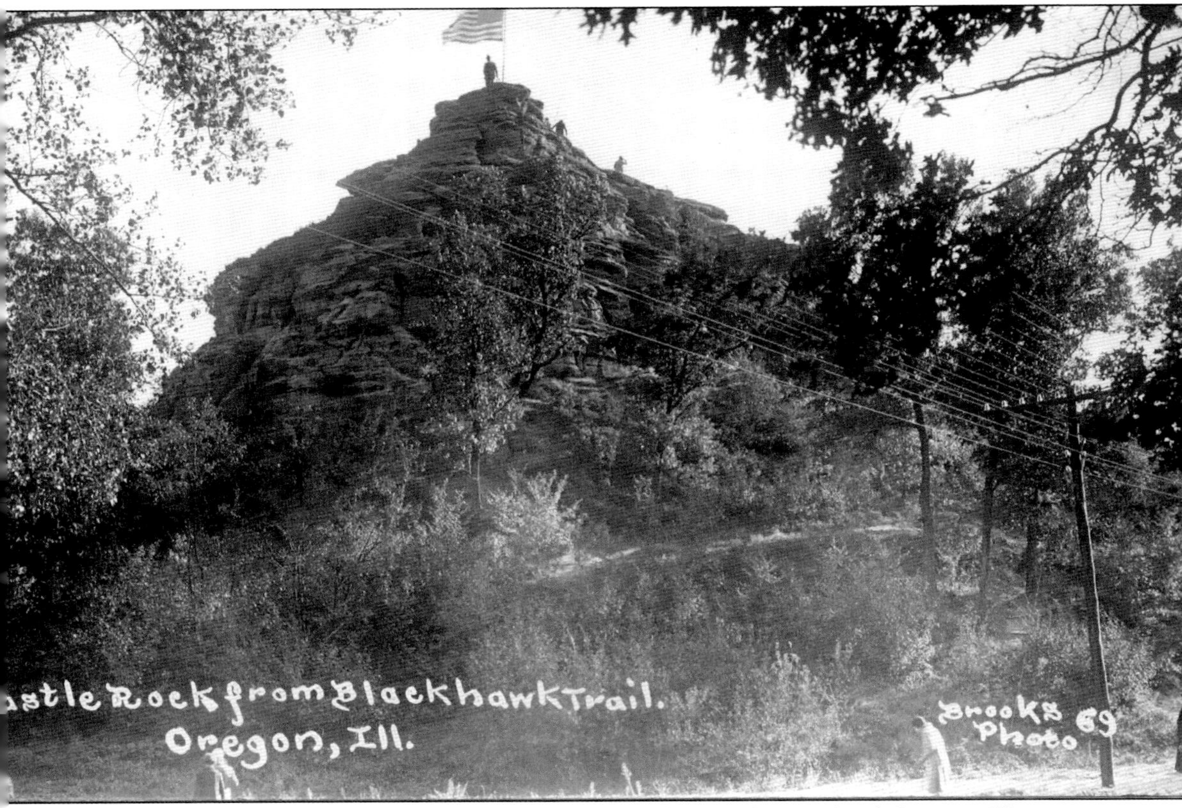

Visitors in 1909 enjoy Castle Rock on Route 2, three miles south of Oregon. The massive promontory is a projection of St. Peter sandstone, which undergirds the entire state. The land was first proposed as a state park in 1921. In 1964, the Natural Lands Institute raised funds to preserve it, and shortly thereafter the State of Illinois granted Castle Rock official status. The park comprises 2,000 acres, 710 designated as a wildlife preserve. A wooden stairway leads to the top, commanding a lovely view of the valley. (Courtesy of Grail Storm.)

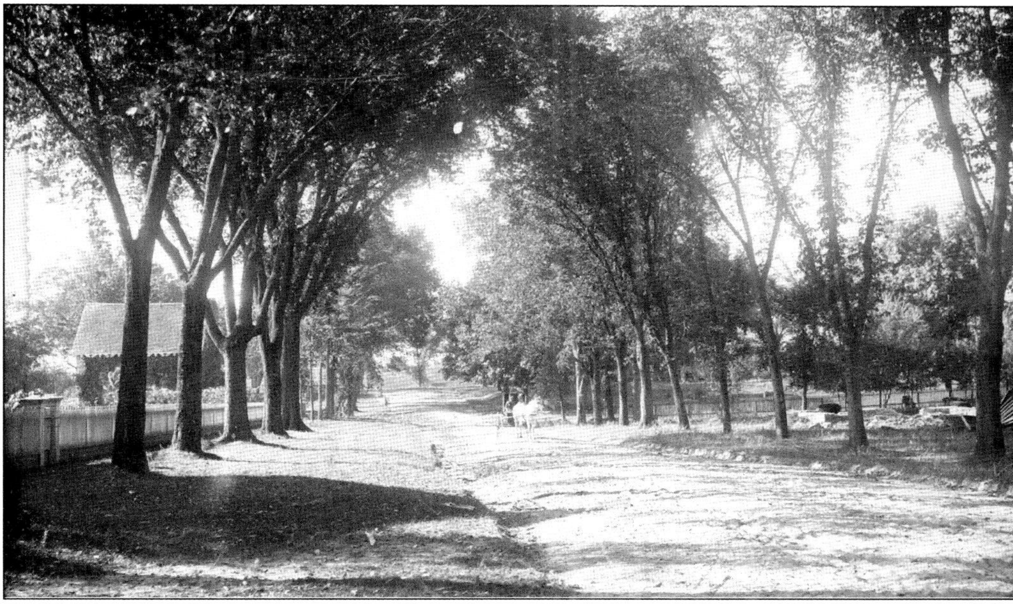

Grand Detour, Illinois, c. 1880. This rustic village derives its name from a deep bend in the Rock River. Founder Leonard Andrus cherished high hopes that a railroad might usher untold wealth and expansion to the region, creating an industrial wonderland. To his chagrin, the tracks were laid in Dixon, and so Grand Detour remains, as biographer Simon Callow succinctly puts it, "just that." (Courtesy of the *Oregon Republican-Reporter*.)

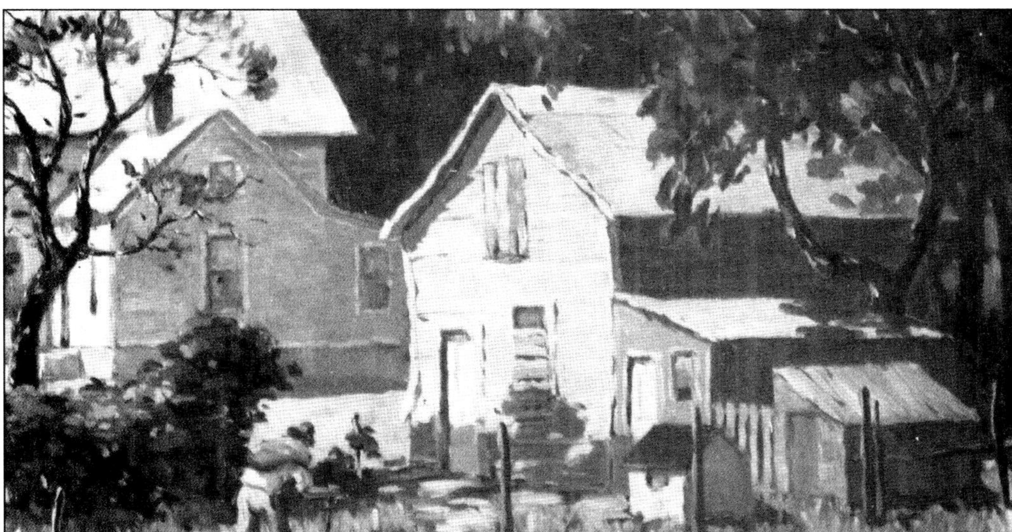

This work, *Oldest House in Grand Detour*, was painted by Holger Jensen. Born in 1878 in Copenhagen, Jensen immigrated to the U.S. in 1886. Studying at the Art Institute, the Chicago Academy of Fine Arts, and Smith's Academy, he was soon exhibiting work at galleries and other venues, including the 1933 Chicago World's Fair. He lived variously in River Forest, Chicago, and Dixon, Ill. The painting is displayed at Oregon Public Library. (Courtesy of the Arts Alliance of Ogle County.)

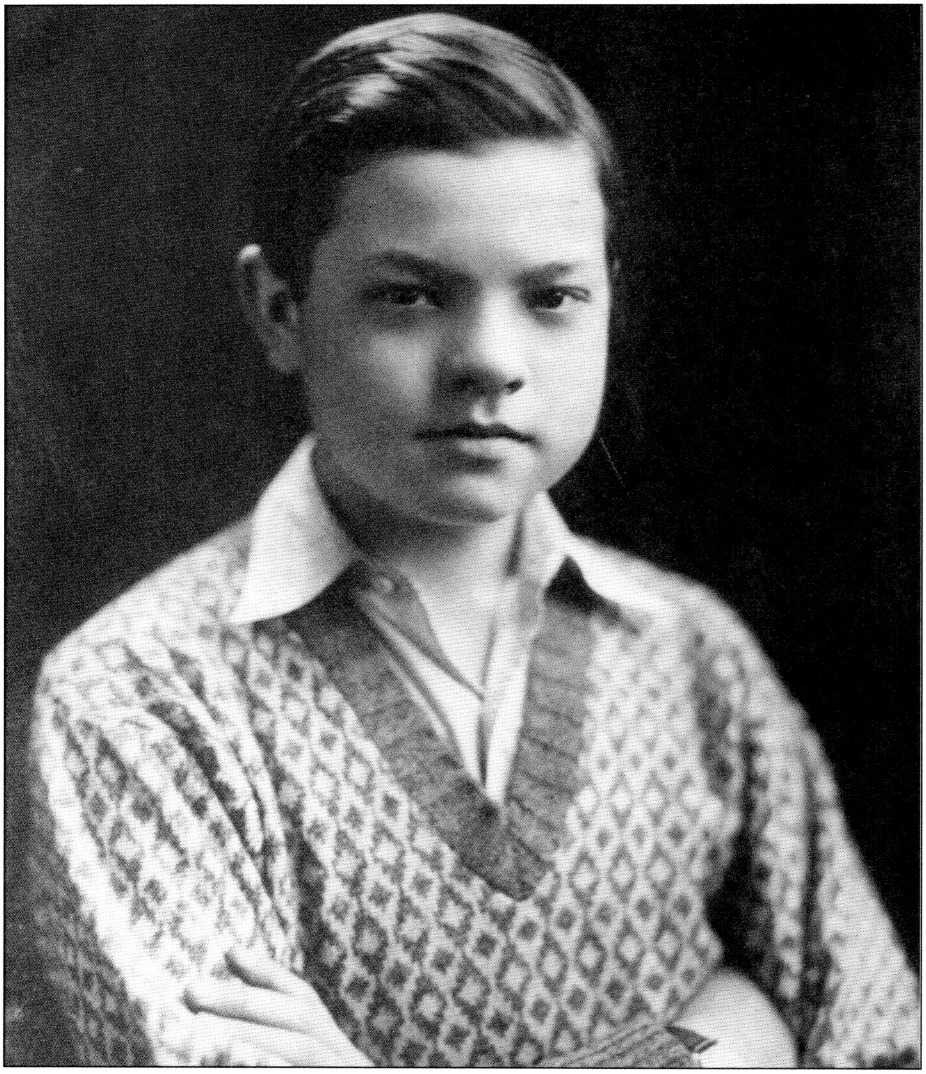

Orson Welles (1915–1985), imperious even as a tyke, attended the Todd School in Woodstock, Ill., in the mid-1920s. During summers he traveled west to father Dick's Sheffield House Hotel in Grand Detour, an attractive retreat for Eagle's Nest colonists and other Chicago artists and entertainers. The Sheffield was widely celebrated for its excellent food and service. Dick also owned a general store with a small dance hall above where little Orson was seen dancing in the moonlight. One contemporary remembers Welles as ". . . a short fat kid who was mean and did not mingle much with the other children." Regardless, in *This Is Orson Welles*, a collection of interviews with Peter Bogdanovich, the maverick actor/writer/director reminisces, ". . . Grand Detour was one of those lost worlds, one of those Edens that you get thrown out of. . . . It really was a marvelous little corner of time." The Sheffield House burned to the ground in 1928 and the Welles family never returned. He told Bogdanovich that if offered the opportunity, this was the only portion of his life he'd care to repeat. Although his ashes were ultimately scattered on a countryside in Spain, he considered Grand Detour his "Rosebud," an emblem of an innocent, lost past, themes further explored in his film *The Magnificent Ambersons*. (Courtesy of Indiana University, the Lilly Library.)

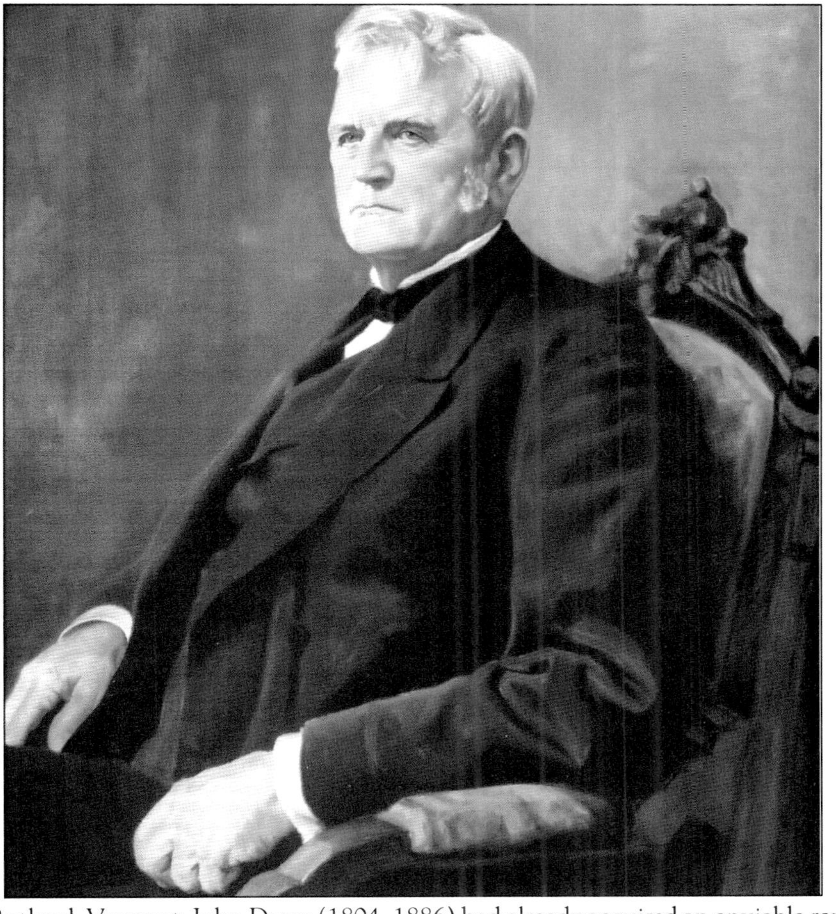

Born in Rutland, Vermont, John Deere (1804–1886) had already acquired an enviable reputation as a meticulous, inventive blacksmith when he ventured west in 1836 to explore the West's blossoming opportunities. Hearing tales of Grand Detour's great potential, he pushed arduously alone across the frontier until he settled properly and paid some debts; later he brought his family. He established a forge two days after his arrival, and in no time his businesses buzzed, shoeing horses, mending pots and pans, and manufacturing rakes, forks, and scythes. As he labored, Deere heard from disgruntled farmers that the thick Midwestern soil clung to their plows, creating insurmountable difficulty. In response, he developed a self-scouring plow, highly polished and uniquely-shaped, importing steel from Pittsburgh and England. The device functioned brilliantly. Elated farmers claimed that the plow merrily sang as its blade sloughed into the earth. An early history of Ogle County relates a tale in which Deere, peddling his wares in the Sinnissippi valley, stopped at a supply shop in Oregon. He stood on the tines of his pitchforks, which did not break. The shop's owner asked if he too could step on the pitchforks, suspecting a trick. The two men agreed that if the implements broke, Deere would bear the loss. The tines did not break, and the merchant bought the entire lot. In 1848, Deere moved his forge to Moline, Ill., on the Mississippi River, availing his operation of its unlimited possibilities for water energy and transportation. A much-respected citizen of Moline, he was elected mayor in 1873. Deere's home is maintained in Grand Detour, with tours available. In 1962, archeologists from the University of Illinois uncovered his original blacksmith shop and cleverly reconstructed it. The epic of John Deere perfectly encapsulates the story of American ingenuity and determination. (Courtesy of the Deere & Company Archives.)

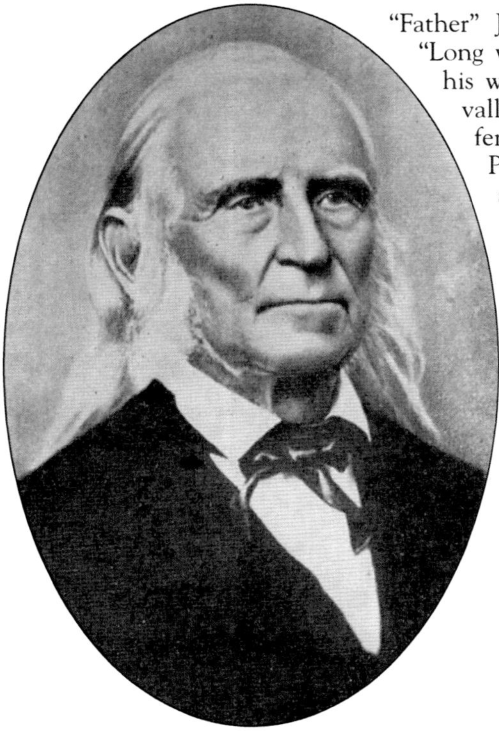

"Father" John Dixon, nicknamed "Nachusa," or "Long white hair," by the Winnebago, brought his wife and five children to the Sinnissippi valley in 1830 where he operated a much-used ferry on the Rock River, servicing the Peoria-Galena Trail. Abraham Lincoln was stationed in Dixon during the 1832 Blackhawk War as Captain of the Sangamon County Volunteers.

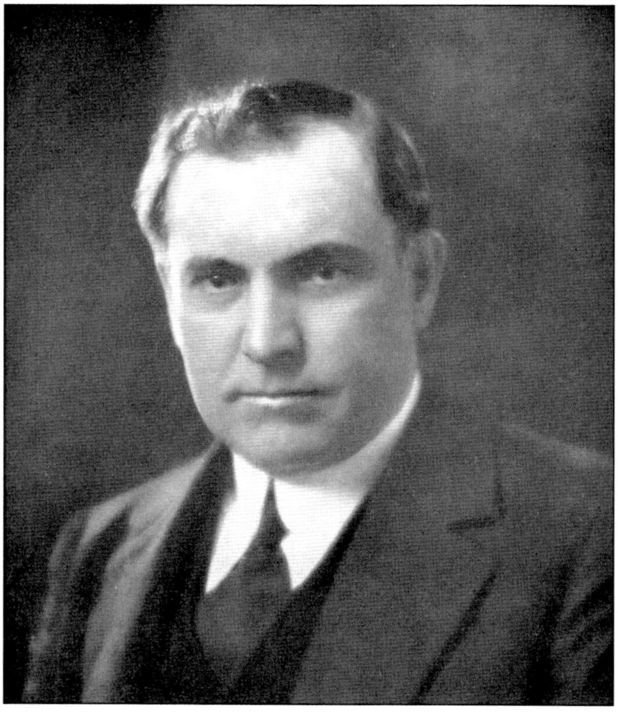

In his autobiography, *River of Years*, liberal preacher Joseph Fort Newton writes of ". . . my destination, Dixon, a community sitting astride the Rock River. The spring thaw was busy melting the ice. . . . it looked its ugliest—drab, unkempt, forlorn, like a station on the way to somewhere else." He pastored from 1903 to 1909 before transferring to Iowa, achieving the rank of Grand Chaplain within the Masonic Lodge; there he wrote *The Builders*, a popular history of Freemasonry. His next charge was the City Temple in London.

Two

THE TRAIN DEPOT

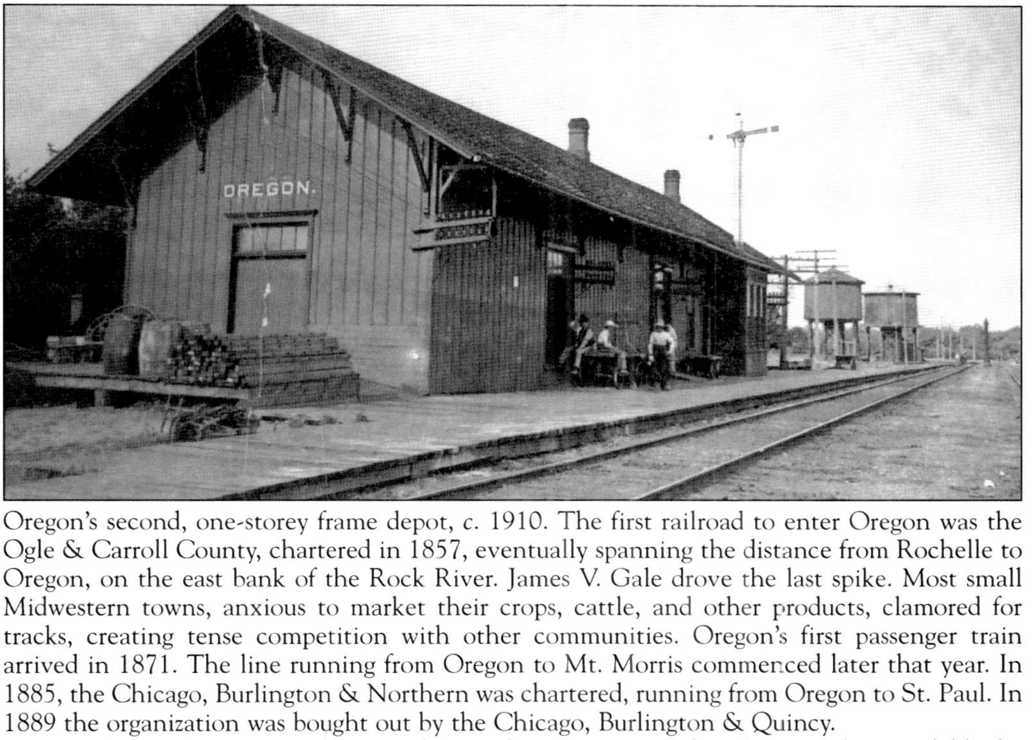

Oregon's second, one-storey frame depot, *c.* 1910. The first railroad to enter Oregon was the Ogle & Carroll County, chartered in 1857, eventually spanning the distance from Rochelle to Oregon, on the east bank of the Rock River. James V. Gale drove the last spike. Most small Midwestern towns, anxious to market their crops, cattle, and other products, clamored for tracks, creating tense competition with other communities. Oregon's first passenger train arrived in 1871. The line running from Oregon to Mt. Morris commenced later that year. In 1885, the Chicago, Burlington & Northern was chartered, running from Oregon to St. Paul. In 1889 the organization was bought out by the Chicago, Burlington & Quincy.

According to historian Bob Rees, three ticket agents served 24 hours a day, available for morning eastbound and evening westbound passengers. During the mid-1930s, the Zephyr dashed through the valley, escorting visitors from Chicago, including bicyclists who would ride the 20 miles north to Davis Junction before loading onto a different train for the ride home. In 1971, President Nixon signed an act creating the National Railroad Passenger Corporation, establishing Amtrak, which did not include Oregon on its timetable. Thus ended Oregon's glorious passenger era. Too many of the classic depots that once dotted the rails across America are gone; however, many are currently experiencing renewal, recognized as vital components of this country's heritage. (Courtesy of Bob Rees.)

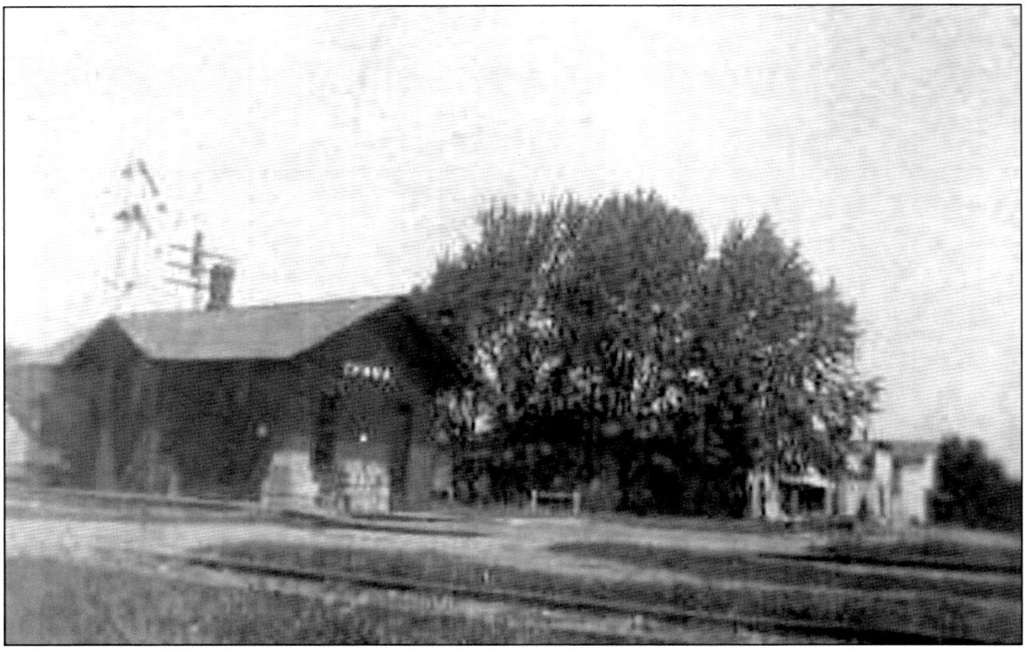

The Chana Depot, the stop just before Oregon, heading west. (Courtesy of Bob Rees.)

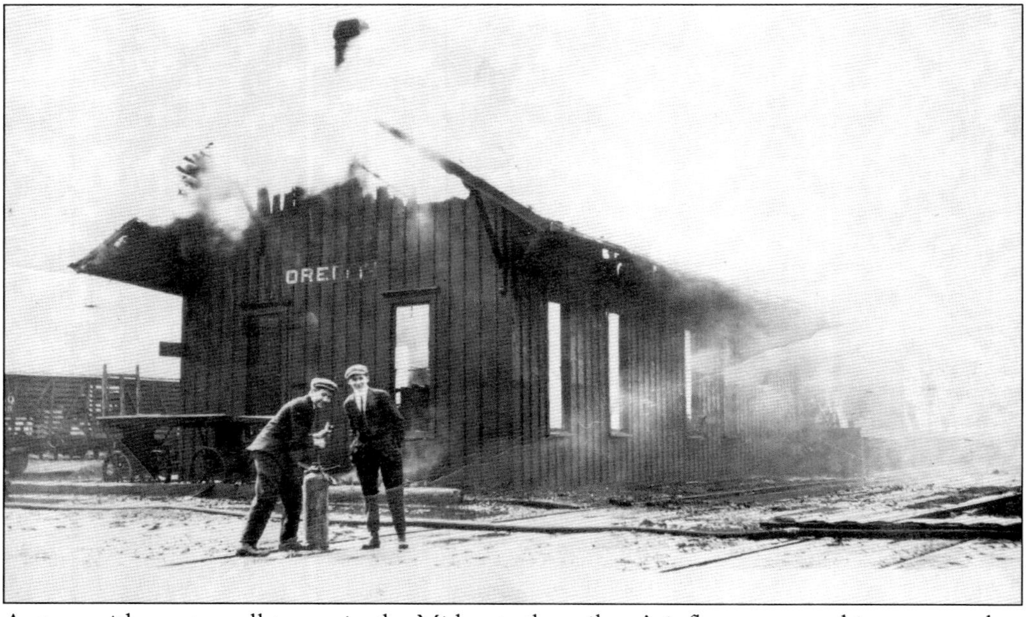

As true with most small towns in the Midwest, the railway's influence proved instrumental to its survival, and losing its connection to the outside world of commerce could prove disastrous. Here, the wooden depot burns in 1910. Considering the circumstances, these unidentified men appear entirely too jolly. (Courtesy of Bob Rees.)

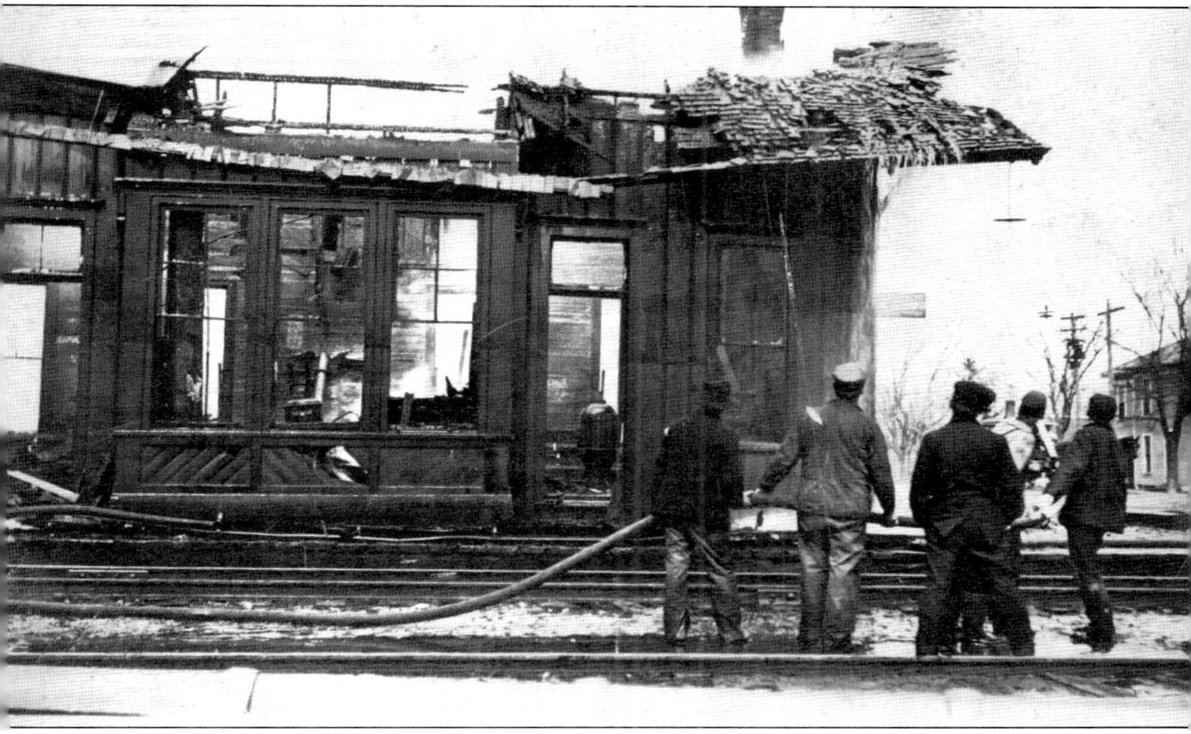

The wooden frame depot lies in ruins after the fateful fire. Quite unexpectedly, its devastation opened a golden opportunity for Oregon. The new station, resultant of Frank Lowden's influence, offered aesthetic pleasure and increased functionality, a classy reception point for distinguished visitors vacationing in the valley. The old structure, partially repaired and moved a few feet away, was used for years as a shed on the freight yard. (Courtesy of Bob Rees.)

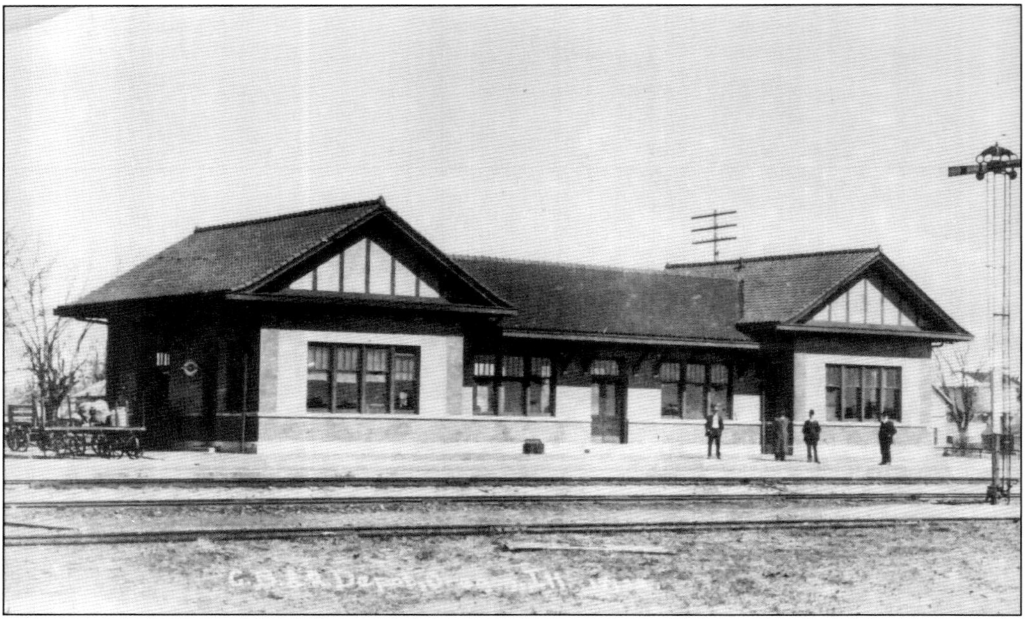

After the fire, the Chicago, Burlington and Quincy Railroad considered canceling the Oregon stop. Fortunately, Congressman Lowden's wife was Florence Pullman, daughter of railroad tycoon George Pullman. Lowden's not inconsequential connections assured this solidly built structure, completed in 1913. (Courtesy of Bob Rees.)

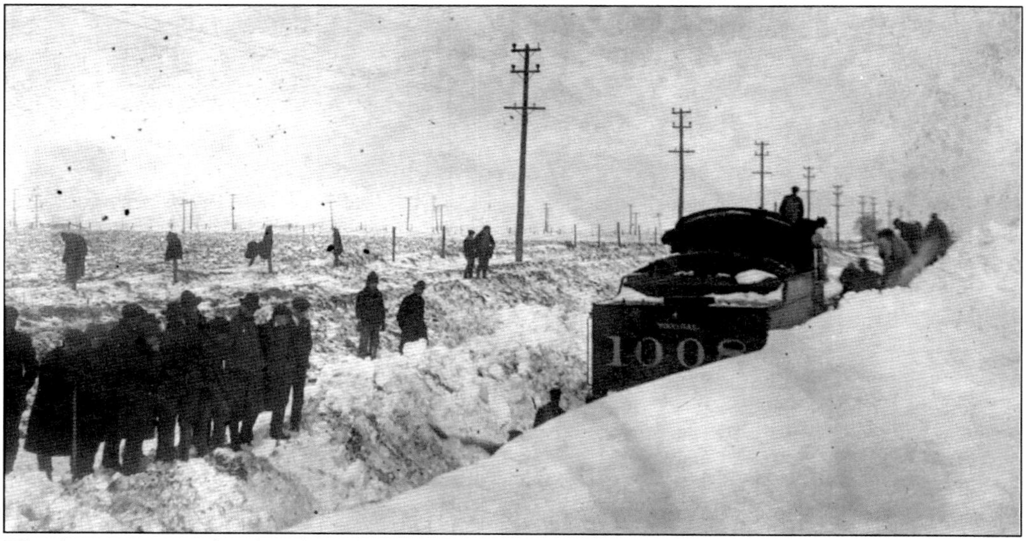

This locomotive is hindered by deep snow, *c.* 1920.

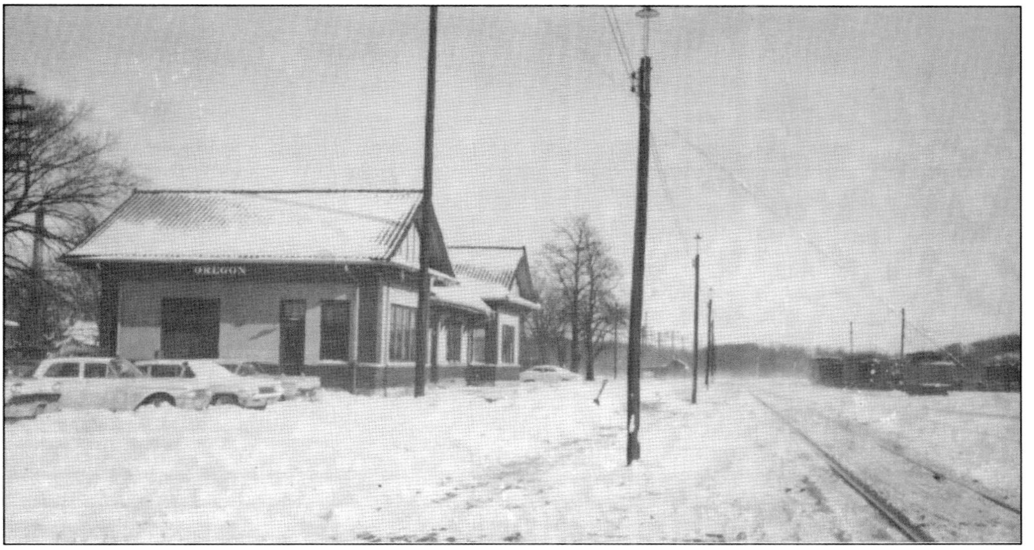

The depot holds stoutly beneath the snow, *c.* 1960. Celebrities known to have passed through include novelists William Somerset Maugham and Ernest Hemingway; Gov. Franklin Delano Roosevelt; poet and editor Harriet Monroe; Professor Albert A. Michelson; actress Judy Garland; a Nobel Laureate in Physics; and Robert Hitt, secretary to Abraham Lincoln, who lived in Mt. Morris. (Courtesy of Bob Rees.)

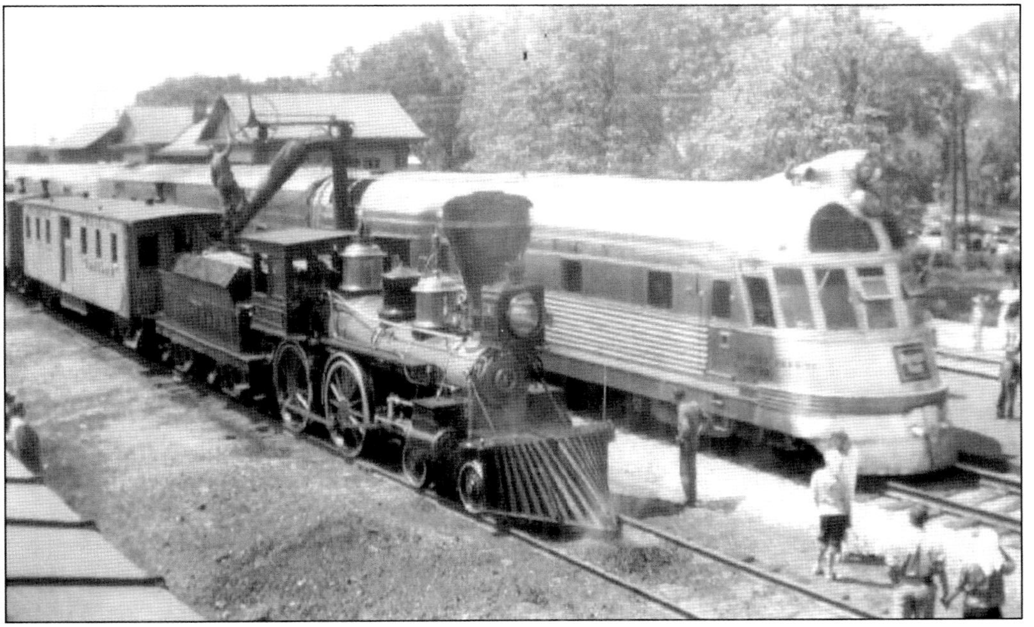

In this wonderful 1950 photo, the Twin Cities Zephyr, headed for Minneapolis, stops next to an old-time steam engine at the Oregon depot. This shot is emblematic of Oregon itself: a dignified past contentedly co-existing with a streamlined, often exotic modernity. (Courtesy of Bob Rees.)

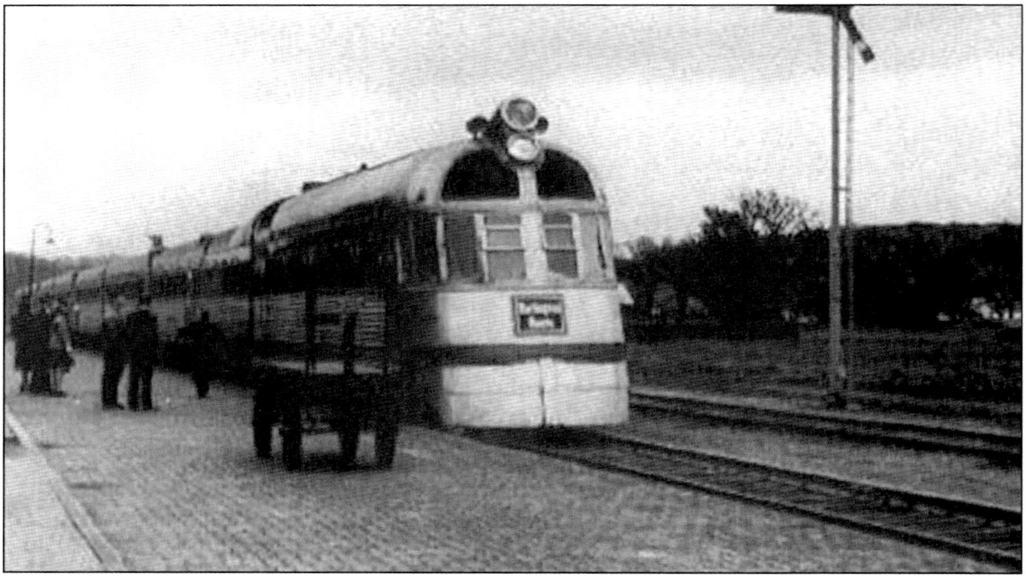

The sleek Twin Cities Zephyr pauses at the Oregon depot, 1950. For almost 40 years, the Zephyr provided luxury transportation until travelers took to the air and the far-reaching superhighways. The route from Oregon to Chicago took one hour, 26 minutes, stopping in Oregon twice a day. The wondrous Zephyr ended its duty in the early 1960s, and is now displayed in the Museum of Science and Industry, Chicago, Illinois. (Courtesy of Bob Rees.)

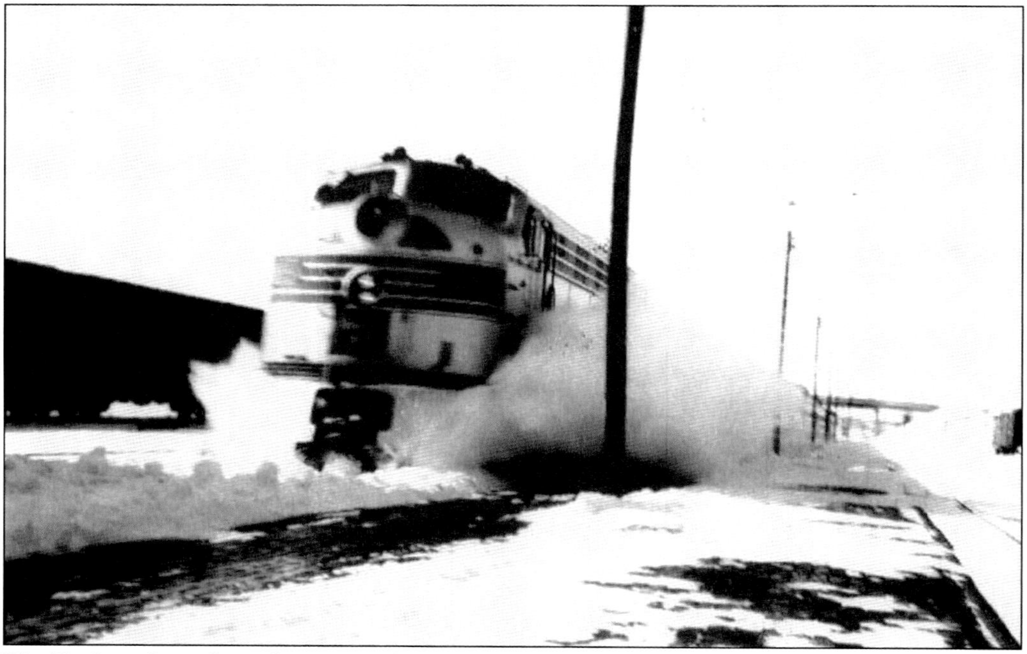

The Zephyr plows through snow in Oregon. In 1947, the New Burlington Northern introduced Vista Domes, containing 24 deep-seated cushioned seats under heat-resistant safety glass. Seats were not reserved, allowing all passengers the pleasure of viewing the rushing sights. Each train boasted five Vista Domes. (Courtesy of Bob Rees.)

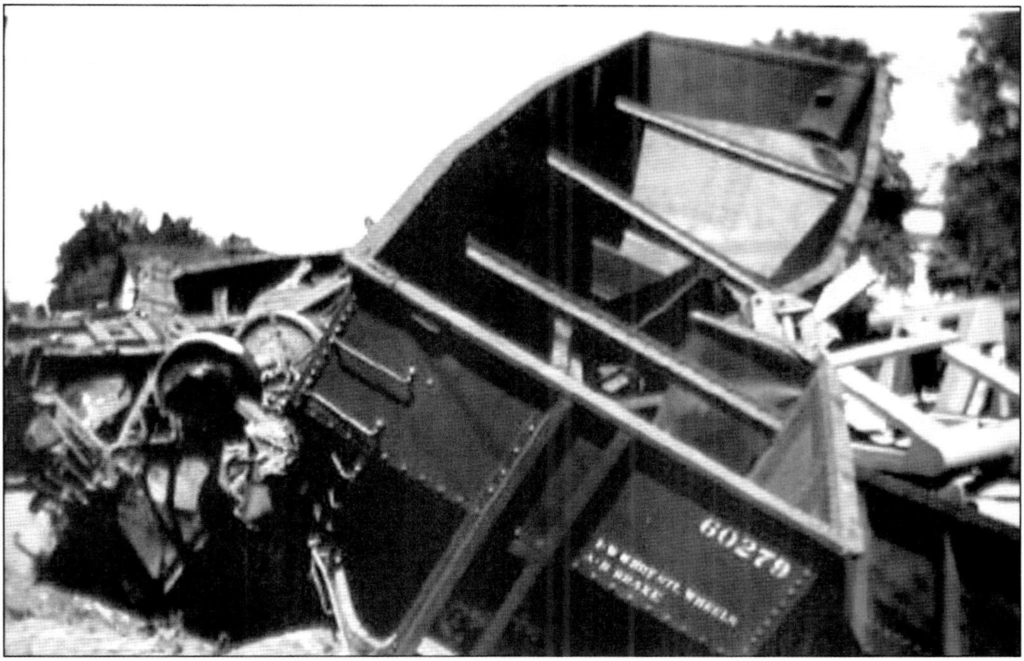

These photos capture a 1953 train derailment. In spite of the abundance of noise and clutter, no one was hurt. (Courtesy Ogle County Historical Society)

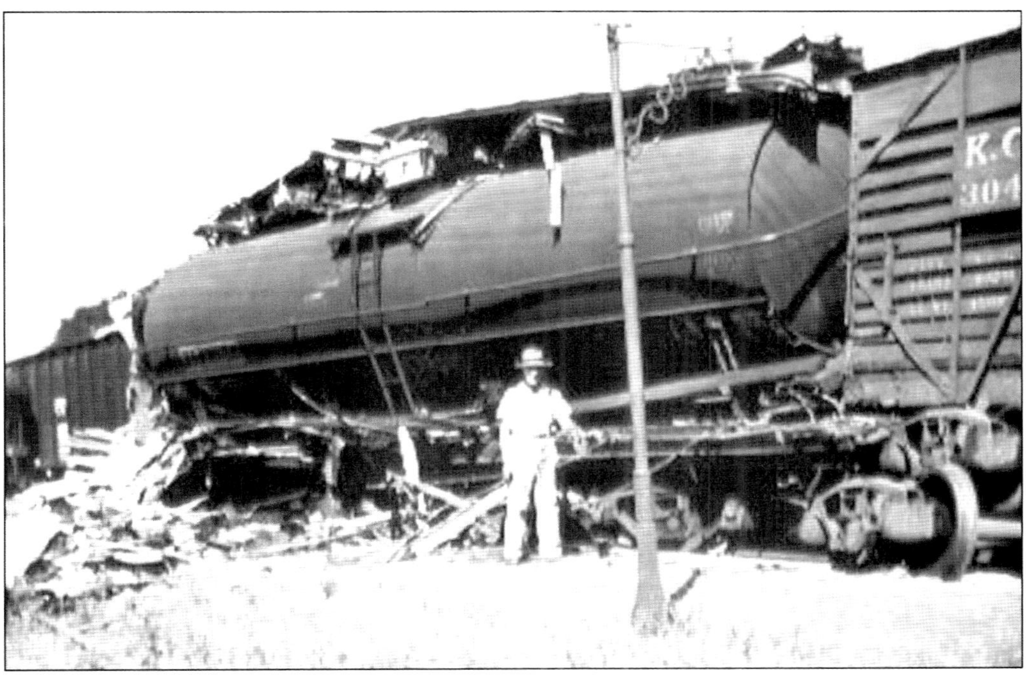

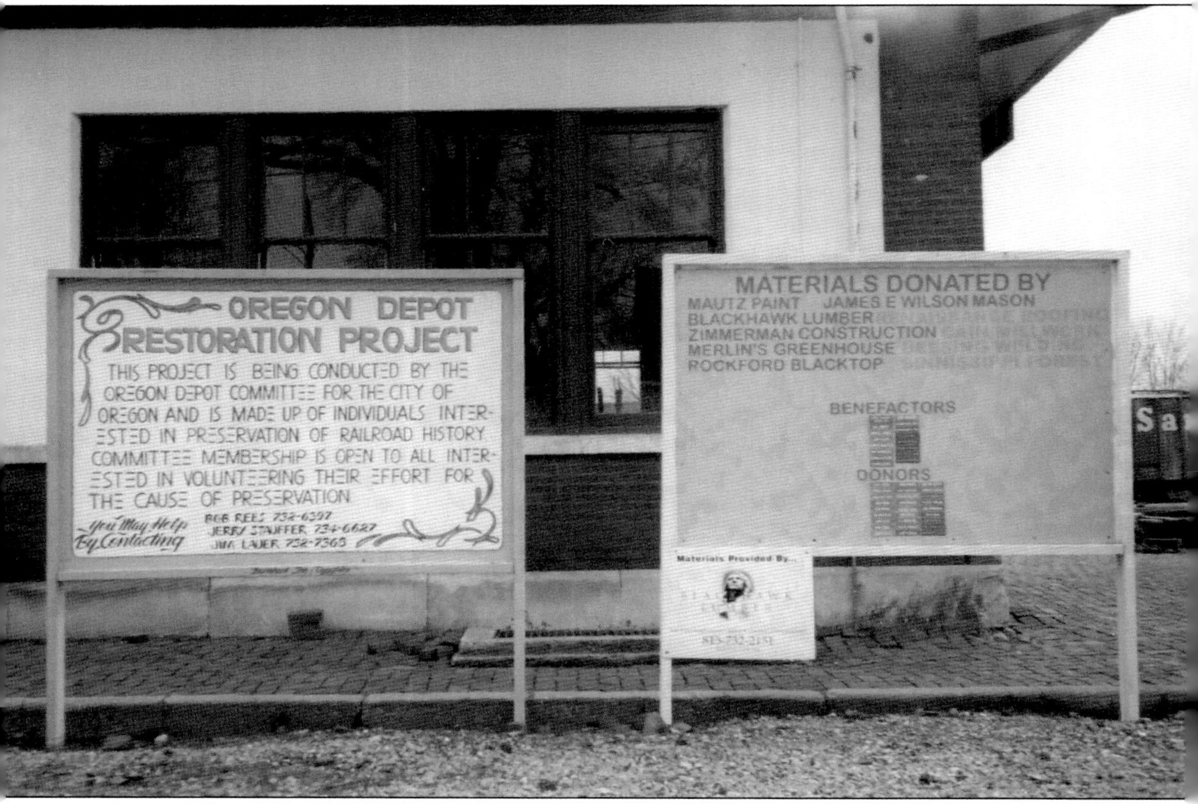

In 1913, Frank O. Lowden successfully campaigned for the construction of the station; once again the cry rings out to preserve and treasure it for a new generation. Considering the importance of America's depot heritage, one recalls North Platte, Neb., where hundreds of heroic citizens during WW II volunteered in days of strict rationing to provide sweets, sandwiches, coffee, and gifts to the thousands of lonely young troops who briefly passed through on their way to either coast for training or transport to foreign theaters of the war. The establishment of Amtrak also did away with that station, which was unforgiveably demolished in 1973. The tale is told by Bob Greene in the heartwarming *Once Upon a Town: The Miracle of the North Platte Canteen* (2002). Similarly, station master Roy Sherick presented a silver dollar to every Ogle County soldier who passed through the Oregon depot, provided the soldier return it to him upon his homecoming. Many silver dollars did not make it back to Sherick's pocket. Fortunately, the depot is cited on the National Register of Historic Places. Efforts are underway to restore its heavy double doors, tiling, roof, restrooms, benches, and ticket booth. Much has been accomplished thanks to the capable attention of project secretary bob Rees, but much labor remains. Completed, the depot will function as a railway museum and library.

Three

Sinnissippi Cincinnatus

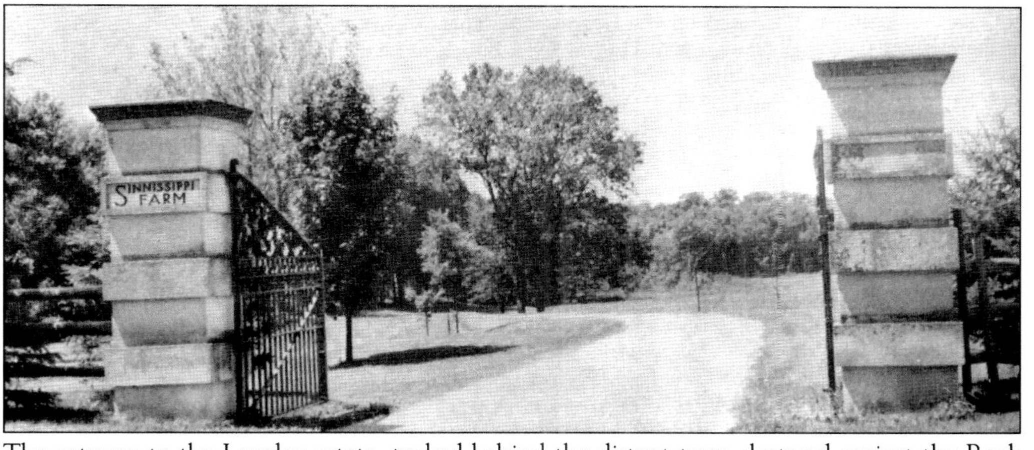

The gateway to the Lowden estate, tucked behind the distant trees clustered against the Rock River, c. 1930. Before white men overtook this region, the Sauk, Fox, Sioux, Pawnee, Winnebago, and Pattawattomie occupied it; objects relating to their tenure, such as arrowheads and beads, are occasionally discovered in the soil. After 1832, a succession of farmers tilled the property, from early frontiersmen to wealthy Chicago landowners, including a Mr. Kneeland of the Chicago Board of Trade, an arrogant man, not suited to country life, and thoroughly despised by the people of Oregon. After his departure, Florence Lowden wrote in her diary: "Frank and I have been on a farm-hunting expedition today. We went in a private car at 8:30 to Oregon, Illinois, to look at a very beautiful farm of 600 acres on the Rock River. We were most pleased and made an offer." They bought the property, and Mrs. Lowden named it Sinnissippi Farm.

According to William T. Hutchinson's *Lowden of Illinois* (1957), the Lowdens couldn't wait to return from springtime in Washington, D.C., to their home where they could "witness the birth of flowers and foliage on the Rock River." Each year, they celebrated Christmas around a blazing hearth, and staged barn dances in the carriage house. The estate provided refuge for quail, pheasants, rabbits, deer, and sometimes wolves.

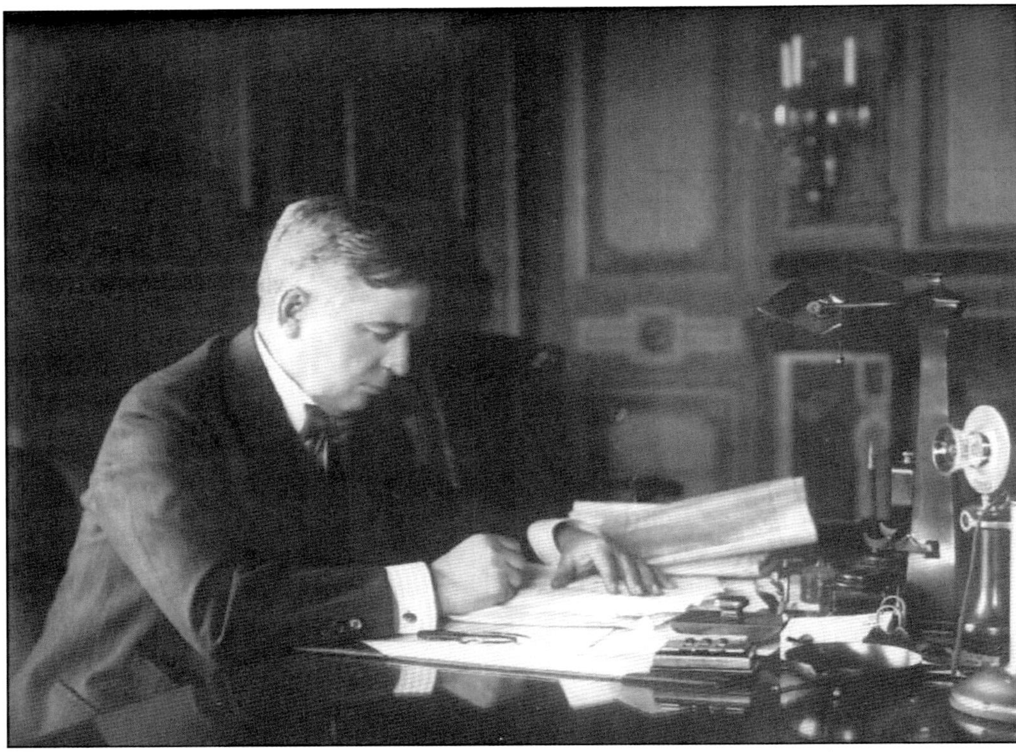

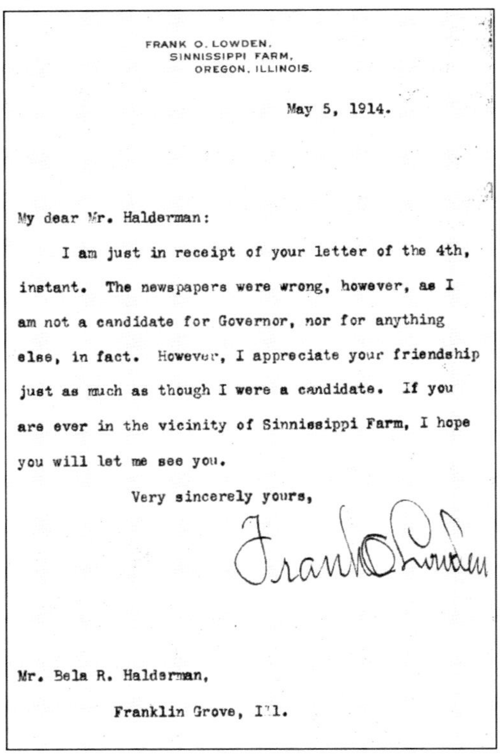

FRANK O. LOWDEN,
SINNISSIPPI FARM,
OREGON, ILLINOIS.

May 5, 1914.

My dear Mr. Halderman:

I am just in receipt of your letter of the 4th, instant. The newspapers were wrong, however, as I am not a candidate for Governor, nor for anything else, in fact. However, I appreciate your friendship just as much as though I were a candidate. If you are ever in the vicinity of Sinnissippi Farm, I hope you will let me see you.

Very sincerely yours,

Frank O. Lowden

Mr. Bela R. Halderman,
Franklin Grove, Ill.

The Honorable Frank Lowden, U.S. Representative (1907–11) and Governor of Illinois (1917–1921) works in his office, c. 1930. A voracious reader and collector of Lincoln memorabilia, Lowden experienced a lean boyhood similar to his hero. At 14 he taught in a one-room schoolhouse for $1 a month. Later he attended the University of Iowa, studying law. He was respected by both Republicans and Democrats. His face graces the cover of the October 23, 1923 issue of *Time* magazine. (Courtesy of the Ogle County Historical Society.)

Lowden's impeccable leadership skills thrust him into constant demand. In this 1914 note he politely denies rumors. A contemporary cartoon portrays him contentedly tilling a field on his farm while a desperate GOP, personified as a portly, well-dressed man, implores the reluctant Lowden to pursue the presidency instead. Actually, Lowden did little or no manual farm labor. (Courtesy of the Ogle County Historical Society.)

This stately portrait of Frank O. Lowden was executed by Ralph Clarkson, a Chicago painter and Eagle's Nest co-founder. Lowden and his wife Florence frequently visited the colony. In 1942, Clarkson donated the painting, hung for years in Clarkson's Loop office, to the Oregon Public Library where it is now displayed. For light reading, Lowden adored Thakeray and Scott; for meatier fare, he enjoyed American history and biographies of statesmen, underlining and adding extensive commentary in the margins. (Courtesy of the Arts Alliance of Ogle County.)

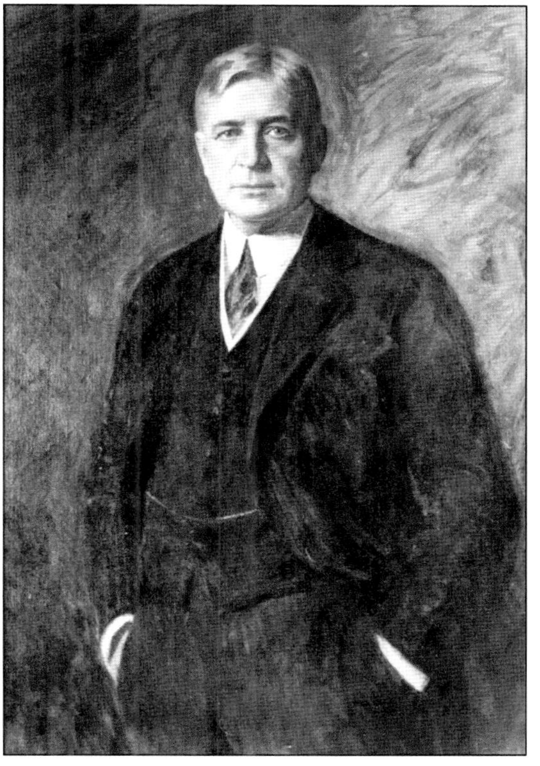

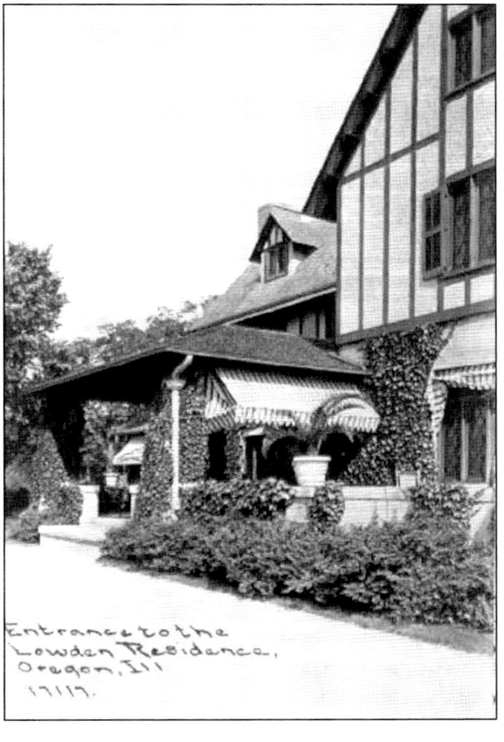

"The Squire of the Sinnissippi" and his wife hosted several passing dignitaries, including Herbert Hoover, who stopped for a visit at Sinnissippi Farm on his way home from delivering a commencement speech in Des Moines. In 1932, Lowden drove the short distance across the river to the train depot to visit with the cheery Governor Franklin Delano Roosevelt, en route to Minnesota. 2000 citizens, Republican and Democrat, showed up to listen to FDR and Lowden briefly discuss reform legislation.

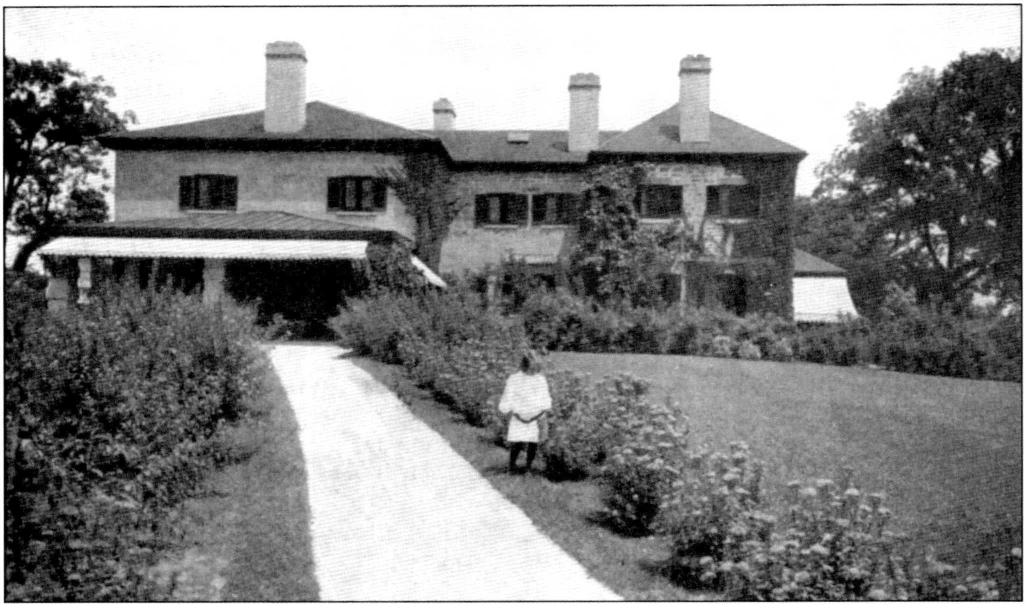

The Lowden home was originally a stone farmhouse secured with thick oak shutters, positioned to protect against Indian raids. The wide lawn narrowed to a woodland path. Remodeling was orchestrated in 1900 by Chicago architects Irving and Allen Pond, members of the Eagle's Nest Art Colony, who also designed the Oregon Public Library. Lowden's no-expense-spared approach to modernizing the grounds stirred some gossip in town. The interior of the house displayed several orginal works by Charles Francis Browne, Lorado Taft's brother-in-law.

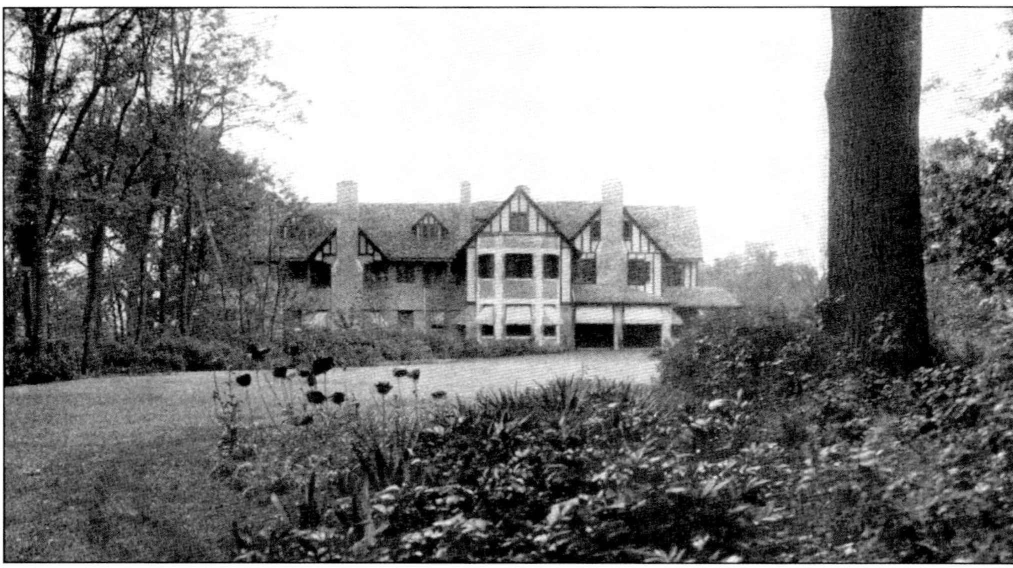

Lowden tied with General Leonard Wood for the presidential nomination; but both lost to Senator Warren G. Harding. Lowden was living at Sinnissippi Farm when he phoned the GOP Convention in Chicago, turning down their vice-presidential nomination. Calvin Coolidge was named Harding's running mate. Interestingly, had Lowden accepted, he would have assumed the presidency upon the untimely death of Harding. Lowden died in Arizona on March 20, 1943.

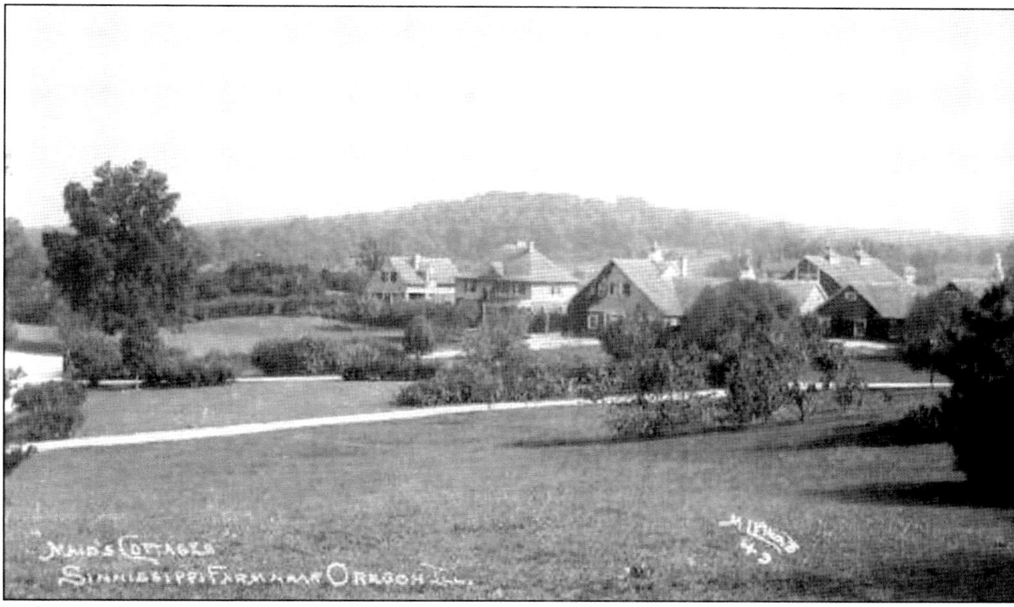

Before his triumphant career in politics, Lowden performed quite well as a lawyer and investor. His vocational success combined with the good fortune of marrying Florence Pullman, daughter of rail tycoon George Pullman, allowed him to employ a small battallion of caretakers, including three nurses, a manager, and a coachman. Pictured here are the maids' cottages, *c.* 1920. The estate also contained a well-equipped playground. (Courtesy of the Ogle County Historical Society.)

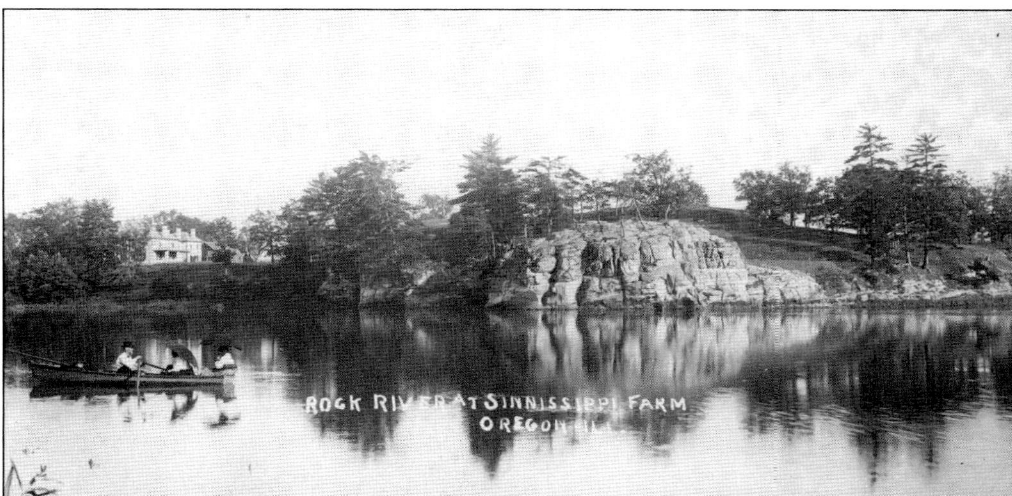

The Rock River at Sinnissippi Farm in the 1910s. The estate's buildings are glimpsed on the sandstone promontory, a favorite spot for Lowden and his guests. The man at the helm of the canoe rows two ladies holding parasols over their shoulders. Lowden bought the property on the opposite side of the river to protect his view. (Courtesy of the *Oregon Republican-Reporter*.)

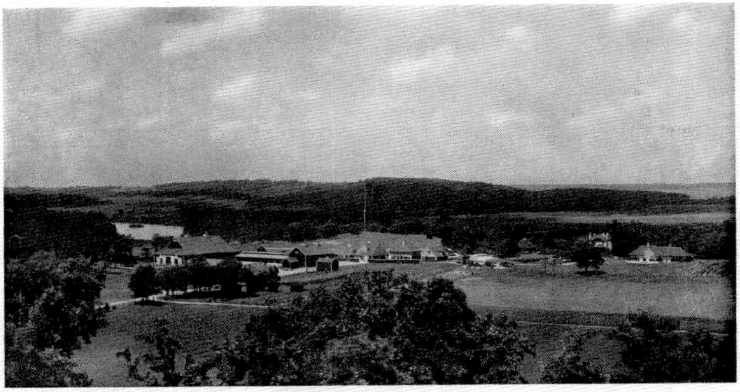

Fig. 1. Sinnissippi Farm, the home of Col. F. O. Lowden, at Oregon, Ill., in the Black Hawk country through which runs the Rock River. Eloquent of rich soil and prosperous farms, it is no longer the wild, black prairie, beautiful and dangerous, but a smiling land of happy, independent homes

A NEW KIND OF WESTERN HOME

BETTER THAN THE FAST LIFE OF A GREAT CITY — BETTER THAN A MERE SUMMER DWELLING — BETTER THAN SPECTACULAR SCENERY — BETTER THAN A SHOW PLACE

By WILHELM MILLER

Photographs by HENRY FUERMANN

FOR five years I have been looking for a great country estate in the Middle West that stands for something better than present-day ideals, and I believe I have found it in Sinnissippi Farm, the home of Col. Frank O. Lowden, at Oregon, Ill. It is better than the fast life of a great city, because it has something of the dignity, calm and satisfaction of English country life. It is better than a mere summer dwelling, and better than spending every summer amid new scenes, because it is a year-round home. It is better than a show place, because it is a real farm, as well as a park, and the farm part of it pays, as it always should do. And above all it is Western. It does not copy Europe literally, as many Eastern places do. It does not copy the East, as most Western places do. It has most of the great merits of the West, and few of its demerits. Finally, the Western character and local color will grow richer every year, and some of it ought to last for centuries.

Having been brought up in the Middle West I know the peculiar merits of the region to which Easterners are so blind. And I have to grit my teeth when cubs who have never been west of Harvard tell me there is no mellowness in the West. That isn't fair. How can you expect big trees on a treeless prairie? How can you expect mature country estates near Chicago when the place had only 100 inhabitants in 1831? The important thing is that a country home should be laid down on right lines. It should be judged by its motives. And here is a place that seems to me on a higher plane than many of the gaudy estates in the East, that reek of sportiness, extravagance, artificiality. It is not like Southampton — all house and no grounds. It is not like Tuxedo — all outgo and no income. It is not like Newport and the Adirondacks with their pretentious "cottages" and "camps." It is simply a big, honest, self-supporting prairie farm plus what the English call a "park," i.e., an ornamental part which,

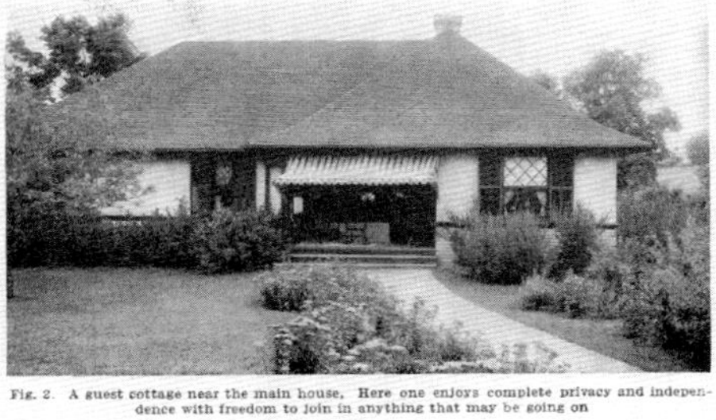

Fig. 2. A guest cottage near the main house. Here one enjoys complete privacy and independence with freedom to join in anything that may be going on

39

In this 1913 profile for *Country Life in America*, Wilhelm Miller of the American Civic Association describes Sinnissippi Farm as ". . . better than the fast life of a great city, because it has something of the dignity, calm and satisfaction of English country life." He chides his effete Eastern colleagues, "never west of Harvard," for not appreciating these Midwestern geographic delicacies. Charmed by this ". . . smiling land of happy, independent homes," he describes the estate's careful arrangement, noting the unsurpassed landscaping skills of Lowden's gardener, O.C. Simonds of Chicago. Miller argues that it is an aesthetic mistake to push together two types of scenery. Ideally, one should appreciate a full look at the river, then a full look at the woods. Therefore the woods must be thickened to best delineate the distinctive views, no spindly trees tolerated. "While one can always see something to criticize," Miller concludes with backhanded admiration, "I have no serious fault with Sinnissippi Farm." In 1881, Lowden's landscaper, O.C. Simonds, surveyed and arranged Graceland Cemetery in Chicago, a graveyard for the city's prominent dead; the job earned him national prestige as the "dean" of American cemetery design.

Four

EAGLE'S NEST ART COLONY

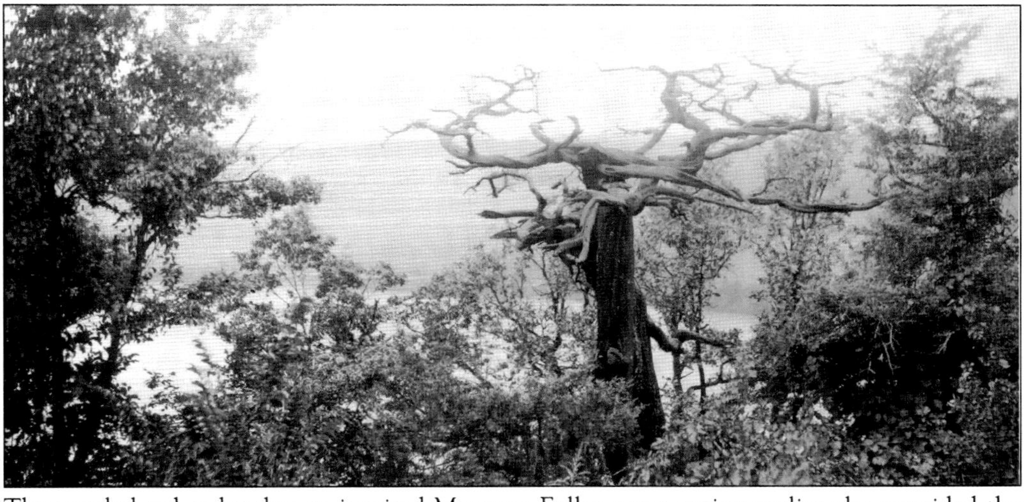

The gnarled red cedar that so inspired Margaret Fuller a generation earlier also provided the rallying point for Lorado Taft and the Eagle's Nest Art Colony. Initially, Taft and his Chicago associates settled in Bass Lake, Indiana, but an outbreak of malaria drove them away. Hearing of their search through James Spencer Dickerson, a colleague from the University of Chicago, attorney Wallace Heckman invited them on July 4, 1898, to visit his country estate, Ganymede Farm, on the Rock River. Taft's wife, Ada, records their first trip: "It was after ten when we arrived, but the moon filled the earth with magic and we, being young, eagerly accepted Mr. Heckman's proposal to walk over to the possible site for our camp." Impressed, the colonists decided to stay. Heckman then drafted a lease, allowing use of his property during summers. In addition to paying taxes and a very reasonable rent, the colonists were required ". . . to deliver or procure to be delivered without charge at least two lectures or addresses on the Fine Arts, or some branch of literature during each year, in the City of Oregon, or on Margaret Fuller Island, or on Ganymede Farm. . . . " The lease was signed and sealed by Heckman, Taft, Ralph Clarkson, Oliver Dennett Grover, Charles Francis Browne, Henry B. Fuller, Hamlin Garland, Horace Fiske, James Spencer Dickerson, and Allen and Irving Pond. The old tree stood near the base of Taft's stature, The Eternal Indian. The tree toppled during a 1972 windstorm and is now displayed on Northern Illinois University's Taft Field Campus. (Courtesy of the Ogle County Historical Society.)

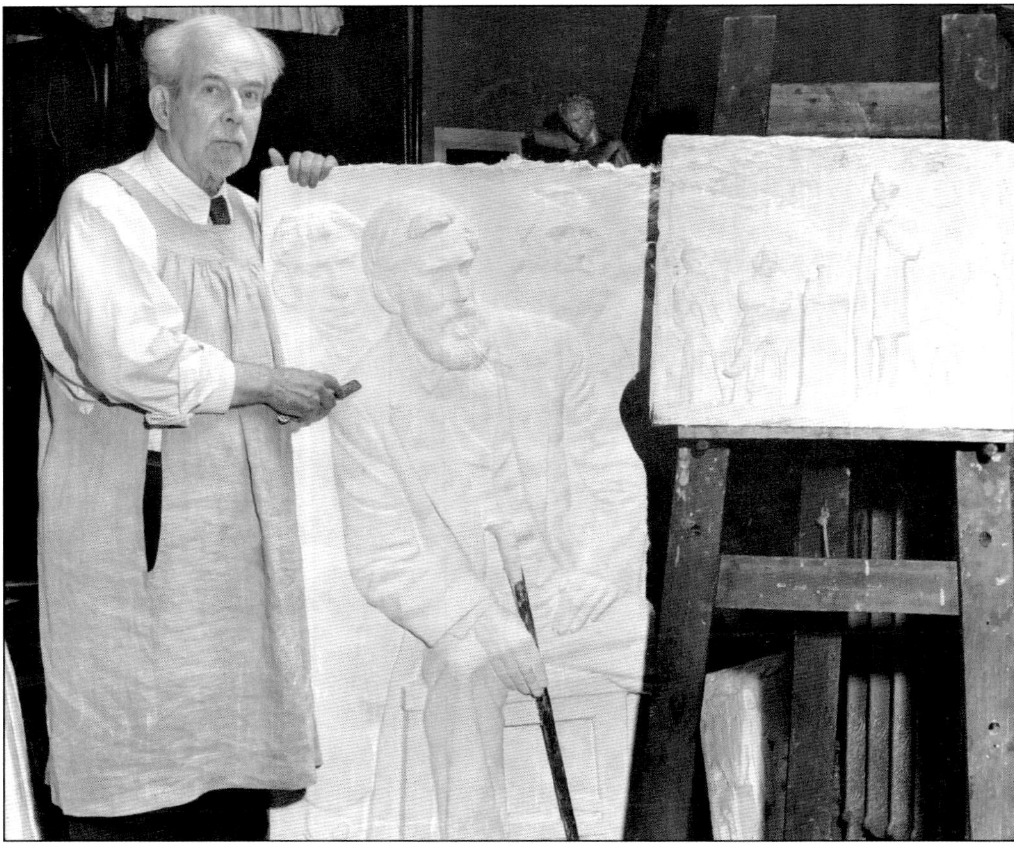

Sculptor Lorado Taft displays his handiwork at the renowned Midway Art Studio, a converted barn adjacent to the University of Chicago. Born in Elmwood, Illinois in 1860, Taft became enamored with his art while unpacking sculptures for the University of Illinois, from which he also graduated with top honors. He studied in Paris for a few years before returning to Chicago where he crafted countless statues, fountains, reliefs, and plaques. Phenomenally gifted, he supervised the sculpture for the wondrous 1893 Columbian Exposition, and later instructed classes at the Art Institute. In addition to fulfilling his academic responsibilities, he traveled across the country, delivering innumerable demonstrations and talks, speaking in memorably eloquent, graceful tones. In 1903, he published the mammoth *History of American Sculpture*, written largely at Heckman's home, Ganymede Farm. As the Eagle's Nest founder, Taft lent energy, focus, and sparkling humor to his peculiar assembly, motivating them to often spectacular creative endeavor, whether it was painting, acting or sculpting. As the son of Professor Don Carlos Taft, a Congregational minister, Taft considered his greatest contribution to be his Christian missionary activity in Paris rather than his civic-minded art, remarking: "It's the best investment I could make!" In an article for the *Christian Century*, he outlined his aesthetic creed, maintaining that intelligent people have a right to: "All the beauty around us which most of us never perceive . . . All of the inheritance of the past, of which we Americans are particularly unconscious," and finally, "The talent which springs up perennially but which America's rushing life is wont to extinguish before it takes root." Taft eagerly looked forward to summers at Ganymede Farm, ". . . that fountain of youth that continued always to refresh him," as his wife observed. He died in 1936 while perfecting the George Washington–Robert Morris–Haym Salomon Monument, located in Heald Square, Chicago, completed by Leonard Cruenelle, Taft's disciple and fellow colonist. (Courtesy of the Northern Illinois University Archives.)

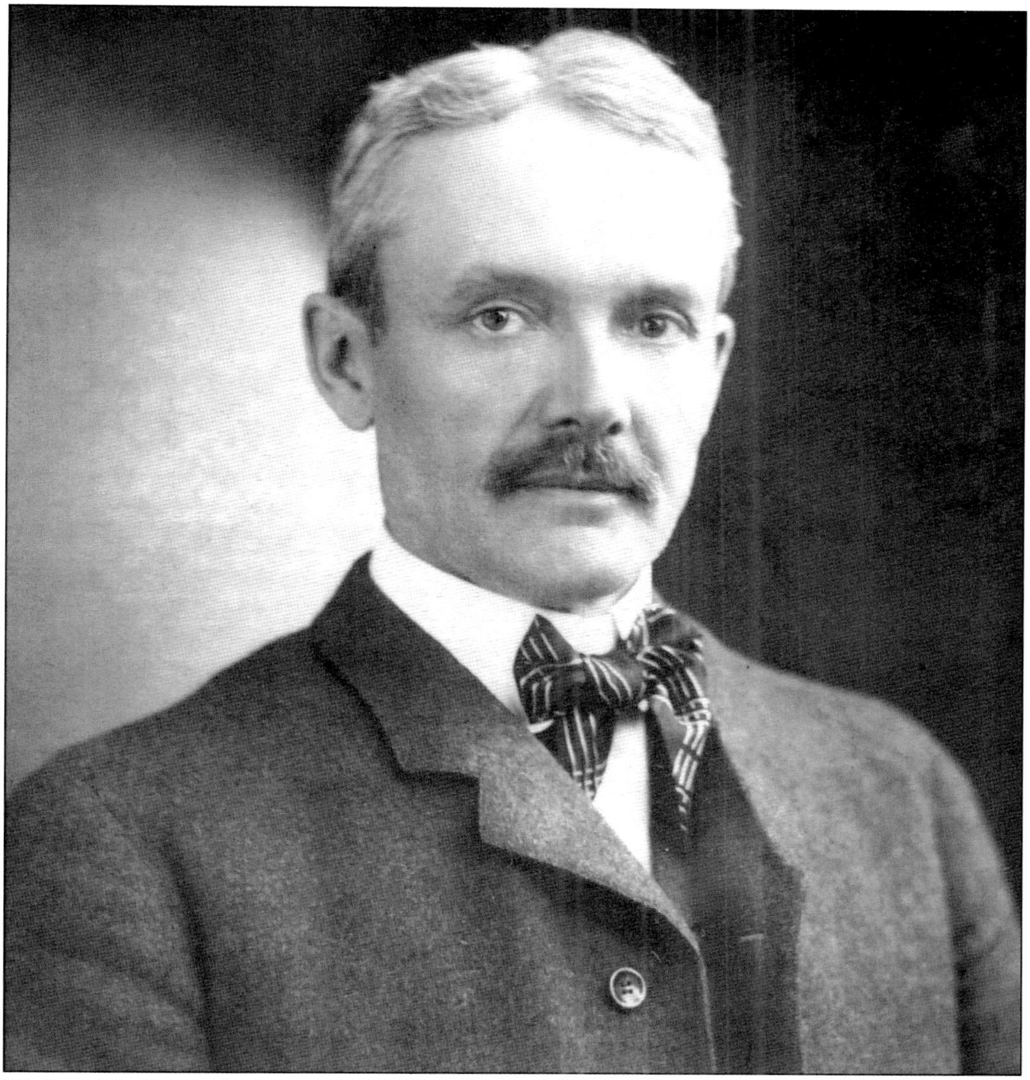

Wallace Heckman, lawyer and president of the Union League Club in Chicago, graciously allowed a small army of eccentric writers, sculptors, dancers and professors to overrun his property once a year for decades. Commenting on his generosity, Ada Taft writes: "He had the talent of putting himself in the place of others and appreciating their different tastes and points of view." In 1912, Heckman published a small book entitled *Lorado Taft's Indian statue "Black Hawk ": An Account of the Unveiling Ceremonies*, containing numerous photos by Dr. Charles Eastman, the advocate for Native American causes. Heckman and Taft spent much time scouting various locations along the bluff to determine the best spot for *The Eternal Indian*, sometimes canoeing on the river. In the early days of the camp, the colonists slept in tents or guest rooms at the Heckman home. Hamlin Garland actually slept in a tepee as a tribute to the Cheyenne; though the others might've considered it an affectation, Garland was attempting a ". . . poetic suggestion of aboriginal life. . . ." Heckman, the camp's patron, was solemnly asked to set a match to Garland's first tinder. Garland then "renewed [his] youth" sitting around the firehole, ". . . smoking the beautiful Pipe of Meditation . . ." given him by a young Cheyenne chief. (Courtesy of the Northern Illinois University Archives.)

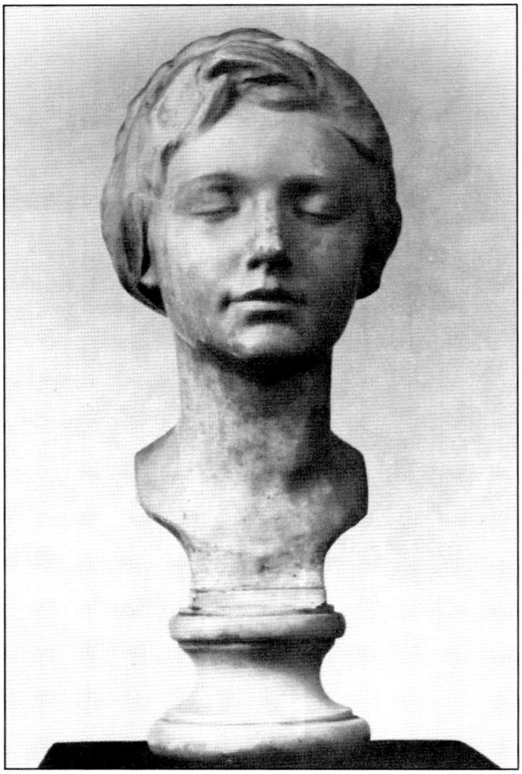

This serene portrait of Tillie, Wallace Heckman's better half, was sculpted by Taft at the colony. Mrs. Heckman was as delighted as her husband to host the carefree colonists, and often rode horseback to visit them. The plaster bust is displayed at Oregon Public Library. (Courtesy of the Arts Alliance of Ogle County.)

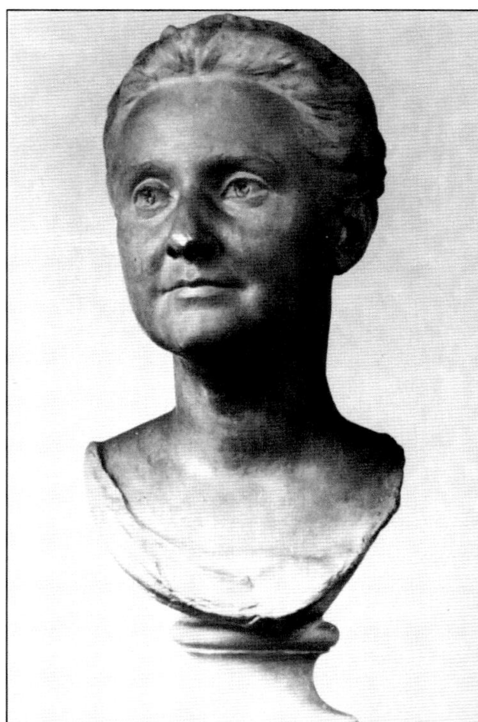

In this sculpture of Ada Bartlett Taft, Lorado's adoring second wife, he forsook his usual cool, classical lines and wisely opted for a rounder, friendlier visage. Ada's invaluable memoir, *Lorado Taft: Sculptor and Citizen* (1946) is a loving, anecdotal account of their life together. The bust is displayed at the Oregon Public Library. (Courtesy of the Arts Alliance of Ogle County.)

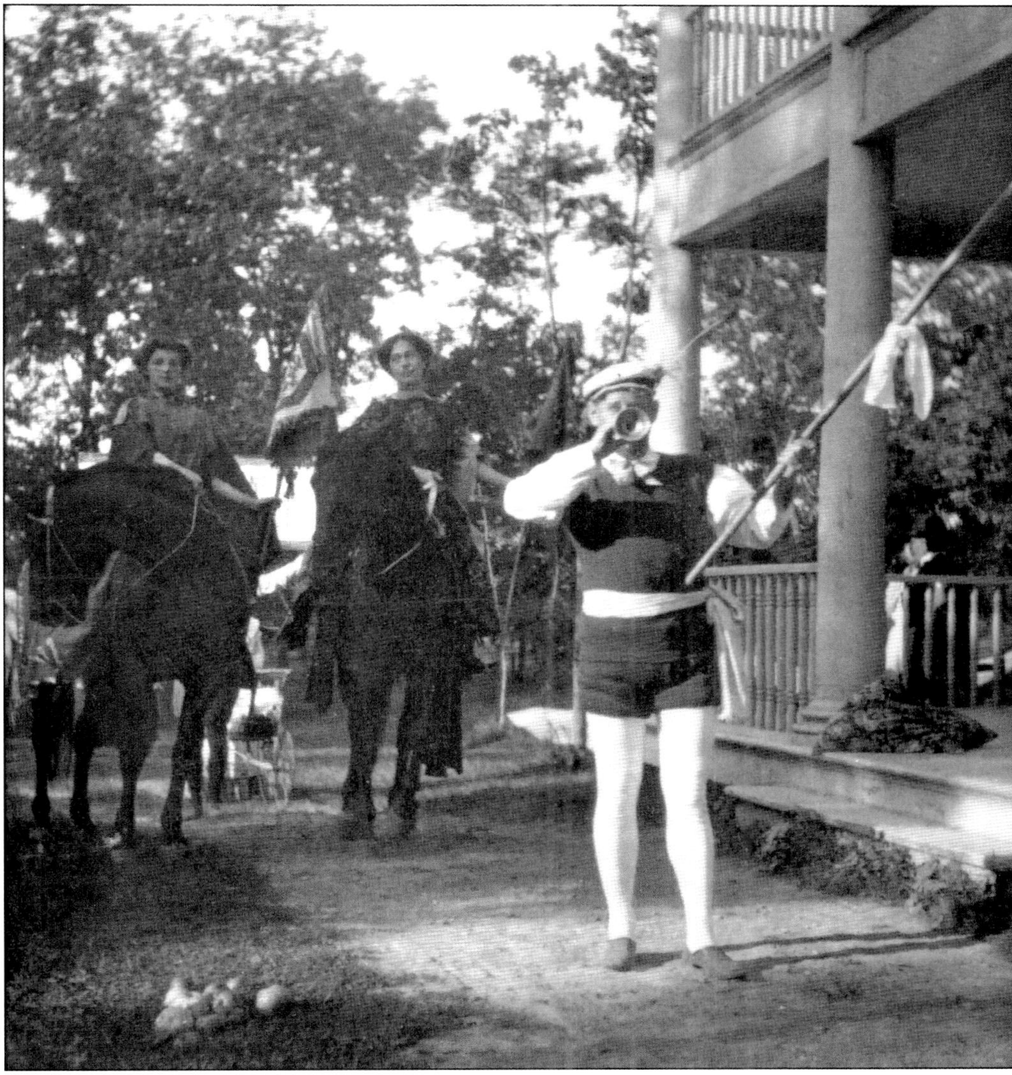

Heckman's lease stipulated that the colony pay $1 yearly for use of his estate, the 15 acre Ganymede Farm. Sometimes the rent was offered in "eighty-nine pennies, two slugs and some postage." Observing custom, the happy colonists are decked in royal regalia, marching triumphantly from the dining hall (Camp House) to his home to deliver payment. Officially due on June 30, the colonists typically paid on Labor Day, the end of summer. "Sometimes carrying banners," remembers Ada Taft, ". . . we followed the edge of the bluff to Tillie's oak from which a wide path was cleared under the trees to the house were the family stood awaiting us." After dinner, the colonists gathered beneath Japanese lanterns and listened to Leonard Cruenelle play guitar. Depending on their whimsy, they dressed as nymphs, ghosts, gypsies, fauns, fairies, or Greeks; their costumes were mostly left over from an event at the Art Institute. At night, full of fun and camaraderie, they often danced in the moonlight. On one occasion the colonists greeted Dr. James Henry Breasted, august head of the Oriental Institute, standing as rows of living statues, depicting the *Colossi of Memnon*. By the end of the day, Breasted was giddily dressed as an Egyptian slave driver, unhesitatingly chiming in with the merriment. (Courtesy of the Northern Illinois University Archives.)

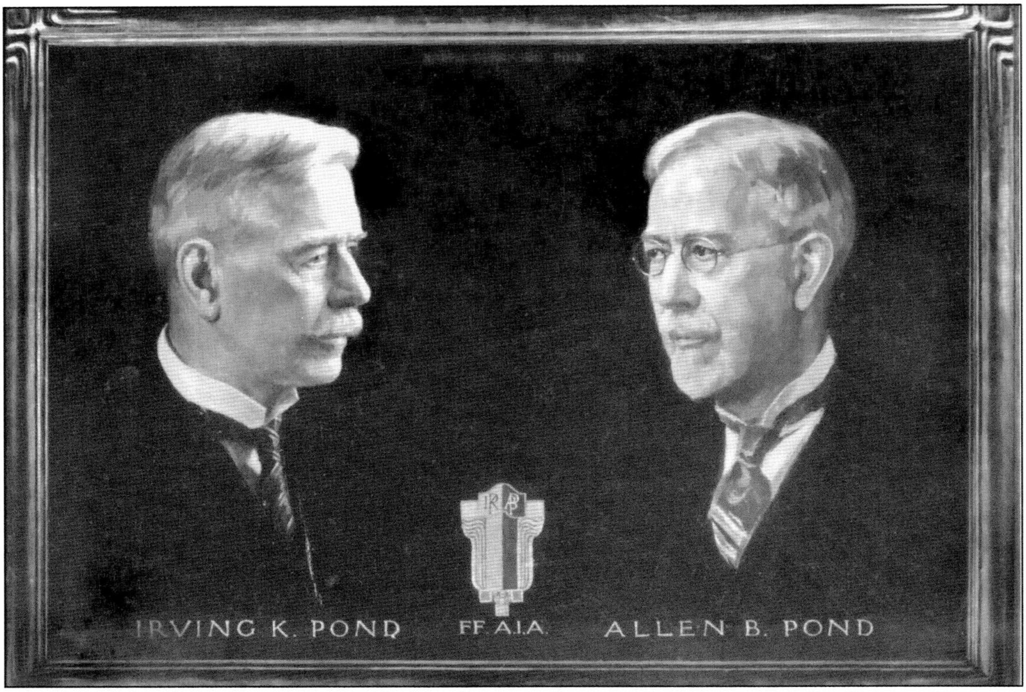

Irving K. and Allen B. Pond formed their architectural partnership in 1885, with offices in Steinway Hall from 1886 to 1926. Known for their detailed craftsmanship, the Pond brothers designed Jane Addams's Hull House; the John Marshall Law School; the American School of Correspondence; and Northwestern University Settlement House. Irving served as president of the American Institute of Architects in 1908. (Courtesy of the Northern Illinois University Archives.)

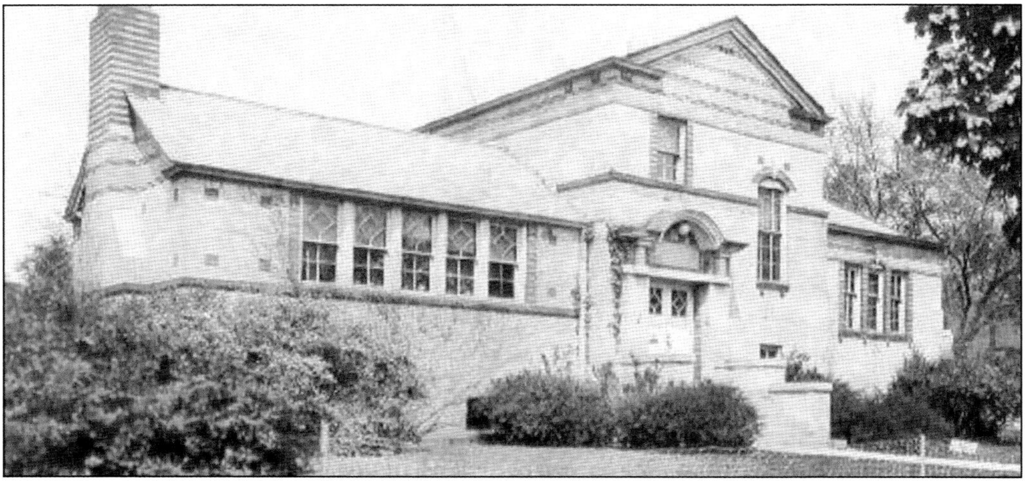

Designed by Pond & Pond, the Oregon Public Library was completed in 1908 with funds from the Carnegie endowment. The upstairs gallery contains artwork donated by the Eagle's Nest Art Colony (1898–1942), and was designed for that purpose. The stairwell displays additional work from local artists. At its opening in 1909, the library held 2,464 volumes; it now it houses 34,000. Though quite efficiently managed, it desperately requires space for expansion. (Courtesy of the Ogle County Historical Society.)

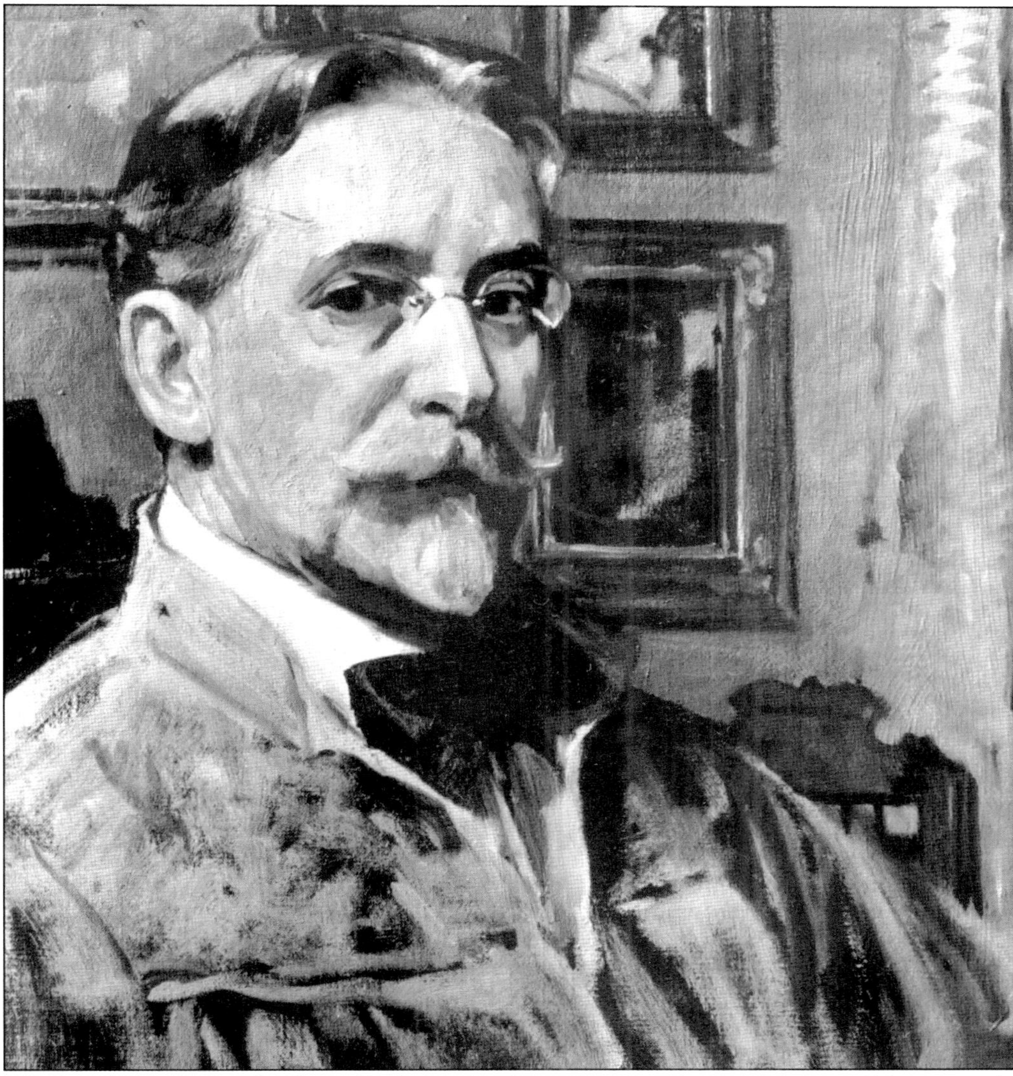

The handsome, exceedingly well-educated Oliver Dennett Grover (1860–1927) graces the cover of this c. 1920 Christmas card sent by his wife, Louise, to friends. Grover was born and raised in Earlville, Illinois, and briefly (and without satisfaction) studied law at the University of Chicago before attending the Chicago Academy of Design, and later the Munich Royal Academy. In Venice, Grover studied under instructor Frank Duveneck and painter James McNeill Whistler, both of whom deeply colored Grover's artistic sensibilities. In Paris, he studied at the Julian Academy before returning to Chicago in 1885 where he accepted a position as senior professor at the School of the Art Institute. As chief instructor, Grover's skillful work heightened the school's international reputation. An Eagle's Nest original founder, many of Grover's masterful paintings portray Oregon and the Sinnissippi countryside. One summer, Grover was the only man at the camp, with 15 or more women. "We were his harem," recalls one, "and he was our fascinating sheik." A work entitled *Thy Will Be Done*, winner of the first Yerkes prize and shown at the Fine Arts Palace of the 1893 World's Fair, was recently rediscovered in New York and obtained by the Illinois Historical Project. (Courtesy of the Northern Illinois University Archives.)

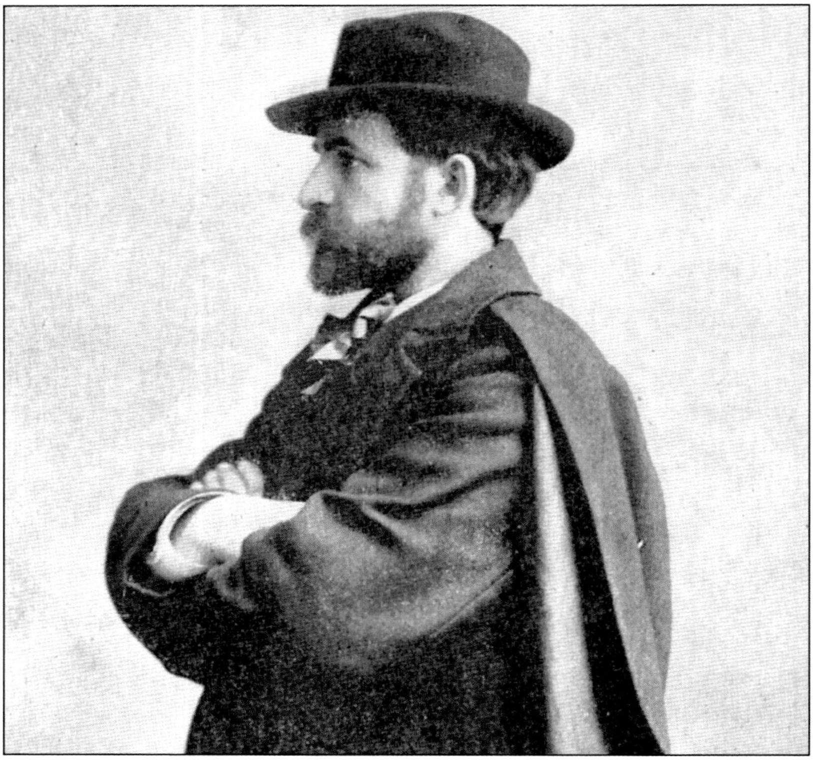

Regional novelist and social critic Hamlin Garland (1860–1940) a trustee of the colony but not a founder, was born in West Salem, Wisconsin. Living the prairie life in Iowa and South Dakota before relocating to Boston in 1884 to pursue a literary career, he published *Main-Travelled Roads* in 1891 to great acclaim. Two years later he moved to Chicago, which was then experiencing an artistic renaissance; there he founded the Cliff Dwellers, a literary club named after the novel by fellow colonist Henry Fuller. In 1899, Garland received an invitation from the Heckmans to visit the Eagle's Nest Art Colony, unaware of their intention to pair him with a young lady named Zulime, sister of Lorado Taft. Garland charmingly relates their courtship in *A Daughter of the Middle Border* (1921), the second volume of an autobiographical series. According to his account, he rode the train to Oregon where Heckman fetched him. Breakfasting at Ganymede Farm, Mrs. Heckman demurely informed Garland that a Miss Taft, the "volunteer stewardess" of the camp, was "not indifferent" to his coming. He recalls, ". . . I had a sense of committing myself to a perilous campaign." That night in the dining hall, the colonists began beating their plates with spoons, singing, anticipating the arrival of Zulime, much teased but surely loved. As the clamor heightened, Garland turned to see ". . . the handsome figure of a girl moving with calm and stately dignity across the little lawn toward the table." As she entered, he noted her quiet amusement. "This entrance . . . was precisely the kind of picture to produce on my mind a deeply influencing impression." The young lady could sew, cook, model, and paint. As days progressed, Garland and Miss Taft walked and talked as circumspectly as possible, "loitering through the magical light of the Harvest Moon," as the colonists sniggered behind their hands and placed bets. At last Garland, nervous about his financial situation, popped the question: "It is monstrous selfishness. It is wrong. But I want you." She consented without debate. Years later Garland fondly reflects, ". . . as I write these lines our silver wedding is not far off. . . . Zulime has met all storms with a brave sweetness. . . If she has regrets, she does not permit me to know them." After Chicago, Garland moved to New York, then to Hollywood where he died.

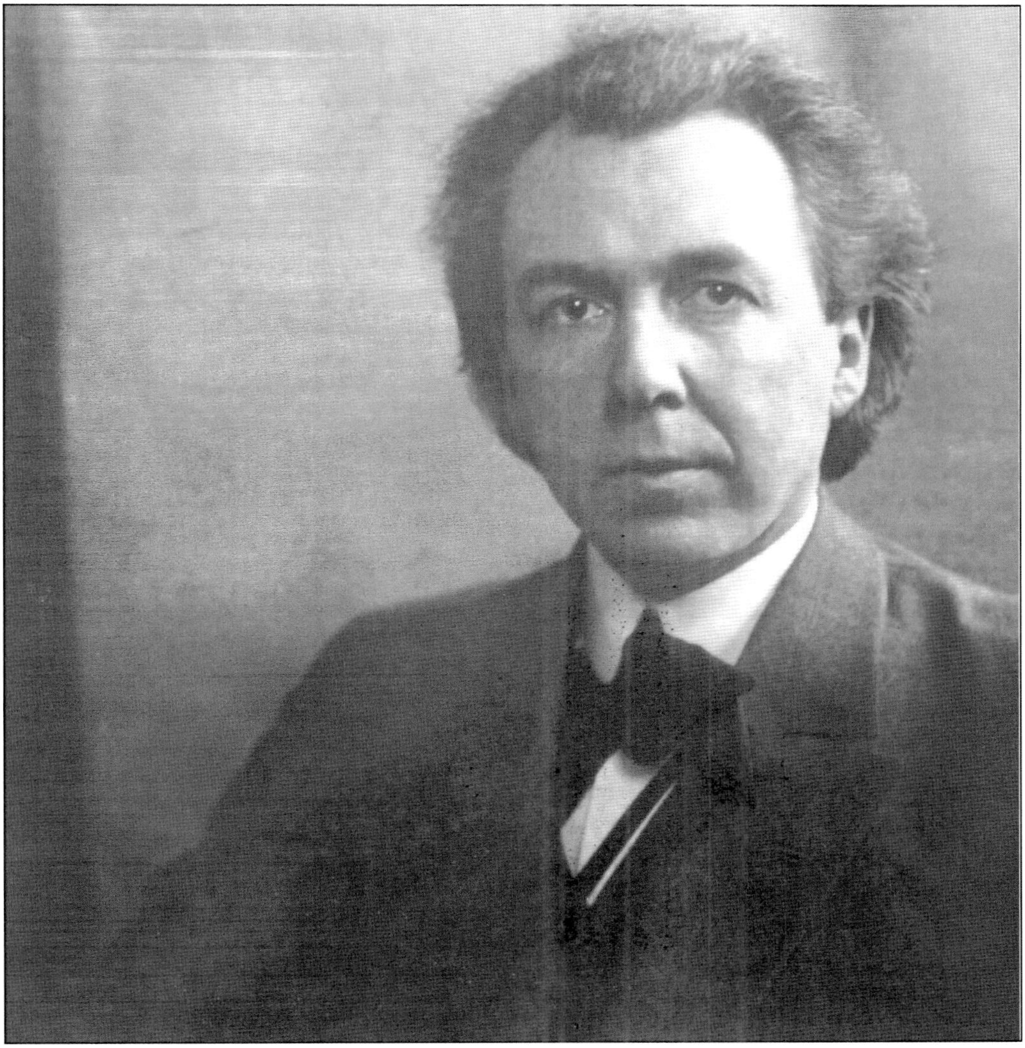

Frank Lloyd Wright (1867–1959) *c.* 1904-06. The formidable architect visited the Eagle's Nest Art Colony at least once, possibly several times. It is likely that he connected with the colony through his beloved mentor, Louis Sullivan, a member of Hamlin Garland's Cliff Dwellers Club in Chicago. One intriguing anecdote lingers relating to his involvement with the colony. Journeying from his Oak Park studio to Oregon, Wright stopped in Rochelle, Illinois, to inspect one of his structures, as was his custom. Discovering that the hapless homeowner had radically altered it to necessarily repair weathering and modernize the kitchen, the enraged Wright stormed into the unfortunate man's downtown bank office and administered rough justice. Later, protesting what he perceived as unconscionable vandalism, Wright destroyed all personal records pertaining to the house, forever disowning it. Owing to its extensive alterations, the FLW Preservation Trust cannot endorse it on their official register. Over the years, further dubious "improvements" were inflicted upon the interior, but its present owners are attempting a faithful restoration of Wright's intent according to surviving blueprints. Oregon boasts two prairie style homes designed by Frank W. Carpenter, a Wright disciple from Rockford, Illinois. (Courtesy of the Collection of Frank Lloyd Wright Preservation Trust, H&S H273, photographer: unknown.)

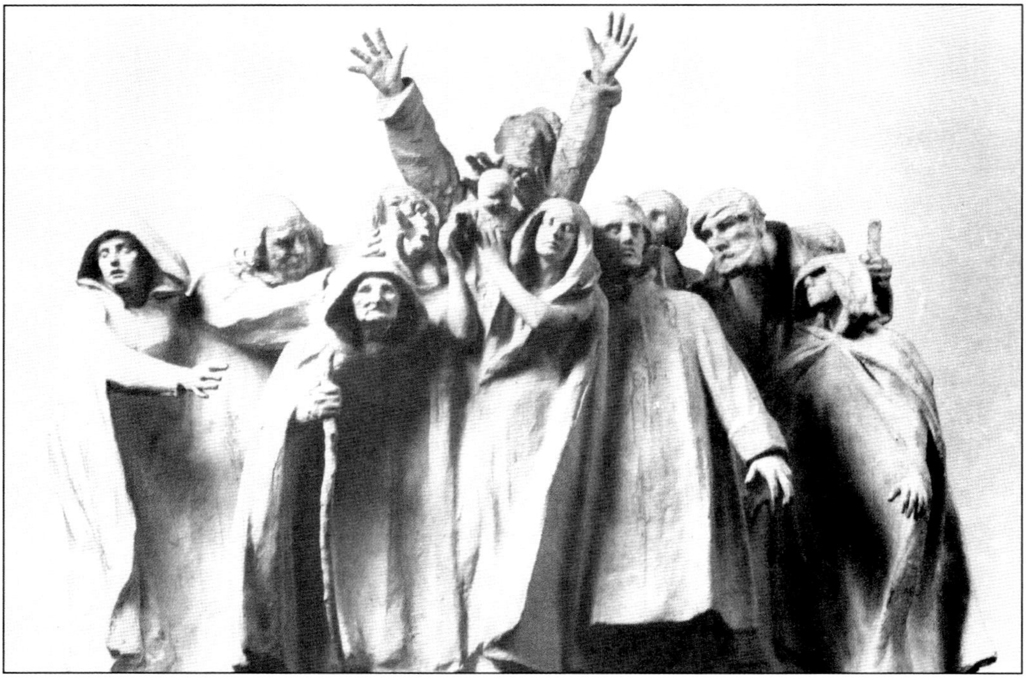

Taft's powerful *The Blind*, a working cast for the finished sculpture at the University of Illinois, resulted from viewing Maurice Maeterlinck's tragedy, *Les Aveugles*. Taft comments: ". . . the figures are drawn together for mutual protection. . . . Then the young girl with the faith of second sight recognizes in the sob of a child a promise of salvation." It is displayed at Oregon Public Library. (Courtesy of the Arts Alliance of Ogle County.)

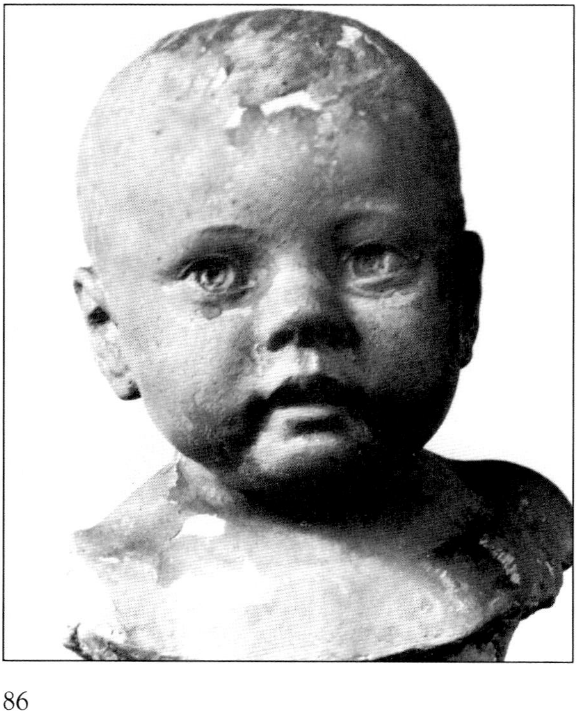

Not much is know about *Nadine* by Leonard Cruenelle (1872–1944). Cruenelle, "as modest as he was gifted," as Ada remembers, met Lorado Taft during a lecture in Pana, Illinois, where he worked in the coal mines. Someone showed Cruenelle's work to Taft, who persuaded him to study at the Art Institute. Cruenelle assisted the master with supervising the sculptural ornamentation at the Columbian Exposition. The bust is displayed at Oregon Public Library. (Courtesy of the Arts Alliance of Ogle County.)

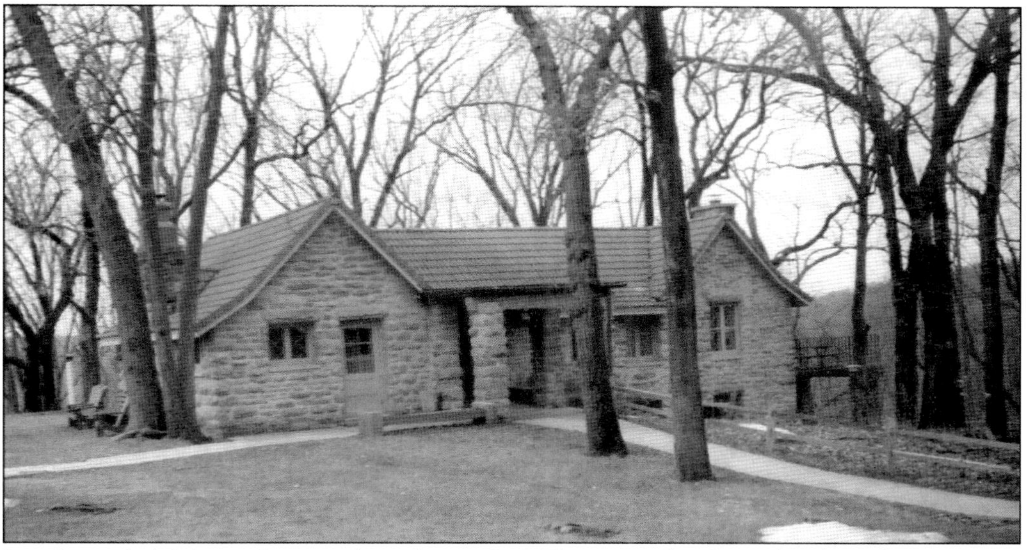

Lorado and Ada's residence, where he crafted *The Eternal Indian*'s head, as his assistant, John Prasuhn, supervised the ten-day round-the-clock construction of the statue's body. The Tafts often remained into autumn, as clay forms could not be moved until cast in plaster. Here Taft sculpted the 15-foot *George Washington* for the University of Washington in Seattle. The cabin's interior has been reconfigured, now serving as a meeting room and offices for Taft Field Campus staff.

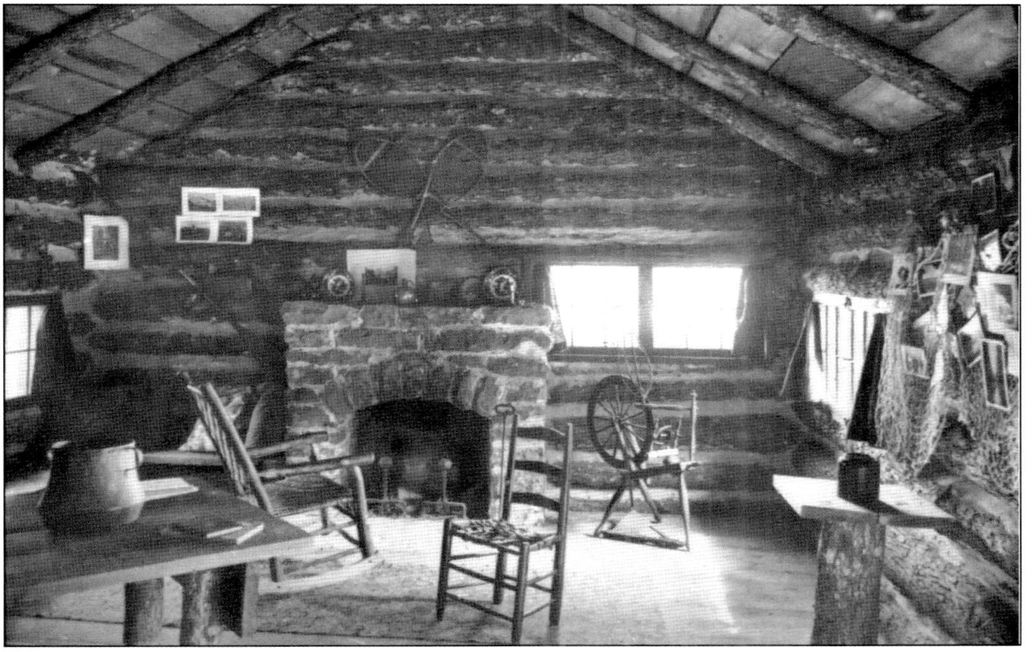

Cottages occupied by the colonists during the summers were small, quaint, and self-consciously rustic. Note the logs serving as table legs, and the spinning wheel beneath the window. The remaining cottages have been converted into offices, residences, or assembly rooms for the Taft Field Campus. This photograph is *c.* 1910. (Courtesy of the Northern Illinois University Archives.)

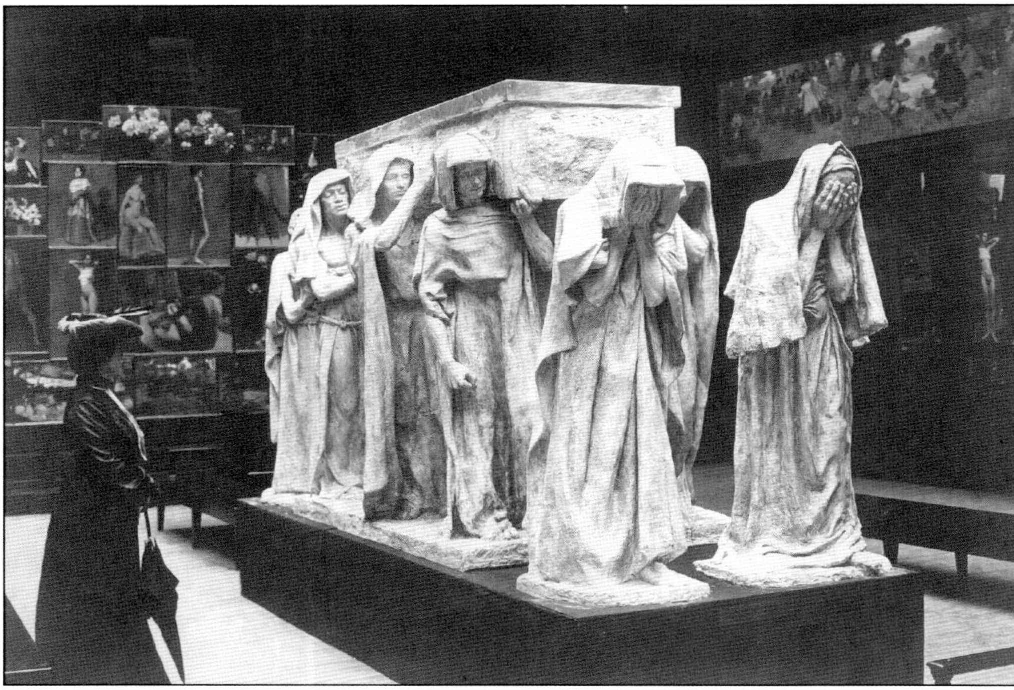

In 1906 Taft's disciples sculpted *The Mourners*, depicting six forlorn, hooded figures bearing a casket, seen here in his Midway Studio. This was one of many large-scale projects assigned by the master. Supposedly its faces are his students' self-portraits. Note the freestanding figures preceding the mourners, absent in the version below. (Courtesy of the University of Illinois Archives.)

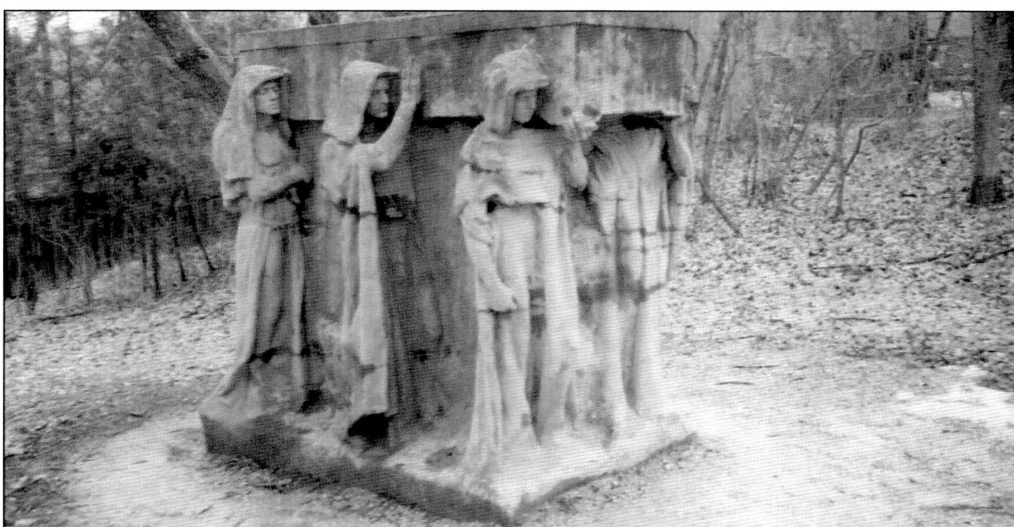

Here is an apparently identical sculpture seen outdoors at the NIU Taft Field Campus. Though it is entirely possible that Taft and his students crafted the piece from local materials, the studio photo suggests that *The Mourners* might have been transported to the Eagle's Nest Art Colony. It is now popularly known as "The Seven Muses." Standing alone on a wooded path, the piece is a marvelously spectral sight after a snowfall.

The *Fish Boys*, c. 1880, kneel beside a shallow pool in Mix Park on South 4th Street. Mrs. Mix presented the land to the city in 1920. The whimsical boys clutch fish out of whose mouths water spouts into the pool. (Courtesy of the Ogle County Historical Society.)

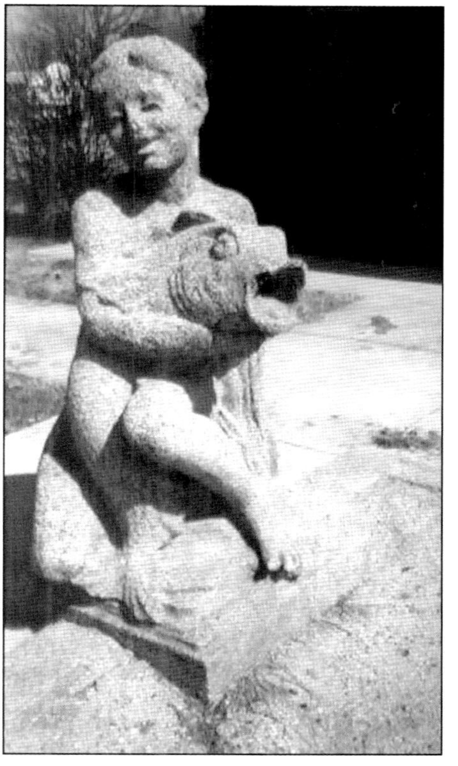

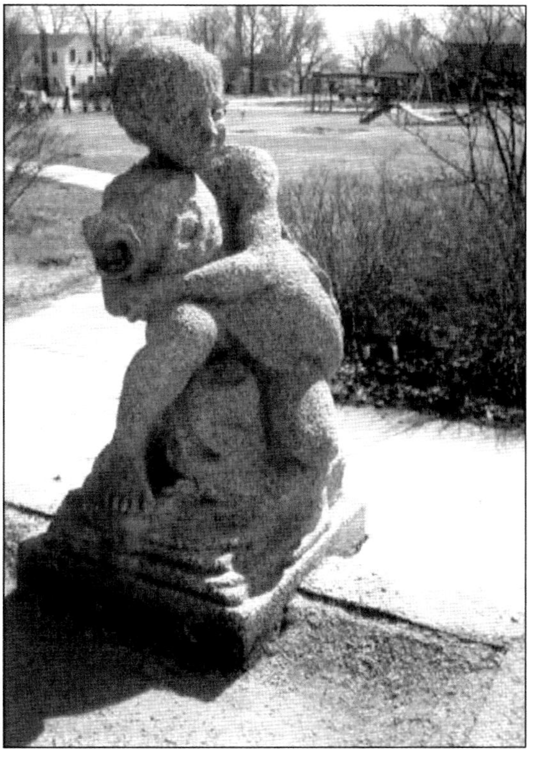

Designed by Lorado Taft, the boys are based on figures seen in his *Fountain of Great Lakes* in Chicago. The statues are composed of concrete and crushed quartz, mixed with pebbles from the Potomac River. (Courtesy of the Ogle County Historical Society.)

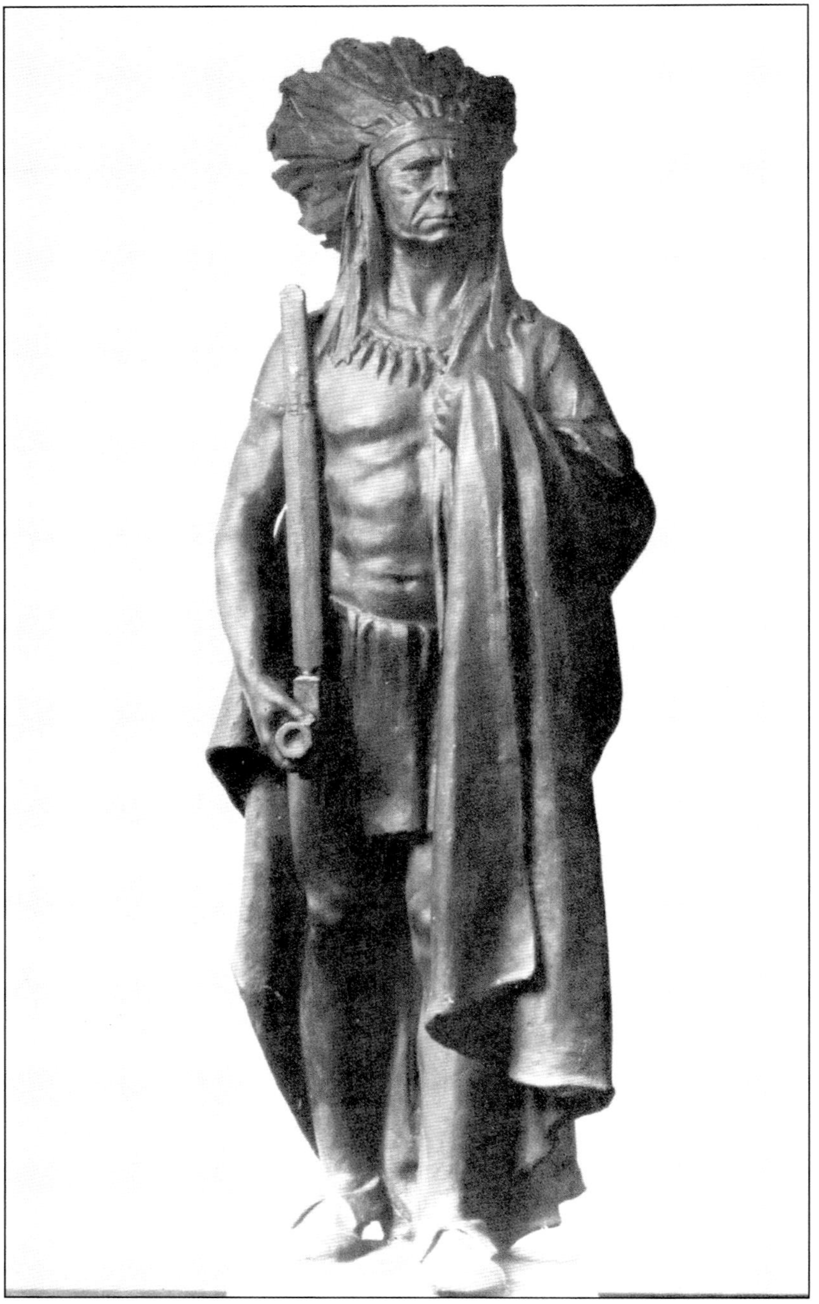

Chief Keokuk, by the awesomely talented Nellie Verne Walker (1874–1973), was probably a working model for the completed Chief Keokuk Monument in Keokuk, Iowa. The Sauk chief's indecision in the face of encroaching white settlement caused Blackhawk to step forward and assume command of his people. Walker studied under Taft at the Art Institute and participated in 16 Institute exhibitions, garnering numerous prizes. She maintained workspace at his Midway Art Studio. The model is displayed at Oregon Public Library. (Courtesy of the Arts Alliance of Ogle County.)

A staunch supporter of Native American causes, as were all of the colonists, Taft desired to create a tribute. Inspired by the high concrete chimneys at the Art Institute, he hatched an idea to utilize this easily-obtained material for a statue, instead of using the much costlier stone or bronze, and commenced figuring the dimensions for the 50-foot figure. The six-foot plaster working model is displayed at Oregon Public Library. (Courtesy of the Arts Alliance of Ogle County.)

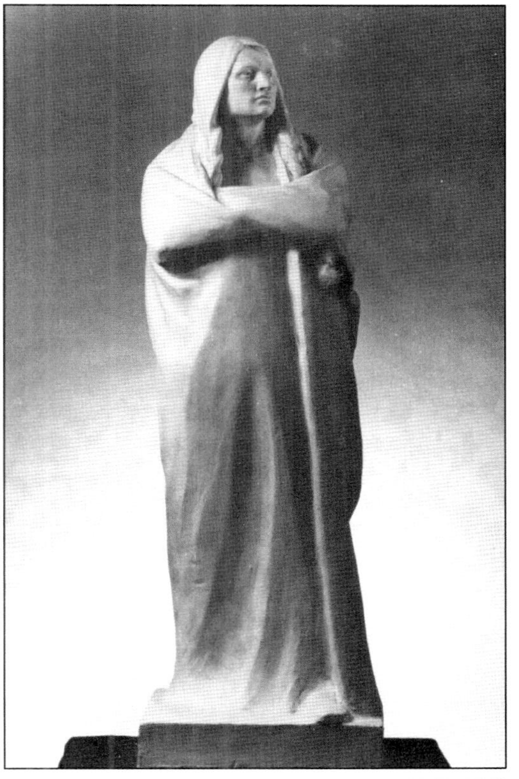

These girls recline in the plaster folds of the mold's neck as Taft and his assistants apply finishing touches before elevating it onto the torso for the first time to determine the head's final positioning. That done, the mold was removed and the piece forms were then erected. Taft rigorously encouraged the presence of children, deriving inspiration from their innocence and playful spirit. Often they posed for sculptures or performed skits. (Courtesy of the Northern Illinois University Archives.)

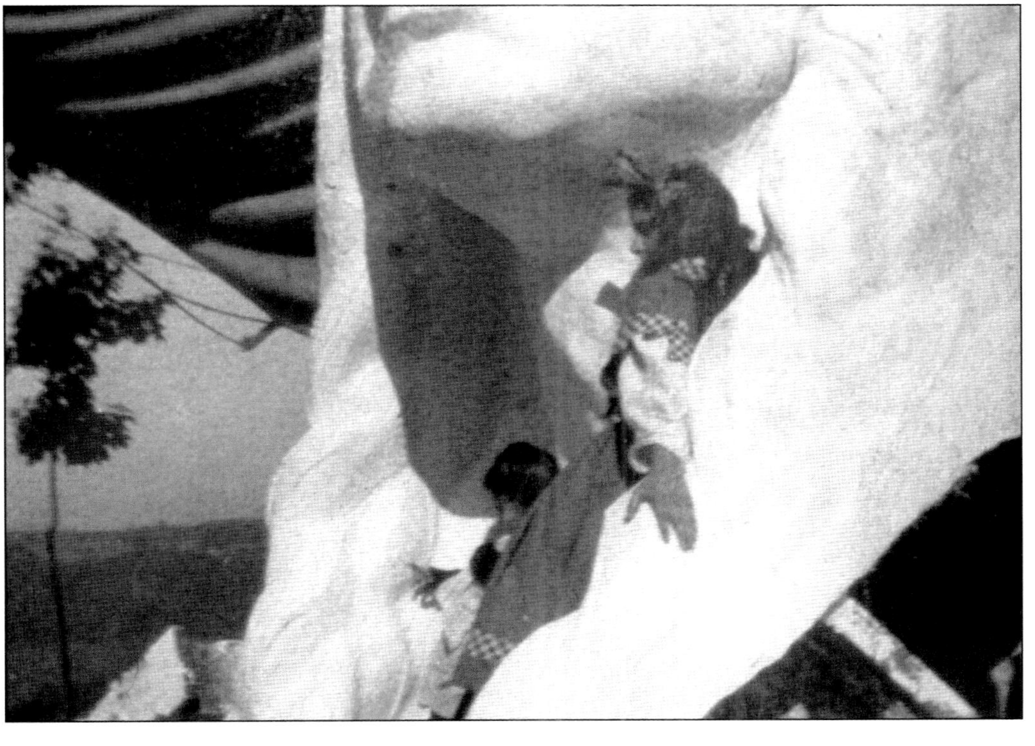

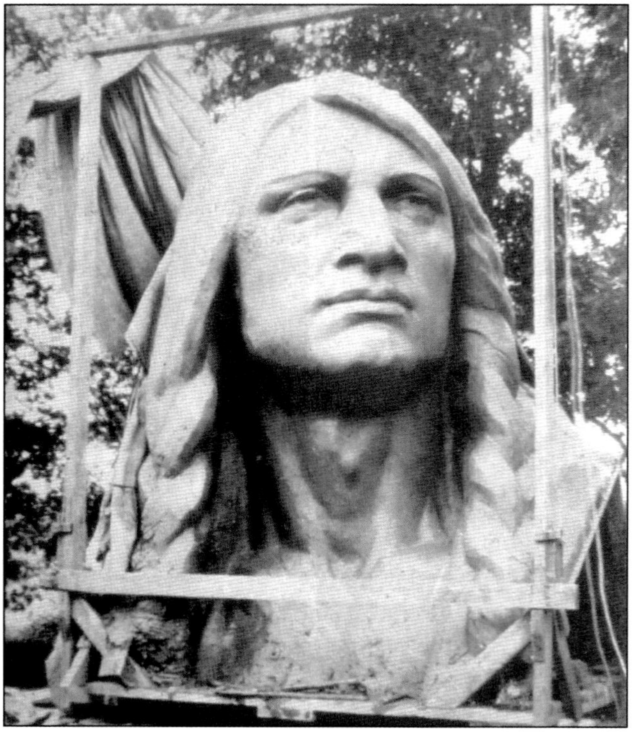

Crafting the statue's face, Taft used the profile of Hamlin Garland, friend and brother-in-law, as his model, in addition to incorporating the features of Roman emperors, and Sauk and Fox Indians. After the plaster cast was detailed, he fitted piece molds over it. For the final step, assistant John Prasuhn positioned it onto the torso for the cement pouring, which contained the crushed plaster. (Courtesy of the Northern Illinois University Archives.)

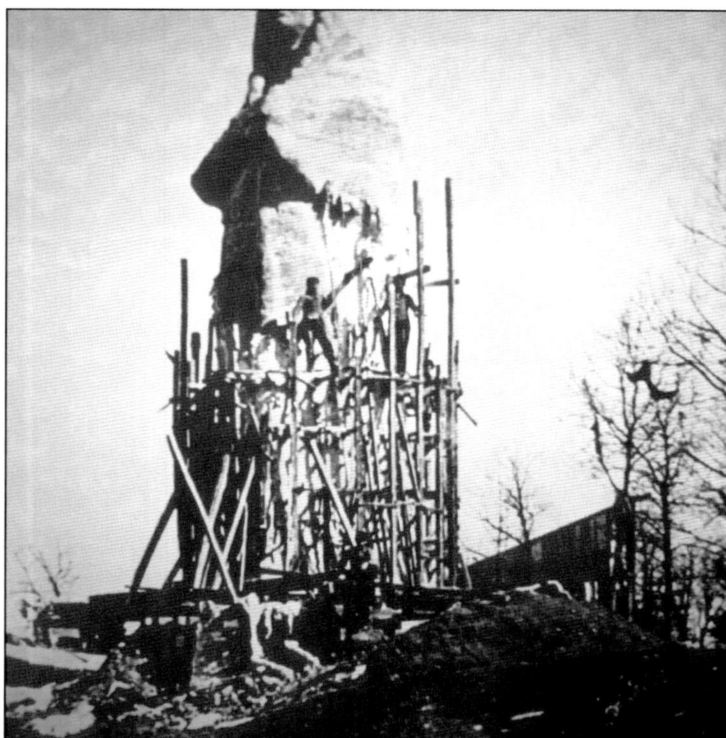

As scaffolding is dismantled, so are the piece molds, revealing the unbroken concrete visage. Ada recalls: "Mr. Prasuhn . . . was able to reach with his chisel a place under the eye and to pry off a block of the mold. It was an ominous moment. . . . One can imagine the relief and joy with which my husband saw this. If the eye, the most carefully modeled part, was perfectly cast, he was reassured as to the large planes of the blanket." (Courtesy of the Northern Illinois University Archives.)

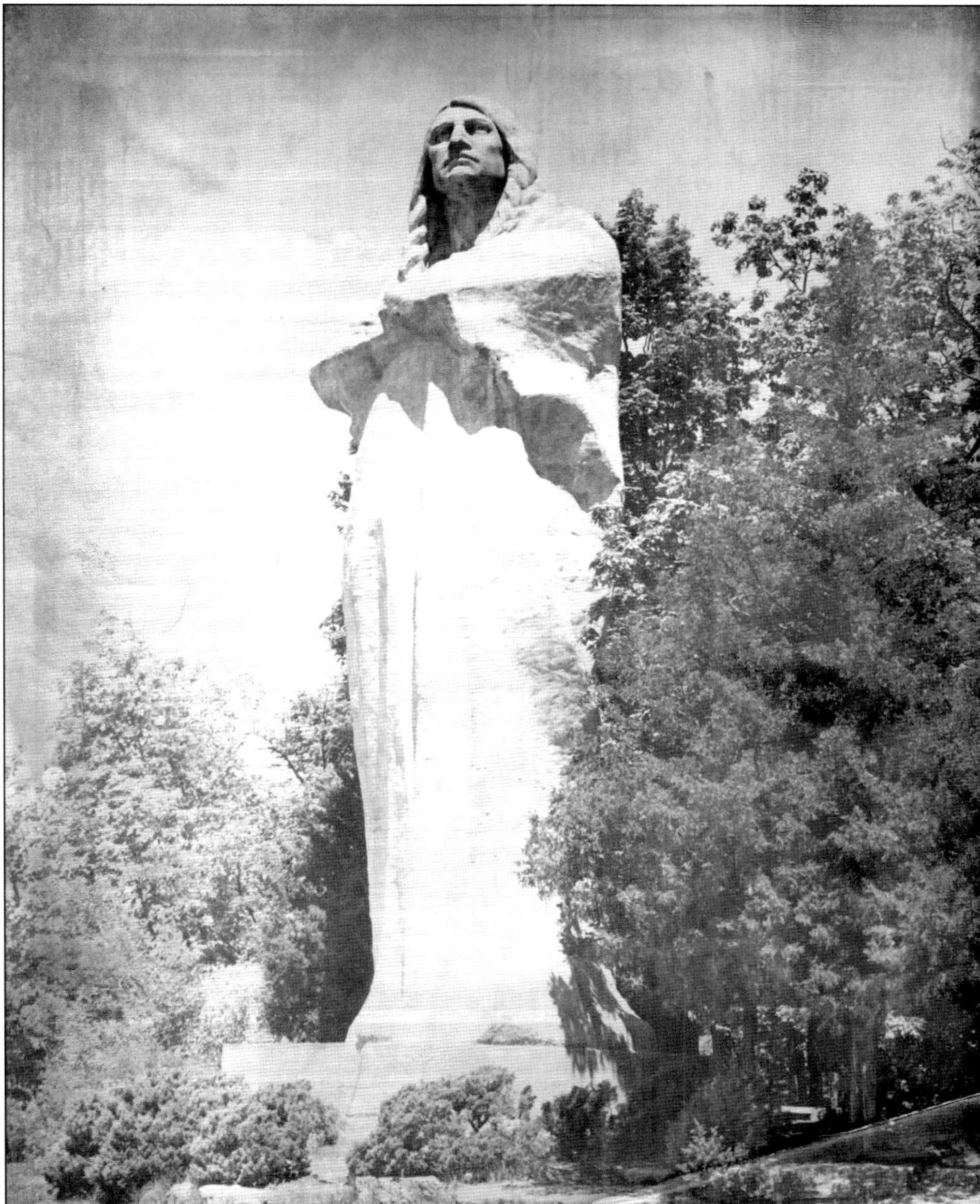

The Eternal Indian, 1920, as it was officially called. The Honorable Frank Lowden presided over its dedication on July 1, 1911. Taft never christened the statue "Blackhawk," the name that has nevertheless stuck in the decades ensuing. (Courtesy of the *Oregon Republican-Reporter*.)

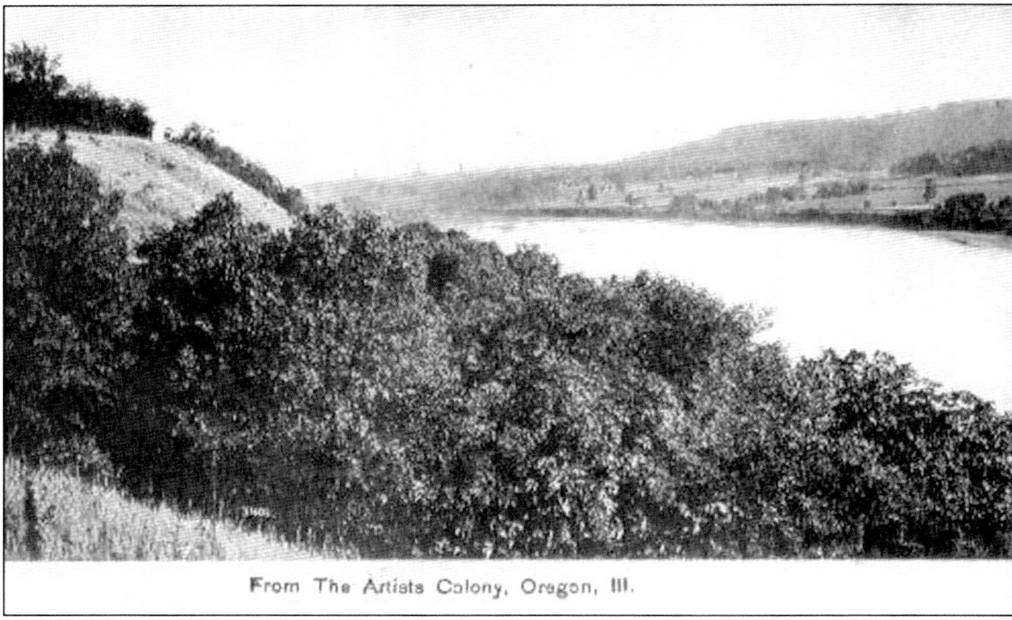

This view looks south from the colony toward Oregon, *c.* 1910. Colony artists frequently painted this view, impressed with the natural vistas, a rarity in urban Chicago. (Courtesy of the *Oregon Republican-Reporter*.)

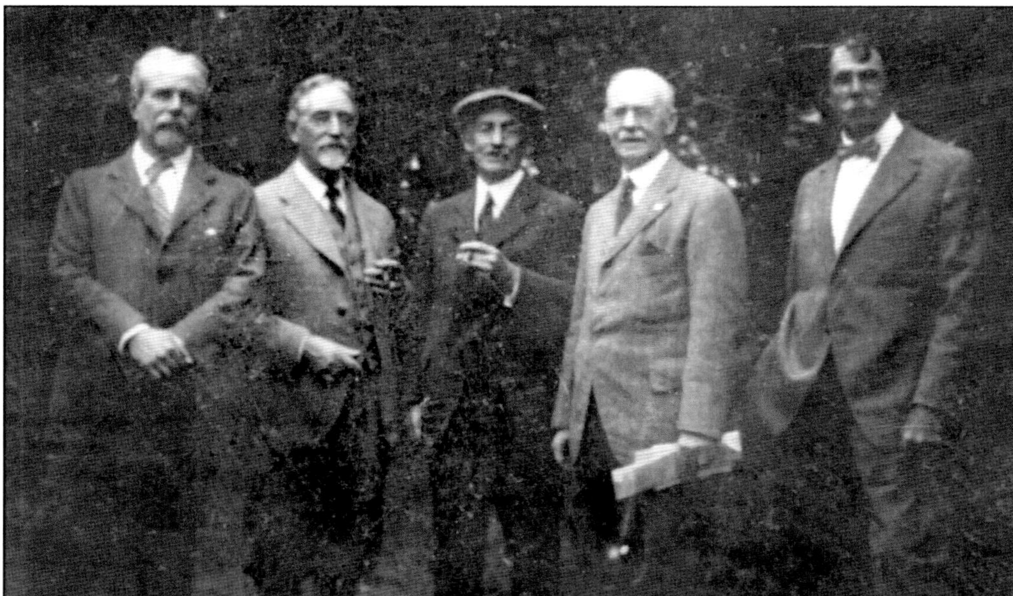

Five of the Eagle's Nest founding fathers are pictured, from left to right: Lorado Taft, painter Oliver Dennett Grover, Horace Fiske, editor and University of Chicago secretary James Spencer Dickerson, and painter Ralph Clarkson. As per Heckman's lease, the colony permanently disbanded upon the demise of its last original member, which happened to be Clarkson, who died in 1942. (Courtesy of the Northern Illinois University Archives.)

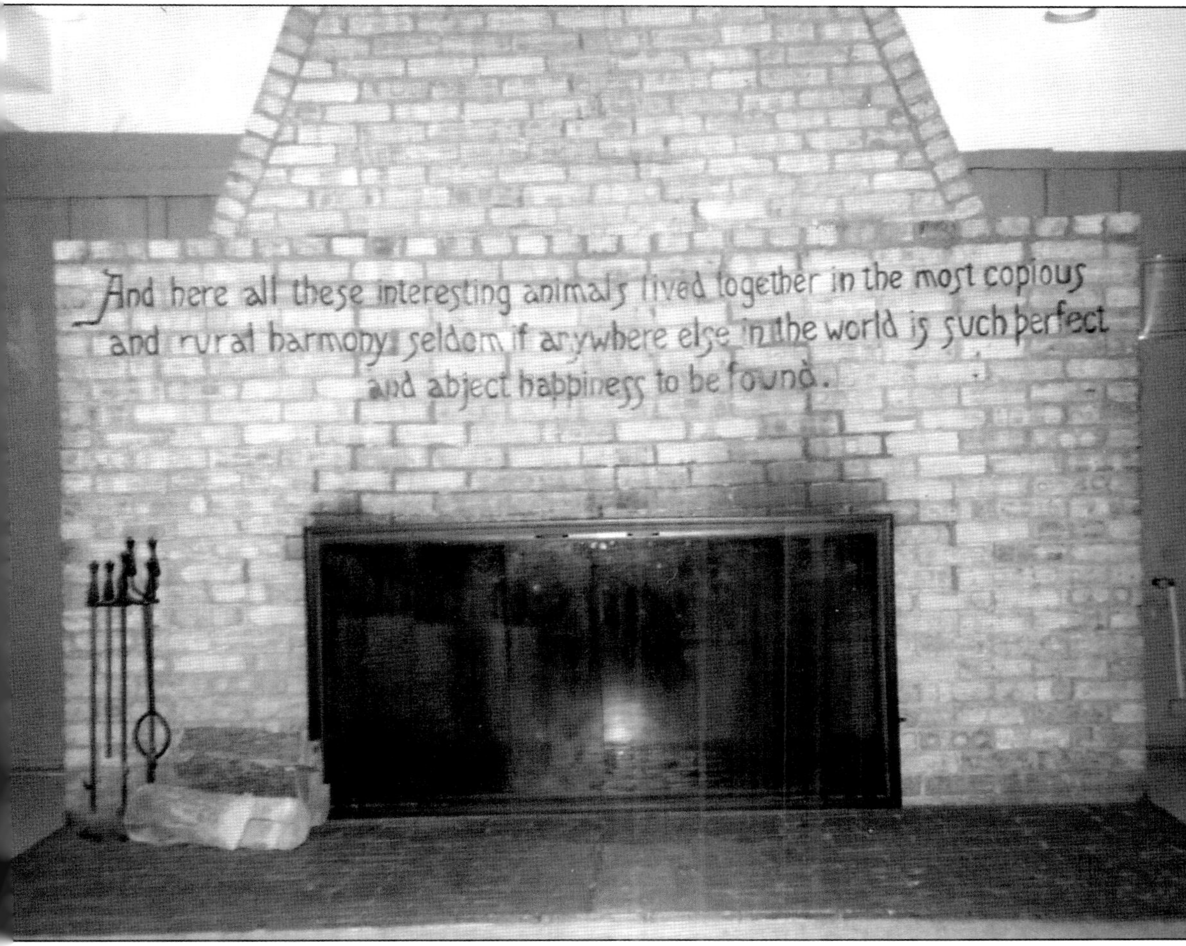

Poley Hall on the Taft Field Campus originally functioned as the Eagle's Nest dining room, then called Camp House. The kitchen was supervised by a black woman named Mary, assisted by her daughter, Ollie Boga. The colonists gathered here for skits and lectures. Other colony guests included Fanny Bloomfield Zeisler, famed pianist, and Lucy Fitch Perkins, noted children's book author and illustrator. The inscription above the hearth, lifted from nonsense poet Edward Lear and limned by Taft's other brother-in-law, Charles Francis Browne, reads: *And here all these interesting animals lived together in the most copious and rural harmony; seldom if anywhere else in the world is such perfect and abject happiness to be found.* Who could argue? After dinner the colonists retired to the patio overlooking the river, now used as a classroom. An inscription in the vestibule declares: *All passes. Art alone endures.* The Eagle's Nest Art Colony is gone, but its legacy remains as bright and pure as the moonlight in which the colonists danced.

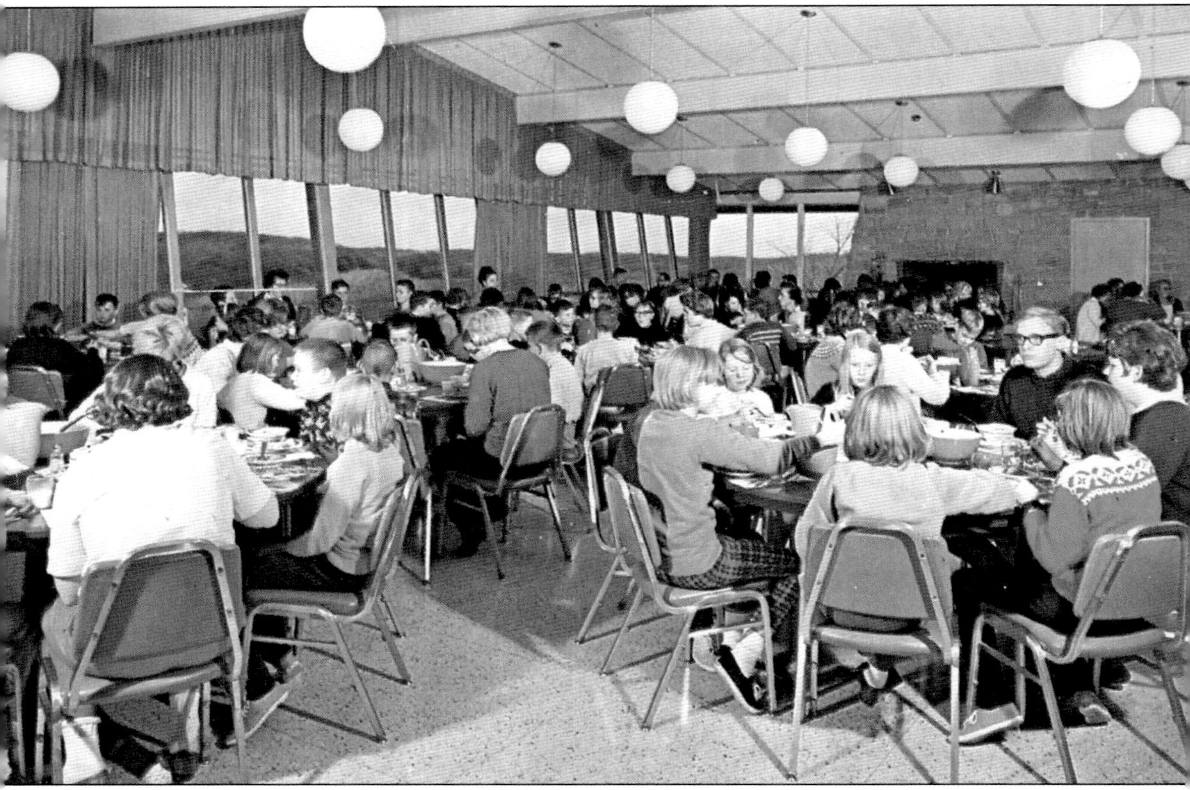

Visiting students enjoy lunch at Harrison Hall on the Taft Campus, as seen in this postcard, *c.* 1970. Observers looking up from the valley often mistake the dining hall for a private residence perched on the high bluff. Here the slanted, wraparound windows afford a breathtaking view of the countryside. An original Oliver Dennett Grover painting of early Oregon now hangs over the fireplace. A few years after the colony disbanded, the state of Illinois bought the Heckman property as a park in 1949; however, the land had fallen under the very interested eye of Dr. Leslie Holmes, president of Northern Illinois University, who advocated a field study camp. In 1951, Adlai Stevenson signed a bill transferring 66 acres to NIU. Three years later, Professor Paul Harrison was enlisted to renovate the buildings for class use. In 1963, a Masters degree in Outdoor Education was approved by the Teachers' College Board. In the years ahead, further renovations were implemented, including additional acreage and staff. In 2000, the College of Education ceased its connection with the campus, now operating under the authority of the Provost's office. The beautiful property continues to offer environmental education programs to thousands of teachers and schoolchildren. Dale Hoppe is the current director of the Lorado Taft Field Campus.

Five

Stronghold Castle

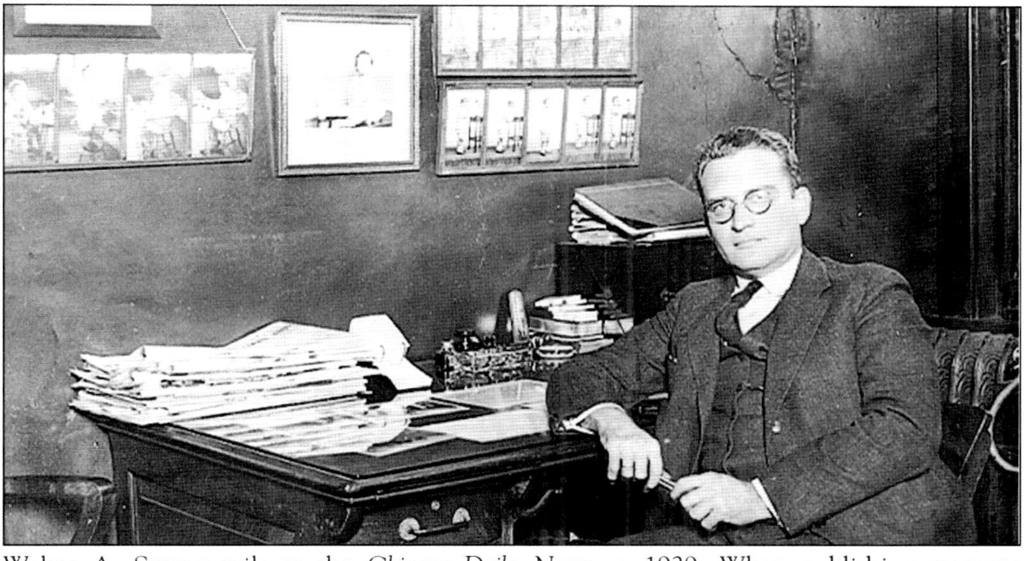

Walter A. Strong toils at the *Chicago Daily News*, c. 1929. When publishing magnate Victor Lawson died in 1925, Strong assembled a party of investors and bought the powerhouse Chicago newspaper for 14 million dollars, replacing Lawson as its editor and publisher. Like many well-to-do Chicagoans, Strong sought a country estate to escape the city heat; so in 1928 he bought 60 acres from Wallace Heckman who owned land west of the Rock River in addition to Ganymede Farm on the eastern bank. The Strong family, based in suburban Winnetka, Illinois, had already enjoyed several summers in Oregon, visiting Mrs. Strong's father, Towner Webster, at Bee Tree Farm north of the city. Walter invested well, and by the end of the year his purchase increased from 60 to 360 acres.

A competent, energetic man, Strong presided over the legendary talent pool that included literary luminaries Carl Sandburg, novelist and poet; William Akin, journalist and rare book collector; Howard Vincent O'Brien, columnist; these offices also inspired humorist Ben Hecht's classic screwball comedy, *The Front Page*. A graduate and trustee of Beloit College in Beloit, Wis. (class of 1905), Strong was posthumously honored in 1934 when his *alma mater* constructed and dedicated the Walter Ansel Strong Memorial Stadium. (Courtesy of the Robert K. Strong family.)

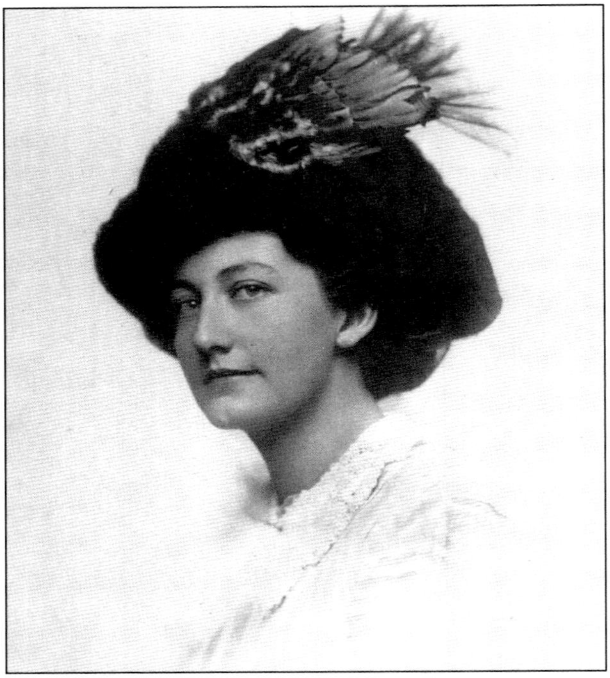

The castle's one and only queen, Josephine Webster Strong, as a younger woman, sporting a peacock-feathered hat. This image is *c.* 1920. (Courtesy of the Robert K. Strong family.)

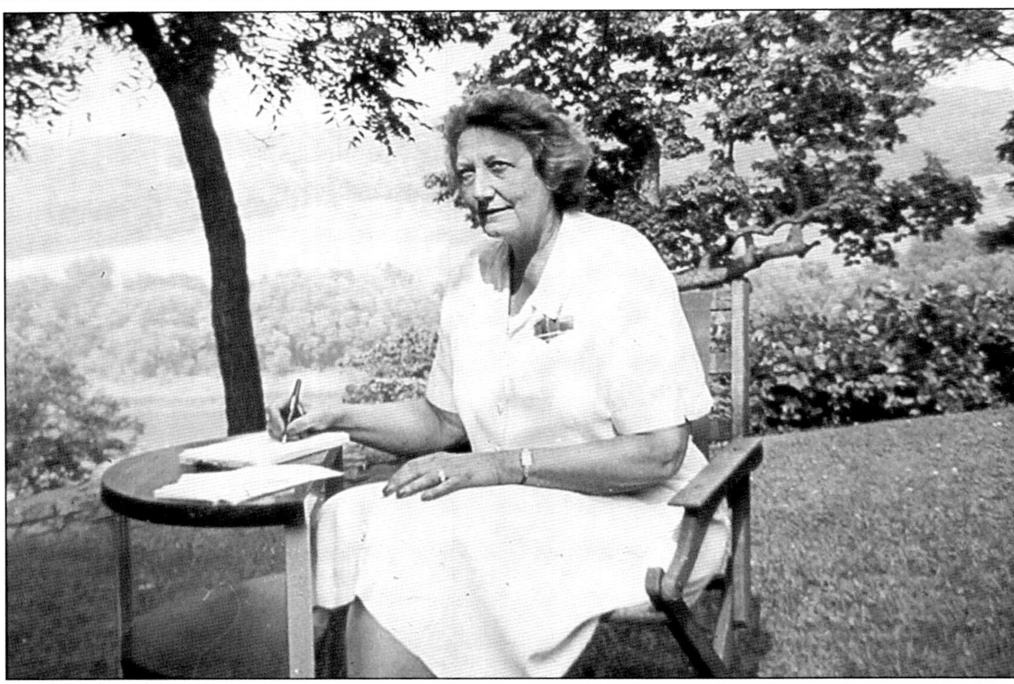

The Rock River is visible behind Josephine Strong, *c.* 1955, relaxing on the western lawn between the castle and the river, now obscured by trees. After Walter's sudden death from a heart attack in 1931, Josephine divided her time between summers at Stronghold, hosting children and grandchildren, and their family home in Winnetka until her death in 1961 at age 80. (Courtesy of the Robert K. Strong family.)

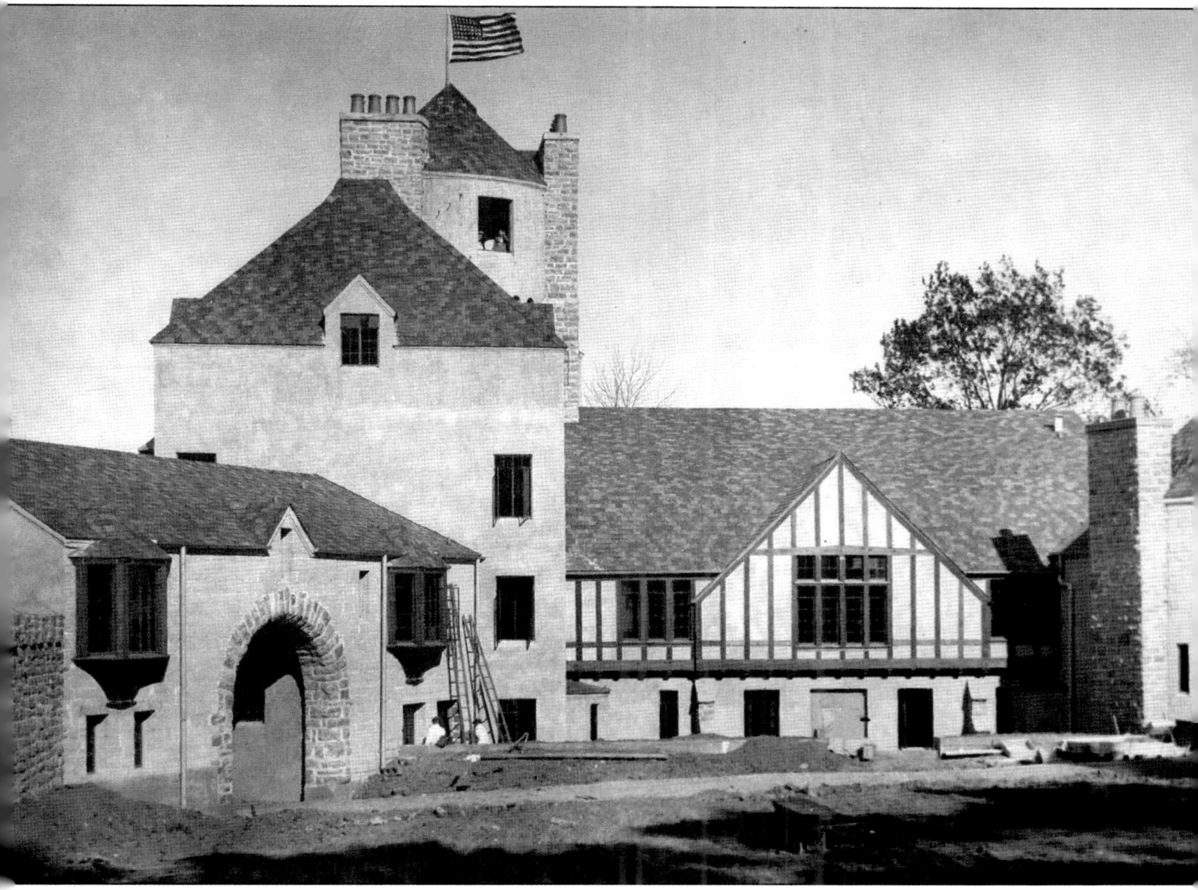

Construction workers finish the walls, *c.* 1930. Originally, the Strong summer estate was a barn and silo-like structure. As matters progressed, the family opted for something a bit more lavish: a French-style castle with Tudor flourishes, designed by Josephine's brother, architect Maurice Webster. Supposedly Walter Strong visited England searching for models, including an ancestral castle. For the two-year construction, he imported most of his workers from Chicago, but also employed local labor and material, including an on-site quarry. The castle's exterior required almost nine months to build, totaling $85,000; the interior took another year to complete. (Courtesy of the Robert K. Strong family.)

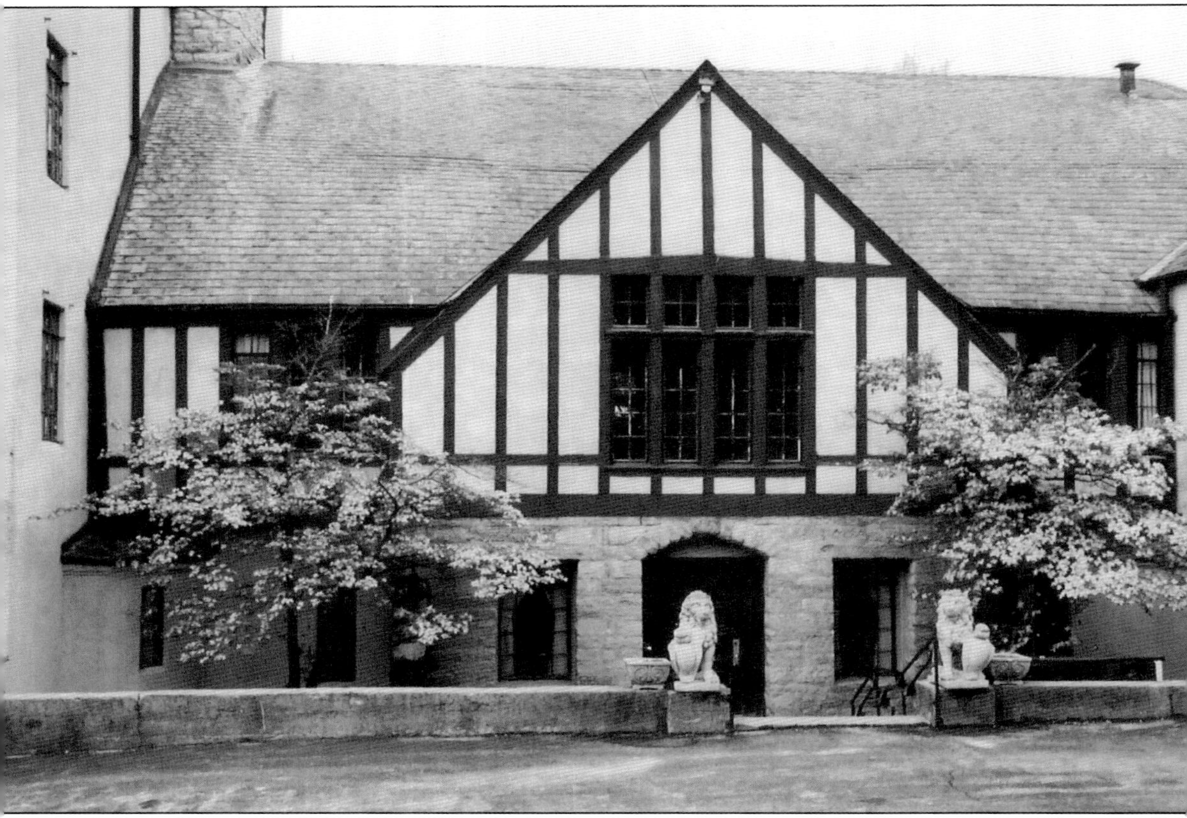

The castle's front door, where tours gather, *c.* 1965. Completed, the building contained 16 bedrooms, 9 baths, 8 fireplaces, and a "great hall." When the family was present and desired company, they flew a flag; if it was not flying, they either were not home or wanted no visitors. (Courtesy of the Stronghold Center.)

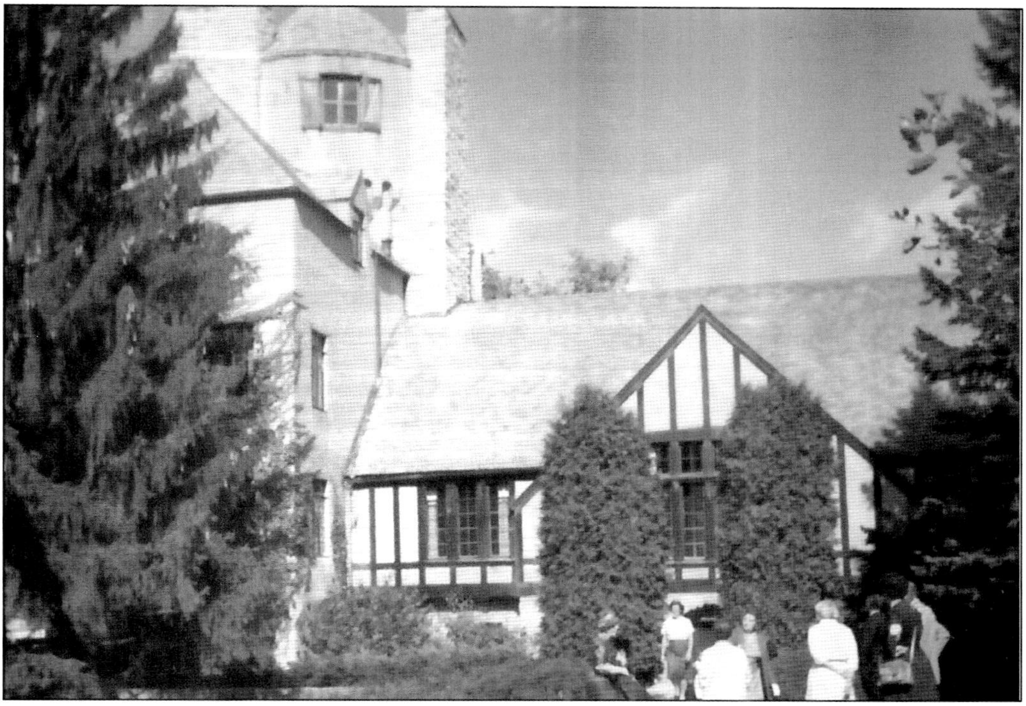

At the top of the tower is the Observation Room. From its height one can spy cornfields on the western side of the Rock River. *The Eternal Indian* is not visible due to a bend in the river, although it is close. Also visible, but somewhat less enchanting, are the gigantic coolant tanks at the Byron Nuclear Power Plant, visible for miles in all directions. This image is c. 1962. (Courtesy of the Stronghold Center.)

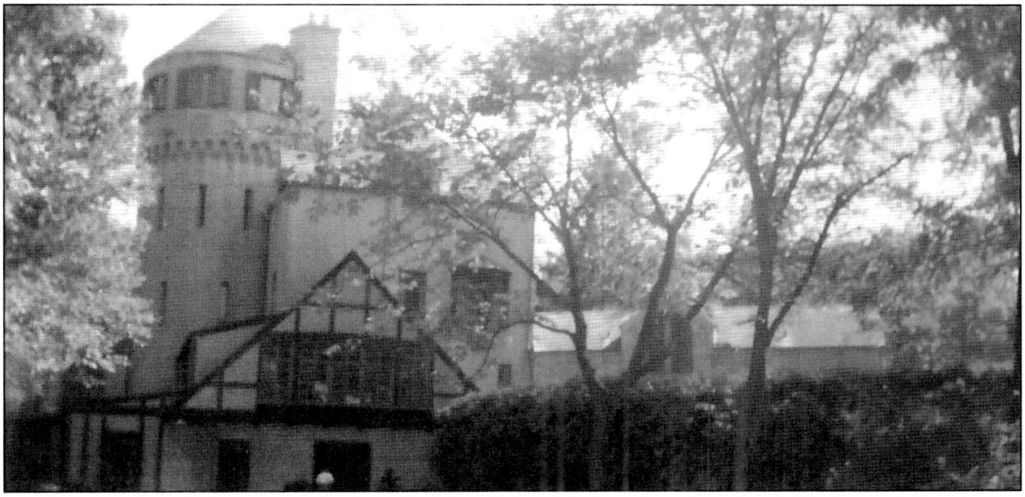

Walter Strong's ashes were spread north of the swimming pool. When their son, David, was killed in WWII, his ashes were spread there as well. The window overlooking the pool is the Sun Room, originally a screened-in porch. Mrs. Strong relaxed here, watching the grounds and pool, as the morning sun warmed the room. This photograph is c. 1962. (Courtesy of the Stronghold Center.)

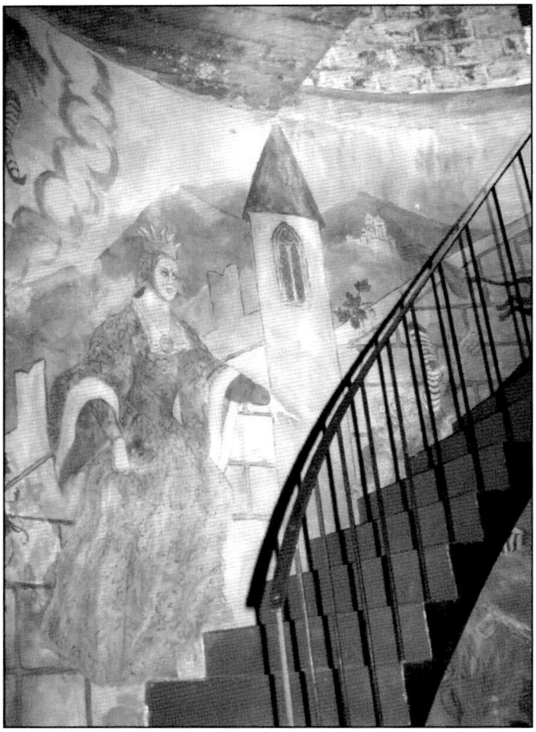

During the Depression, the Strongs hosted an unemployed Russian artist from Chicago named Nicholas Kaissakoff, who painted a fresco in the tower depicting Rumpilstiltskin, of the Grimm's fairytale. The cantilevered stairway leading up the tower was constructed with two layers of cinder blocks; the outer layer is covered in concrete, the inner layer reinforced with steel rods, thus ridding it of unsightly support beams. (Courtesy of Linda H. Strong.)

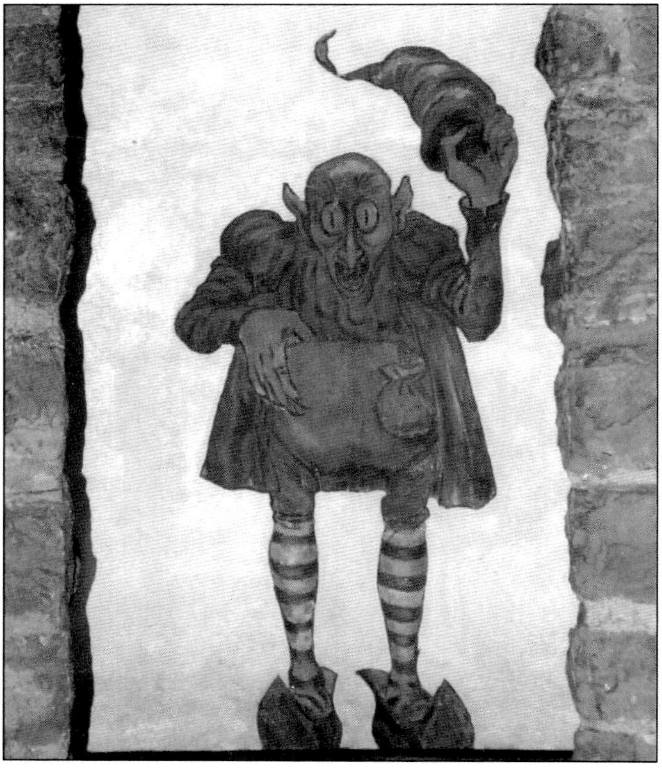

Here is Kaissakoff's rendering of the grotesque, greedy little creature named Rumplestiltskin with whom the miller cut a very bad deal. Kaissakoff modeled the characters' faces on Maurice Webster, Mrs. Strong, and several family pets. Through the years, restorationists have added their own distinctive touches, often incorporating self-portraits. (Courtesy of Linda H. Strong.)

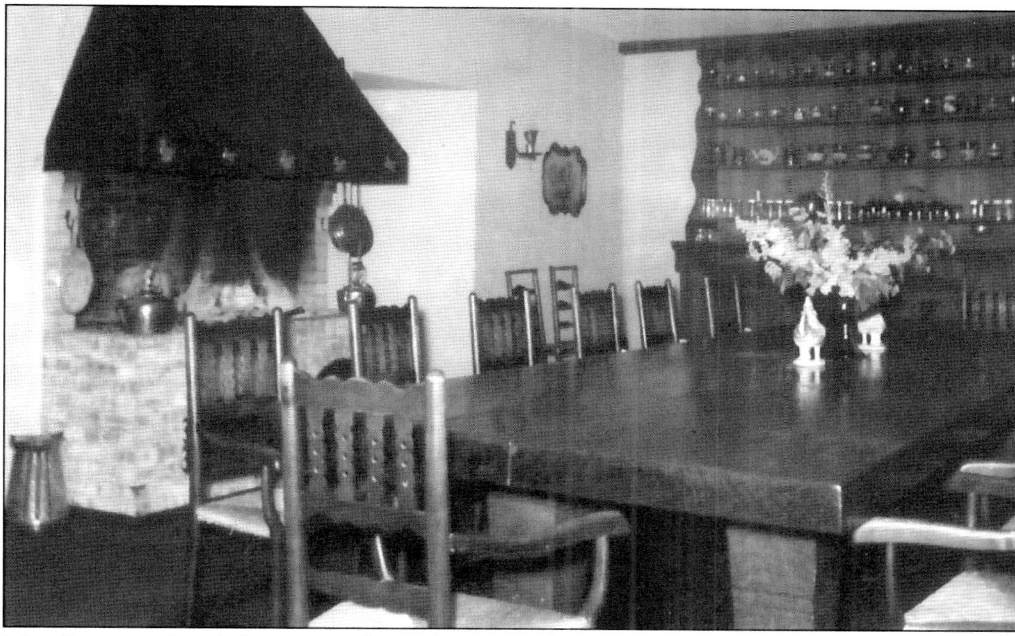

Mrs. Strong ordered this oak table made to specific measurements to best accommodate the entire family. It was sawn into three slabs, two for the top and one for the legs. To fit it, the east wall of the dining room was left unfinished. However, the table proved too heavy for the floor, which required reinforcement before the it could be reinstalled, allowing the wall to be completed. The table weighs approximately two tons. This image is c. 1965. (Courtesy of the Stronghold Center.)

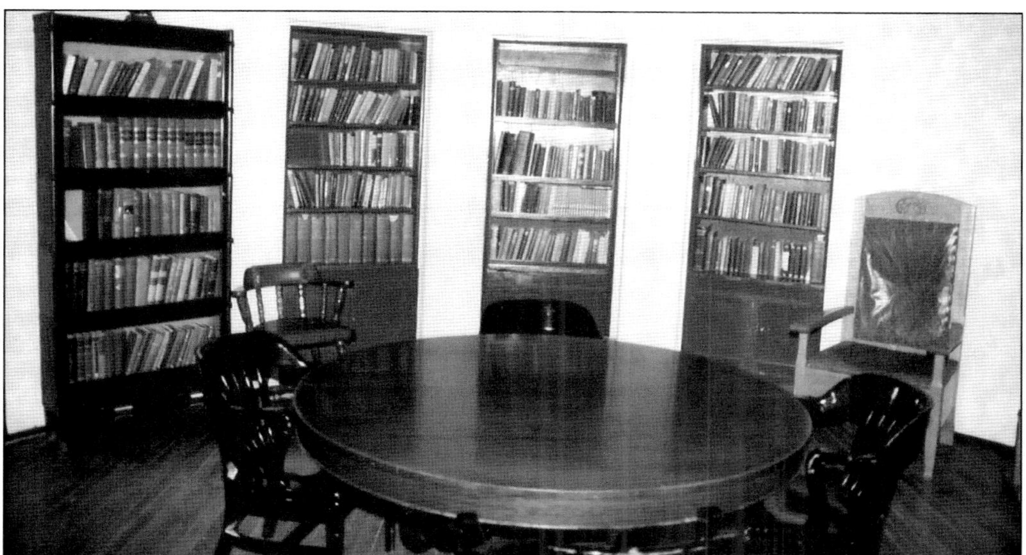

One of these shelves in the Stronghold library swings aside to reveal a secret passageway leading to the chapel. The door's mechanics were designed by David S. Strong and caretaker Henry Tyse, who also built the toboggan tower. The library's ceiling was painted in mock-medieval style by Nicholas Kaissakoff, and has never been repainted. (Courtesy of the Stronghold Center.)

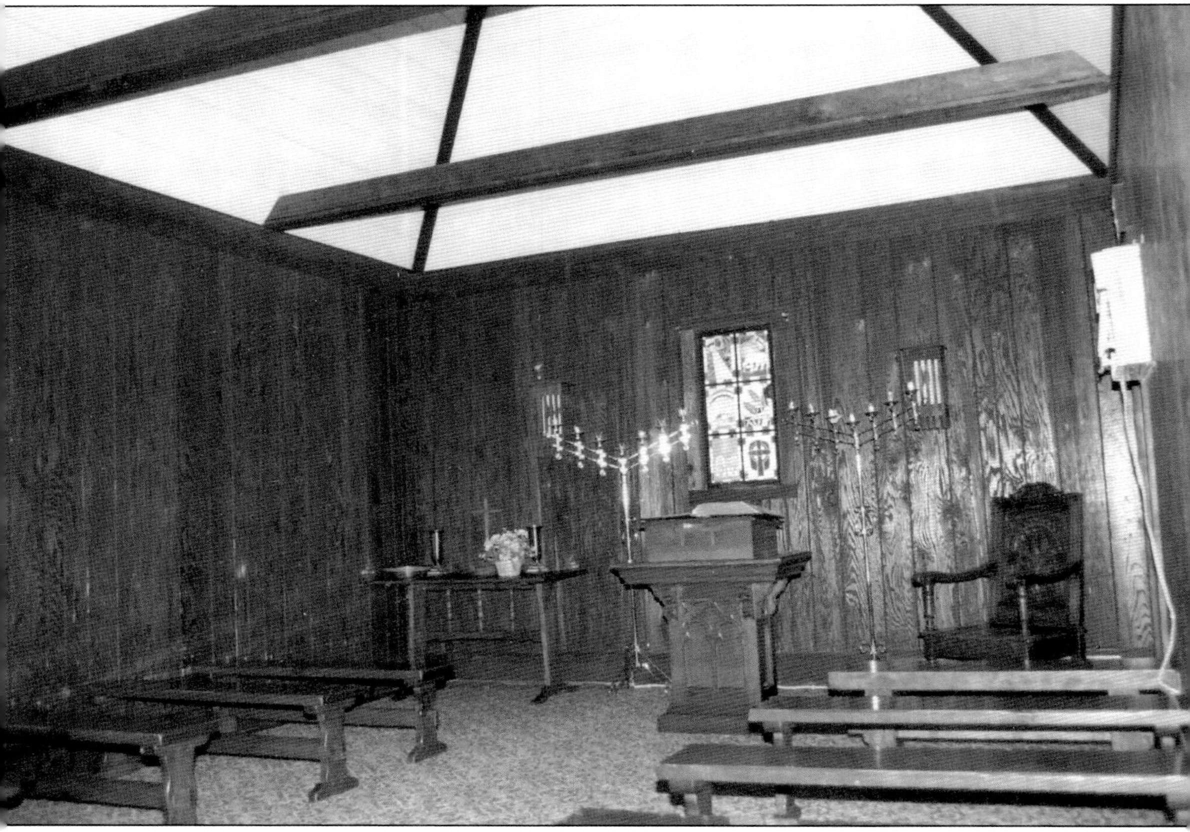

Originally intended as a chapel, this room was used primarily for storage. In 1975, the Middle Creek Church of Winnebago raised funds and offered to complete its decor according to Strong's plans. The benches were handmade, as was the stained-glass window, crafted by Hazel Speer and given by the High School Fellowship of Hanover Presbyterian Church. Its six panels depict Creation, represented by the ray of light emanating from Heaven; Noah and the flood, symbolized by the olive branch and rainbow; the Ten Commandments, represented by the stone tablets; Christ's death, represented by the red Celtic Cross; the Last Supper, symbolized by the wheat and wine; and the Lamb carrying the Cross, symbolizing Christ's sacrifice, and the establishment of the church. The Strongs were devout Episcopalians, and hoped that the castle might one day assist visitors in the nurturing of the spirit. The grounds are now owned by the Presbytery of Blackhawk, and this intent is fully, wonderfully realized. (Courtesy of Linda H. Strong.)

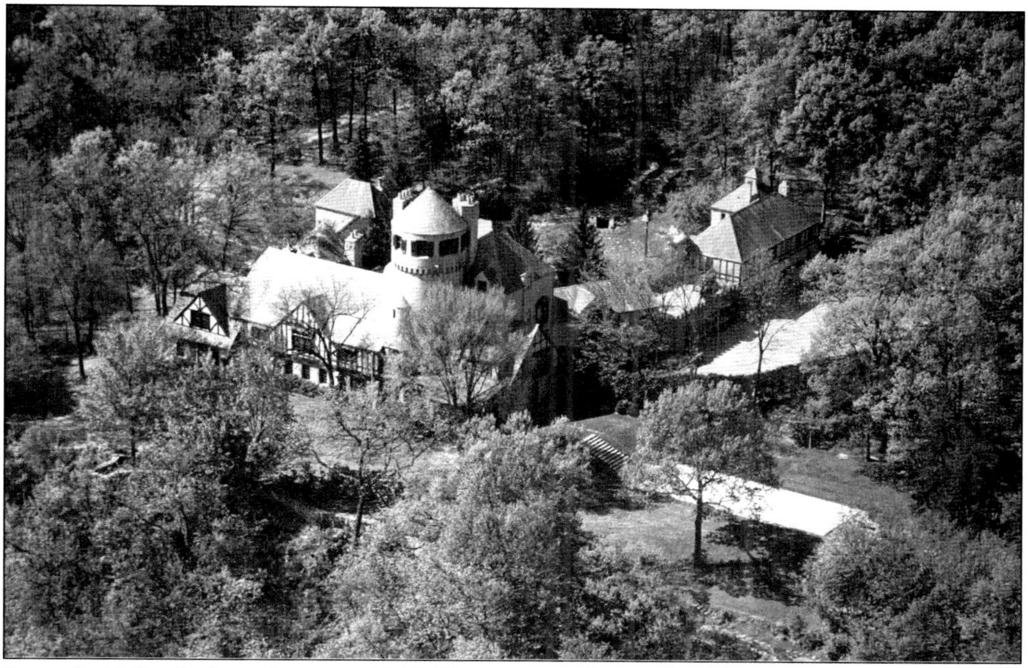

Stronghold Castle from the air, c. 1960. The wing on the south end was originally the Carriage House. Below was the garage, and above were rooms for the cook, caretaker, chauffer, and other servants. In 1971, it was converted into guest rooms for the retreat center, housing up to 30 people. Also attached is the bunkhouse, a favorite getaway for the Strong boys; now used as staff quarters. (Courtesy of the Robert K. Strong family.)

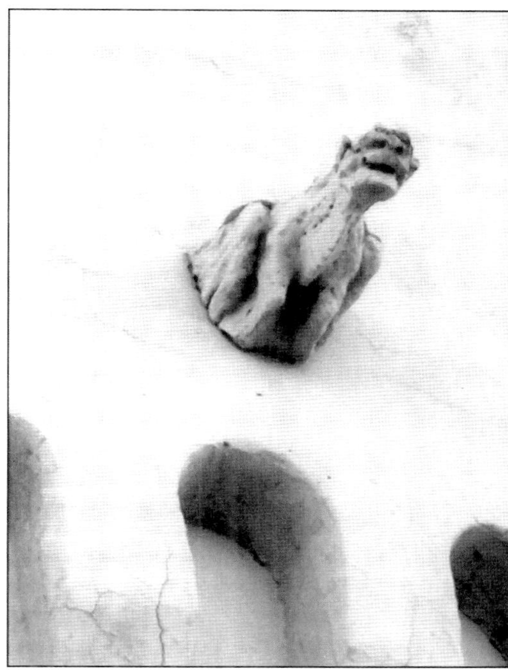

This detail reveals in greater detail the gargoyle attached to the tower, glaring down on the north lawn at the swimming pool. Theories abound concerning the purpose of the medieval gargoyles; one is that they functioned as waterspouts, another suggests that they spooked away wicked spirits. Either way, we love them. (Courtesy of Linda H. Strong.)

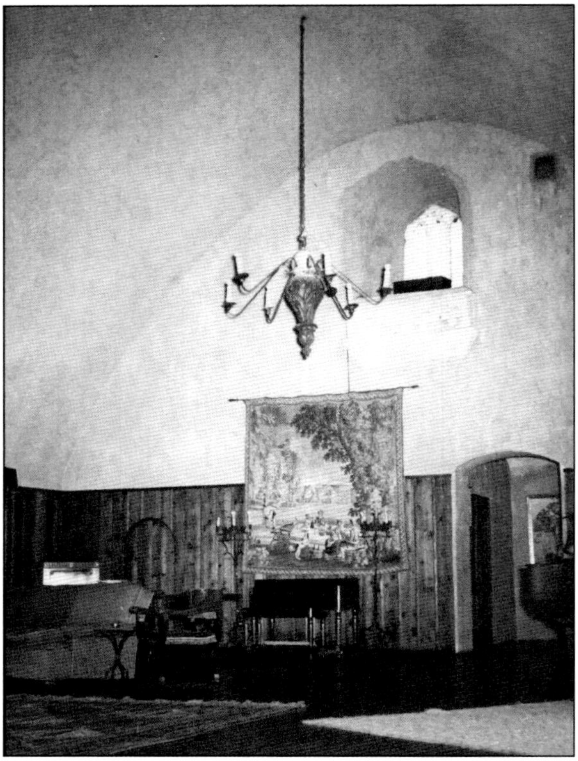

The balcony overlooking the Great Hall is deceptively proportioned, reaching only to the knee of an adult. The space behind is a maintenance passageway, off-limits to visitors. Opposite the balcony is the fireplace. (Courtesy of the Robert K. Strong family.)

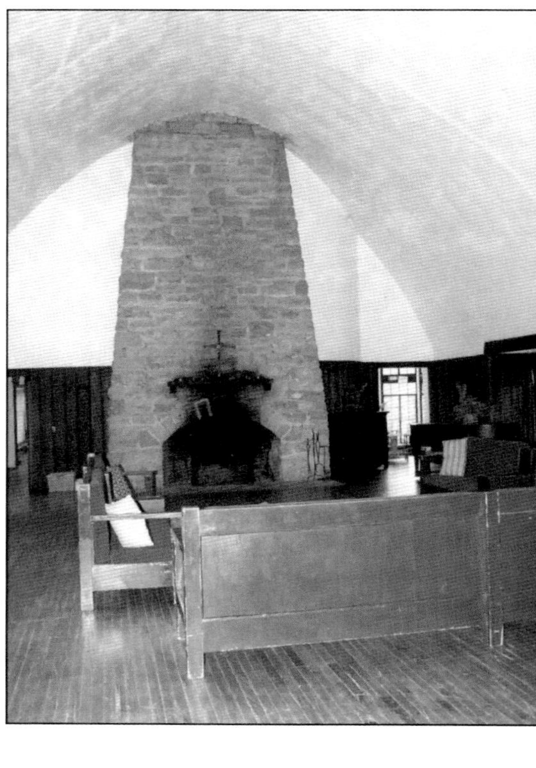

The Great Hall was modeled after a medieval banqueting room where the meals were cooked in the open hearth. Here the Strong family hosted social events, such as dances and elaborate dinners. The hall is now used for weddings, proms, and worship services. Mrs. Strong felt the fireplace hood was too shiny, and had it beaten with a chain to simulate age and usage. (Courtesy of Linda H. Strong.)

The toboggan tower was built by groundsman Henry Tyse, and contains a fireplace inside the first floor. (Courtesy of Linda H. Strong.)

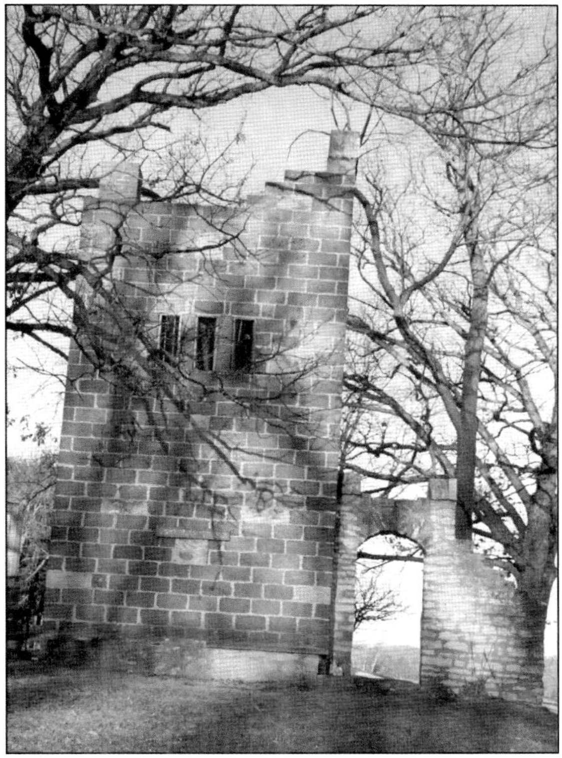

A gleeful boy enjoys the Stronghold toboggan tower, 1965. As pictured above, the wooden sledding ramp is gone but the stone structure remains intact. (Courtesy of the Stronghold Center.)

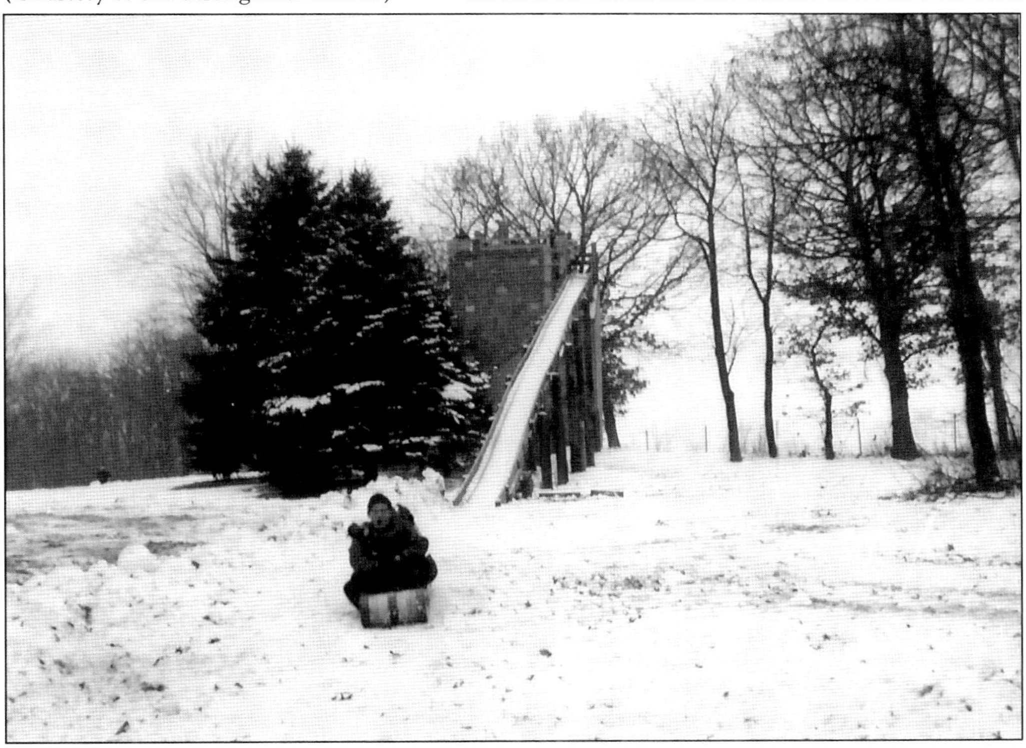

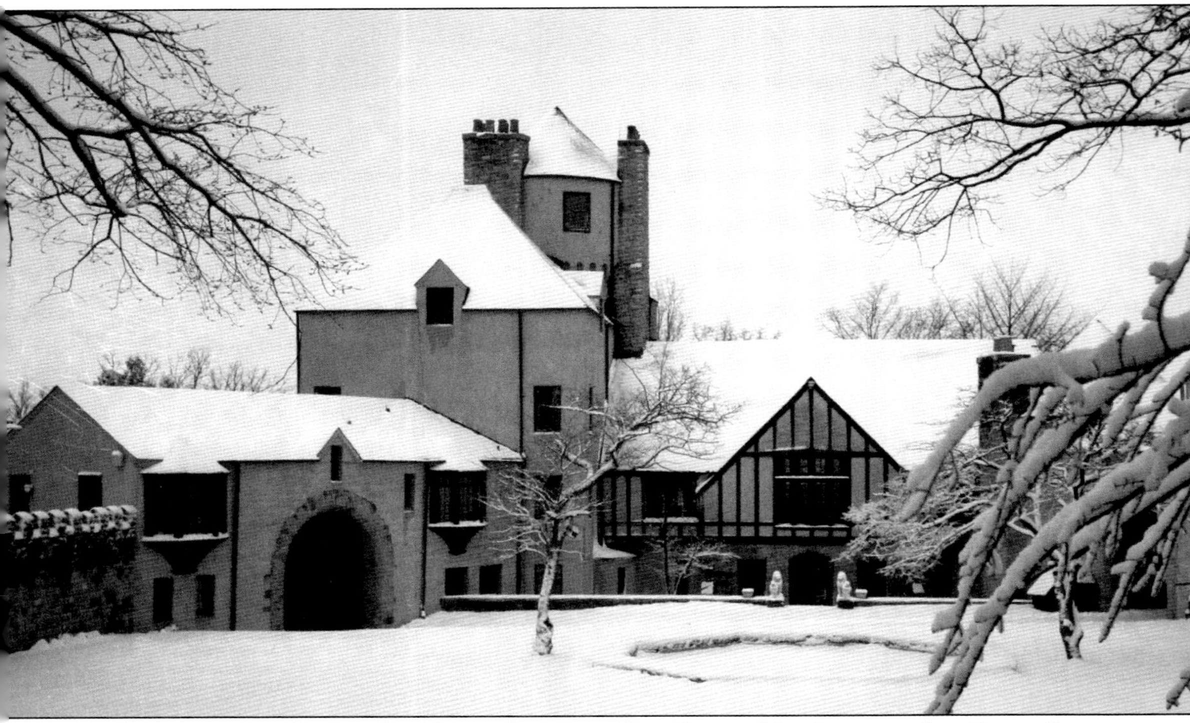

Walter Strong's desire to build a castle was partly influenced by the example of his colleague, William Randolph Hearst, who constructed the magnificent San Simeon in California. Another local boy influenced by Hearst's life and fortunes was Orson Welles, then a lad vacationing at his father's hotel a few miles south in Grand Detour. One is tempted to speculate as to whether Welles and Strong crossed paths somewhere in the Sinnissippi valley, perhaps during dinner at the Sheffield House Hotel. Is it possible that young Welles' fertile imagination was struck by the narrative possibilities suggested by Strong, the powerful empire-building newspaper mogul? Perhaps sometime before Welles composed the script about the fictional, Hearst-like publisher Charles Foster Kane (whose vast estate is called Xanadu) for his 1941 film *Citizen Kane*, he recalled local gossip about Walter Strong's "stately pleasure dome" on the Rock River. However, this is somewhat unlikely considering the fact that Welles departed Grand Detour the day after his father's hotel burned in May of 1928, several months before late autumn construction commenced on Stronghold. (Courtesy of the Robert H. Strong family.)

Six

White Pines State Park

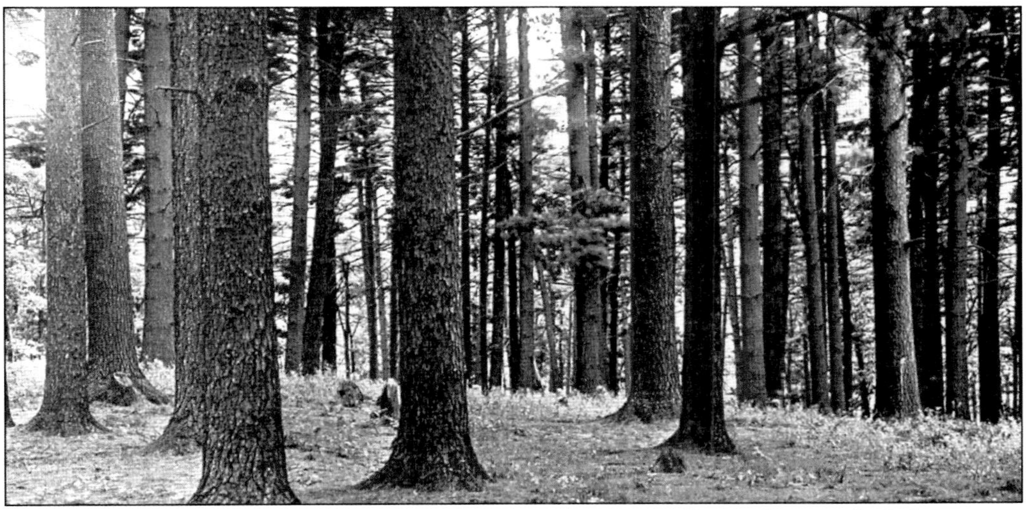

White Pines State Park, eight miles west of Oregon, represents Illinois' last stand of white pines. The southern boundary of the Chicago–Iowa trail, the forest also lay on the historic Blackhawk trail, extending along the east bank of Pine Creek. In the early 1900s, an effort was presented to preserve the land, and a bill was passed appropriating $30,000 to acquire it; however, the measure was vetoed. Further efforts assured the bill, and in 1927, the land was granted nature preserve status. The park harbors plants such as blue-eyed grass, bloodroot, trout lily, and spring beauty; animals include squirrels, chipmunks, raccoons, and deer. It is a favorite haunt of Boy Scouts and church retreats.

Instrumental in securing White Pines' official protection was Jens Jensen (1860-1951), the visionary Danish landscape designer and conservationist. As founder of the Prairie Club and Friends of the Native Landscape, he successfully championed the preservation of Midwestern fields, dunes, and wetlands. One of his most recognized projects is the Garfield Park Conservatory in Chicago. Jensen and his associates often journeyed to the Sinnissippi valley; at White Pines Forest they hosted well-attended lectures and masques, including a presentation by that indomitable lover of Illinois, Vachel Lindsay, who read his poem, *Hawk of the Rock*. Other notable Friends of the Native Landscape included Carl Sandburg, politician Harold Ickes, and Harriet Monroe, editor of *Poetry* magazine. This postcard is c. 1950.

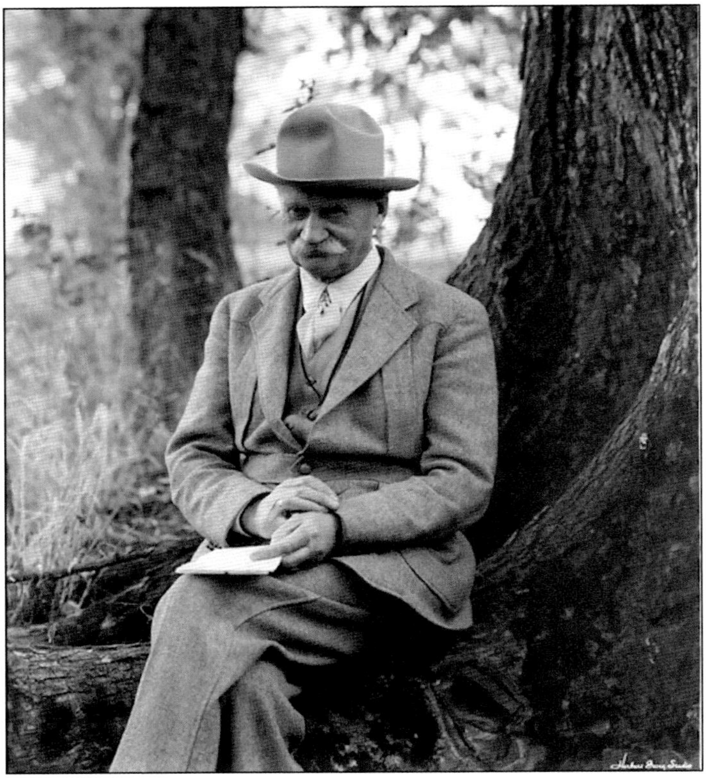

In his ceaseless efforts to preserve park areas, Jens Jensen noted that certain scenic regions possessed little agricultural value but much "museum" value, such as White Pines Forest in Ogle County. Other lands protected by Jensen and the Friends of the Native Landscape include Fort Kaskasia, Giant City State Park, Rock River State Park, and Dixon Springs. (Courtesy of The Suzette Morton Davidson Special Collections, The Morton Arboretum; photo by Herbert Georg Studio, 1935.)

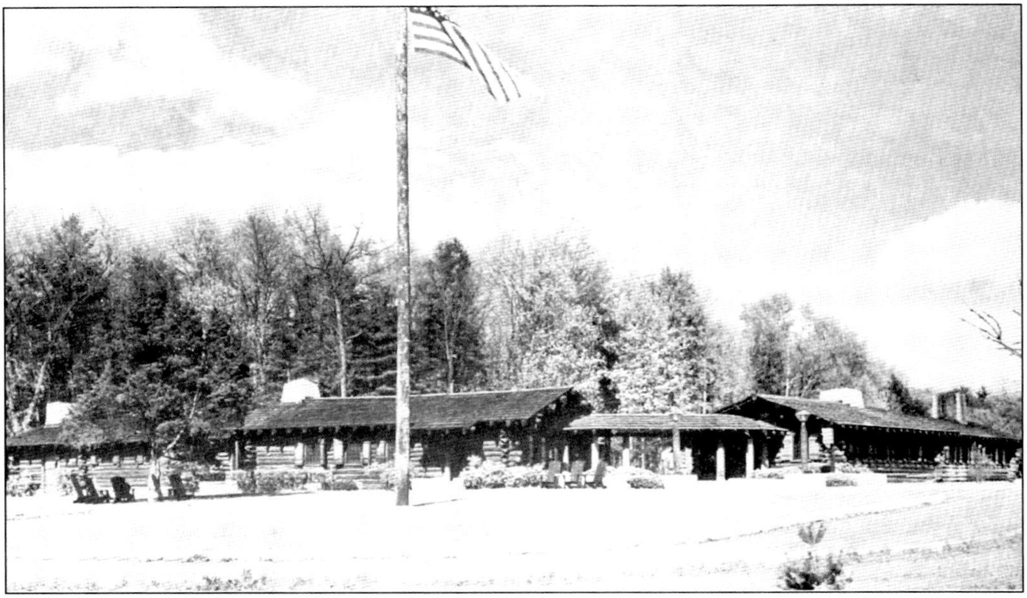

White Pines Lodge and Restaurant, shown on this postcard, *c.* 1960.

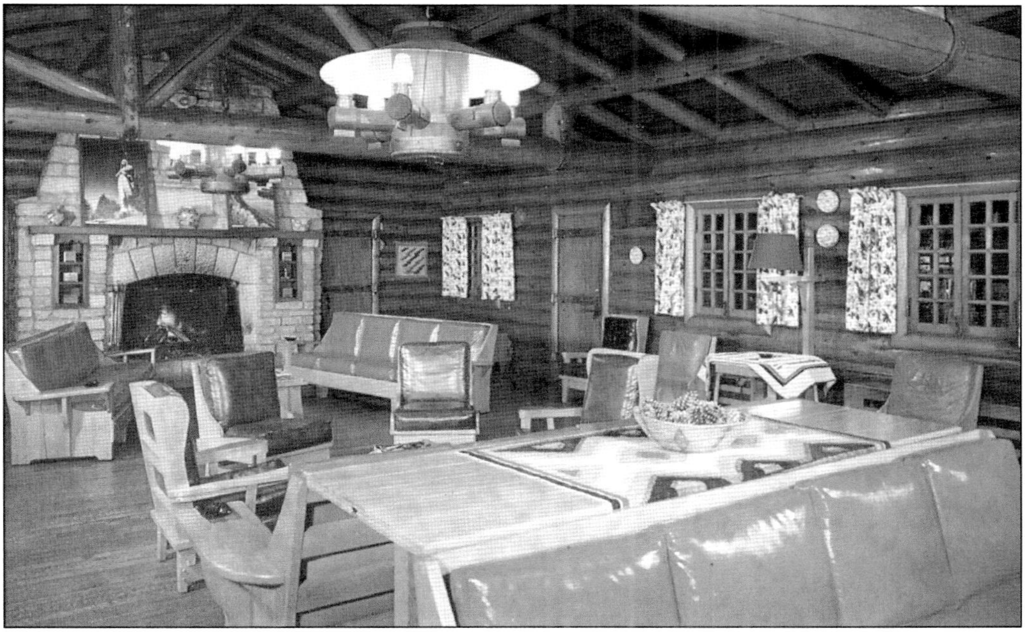

The White Pines Main Lodge, resplendent in glistening 1960s vinyl. Note the statue of Blackhawk on the mantelpiece. This image is *c.* 1965.

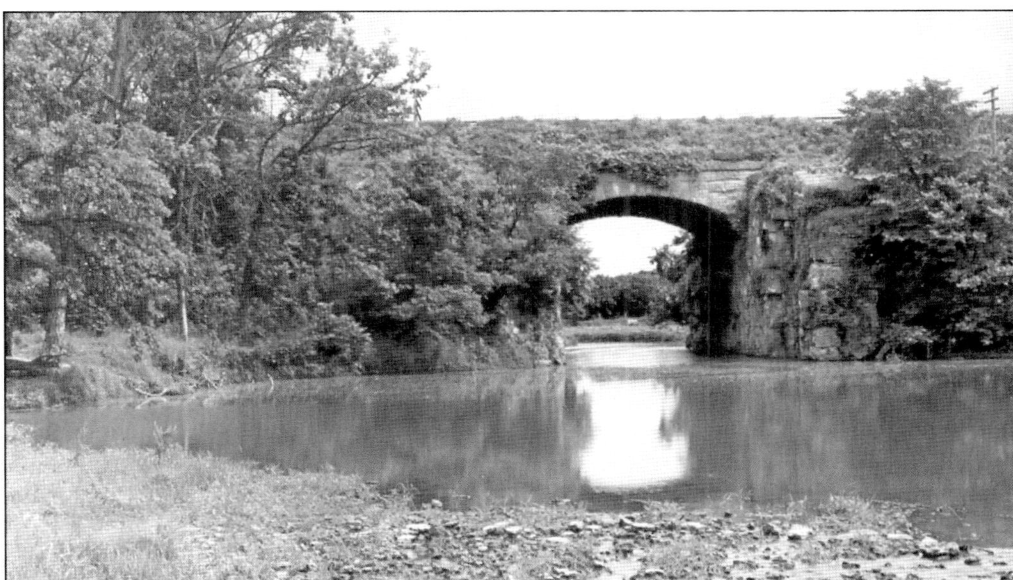

The "Natural Bridge" spanning Pine Creek is shown on this *c.* 1960 postcard.

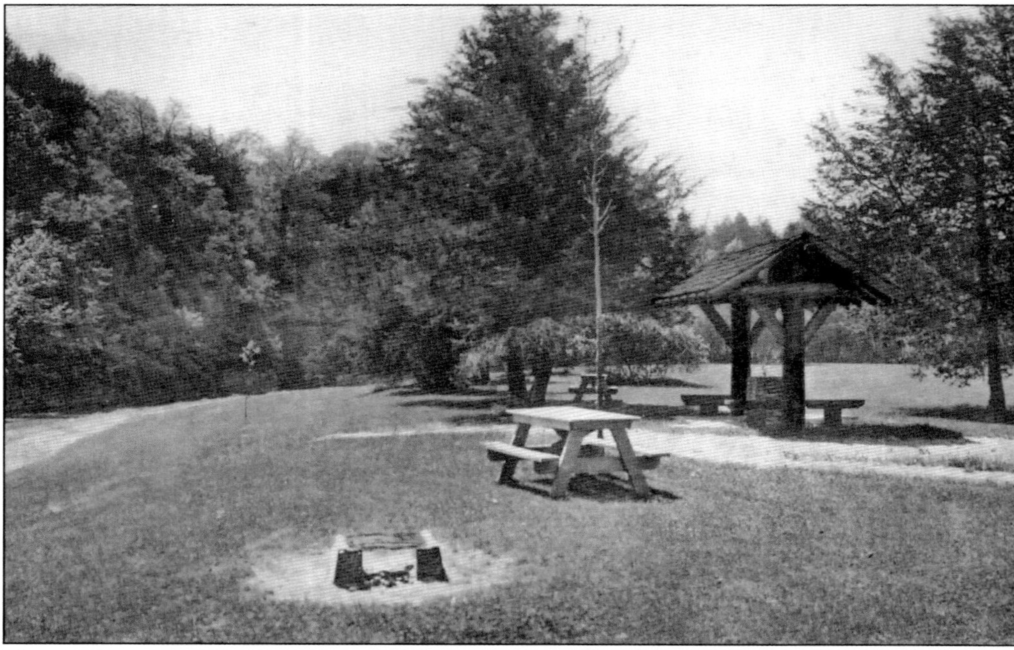

This 1944 postcard displays a sight familiar to innumerable happy campers throughout Northern Illinois: an awaiting picnic table, an open barbeque pit, and green grass on a sunny day at White Pines.

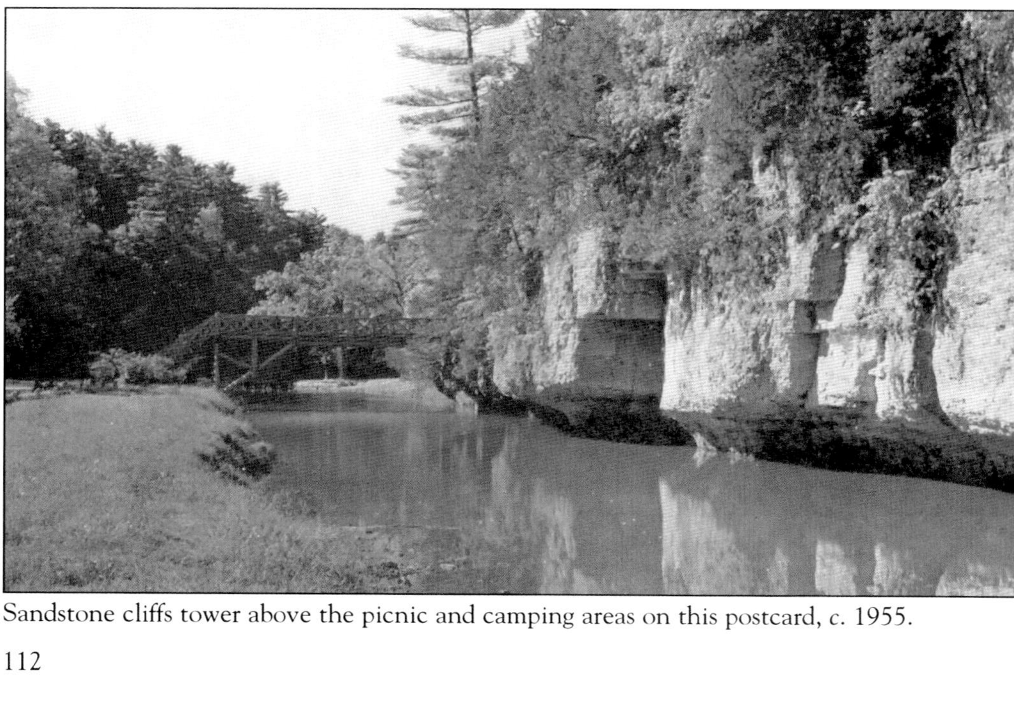

Sandstone cliffs tower above the picnic and camping areas on this postcard, c. 1955.

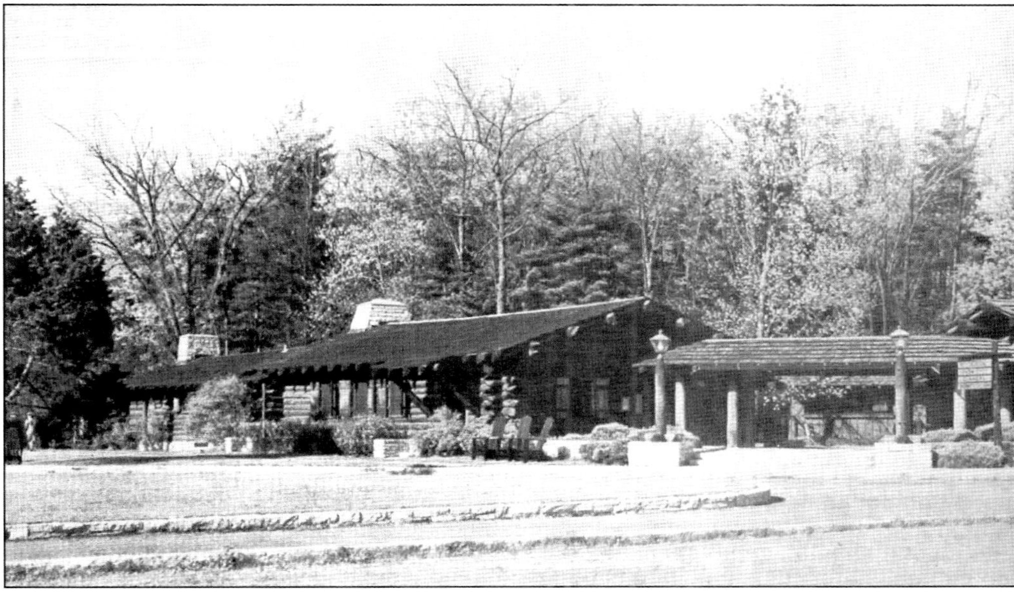

Built by the Civilian Conservation Corp in the late 1920s, the White Pines Lodge and its accompanying cabins have undergone extensive renovation. The White Pines Inn is listed as one of the "15 Best Getaways" by *Midwest Living* magazine. The Lodge is shown on this postcard, *c.* 1960.

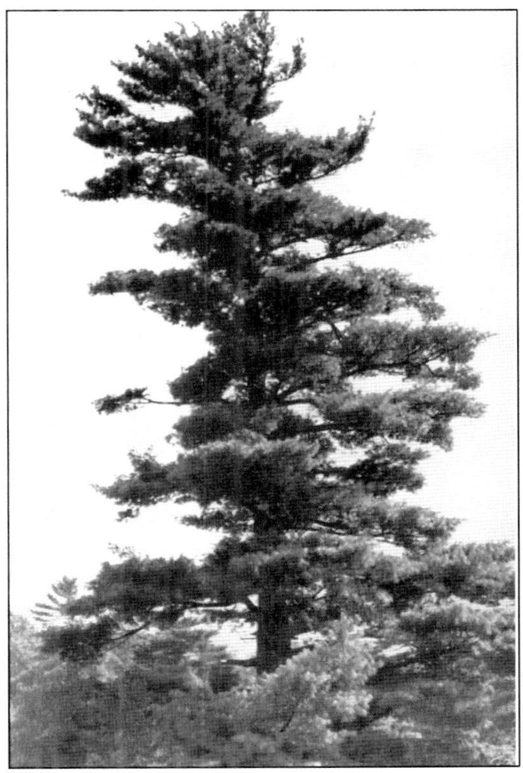

"The Lonesome Pine," postcard, *c.* 1960.

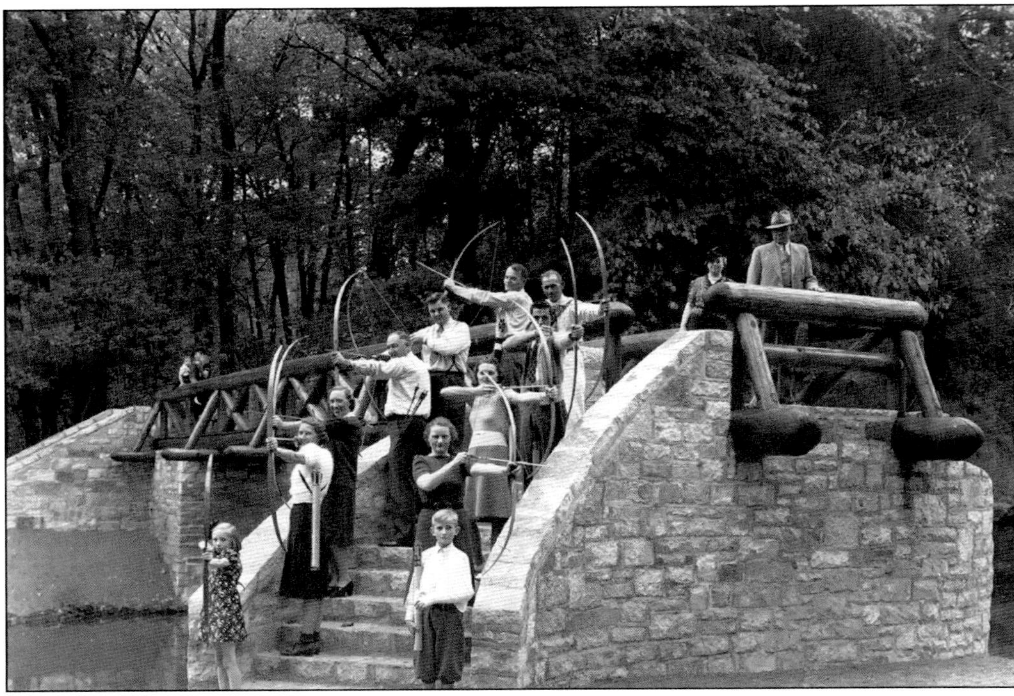

Unidentified archers at White Pines, posing *c.* 1950 on the stone bridge over Pine Creek.

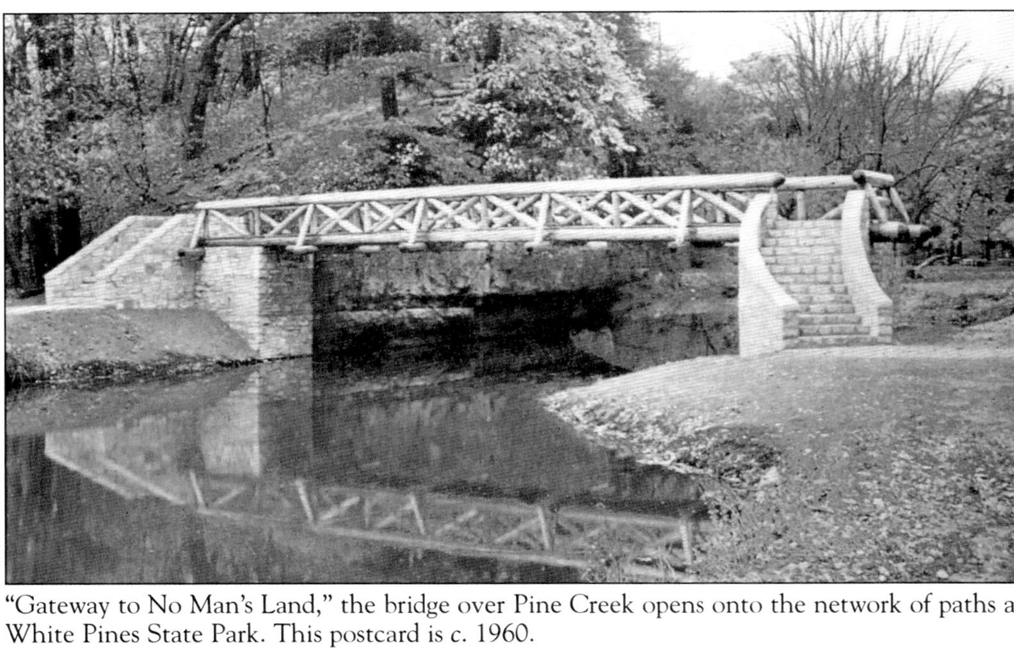

"Gateway to No Man's Land," the bridge over Pine Creek opens onto the network of paths at White Pines State Park. This postcard is *c.* 1960.

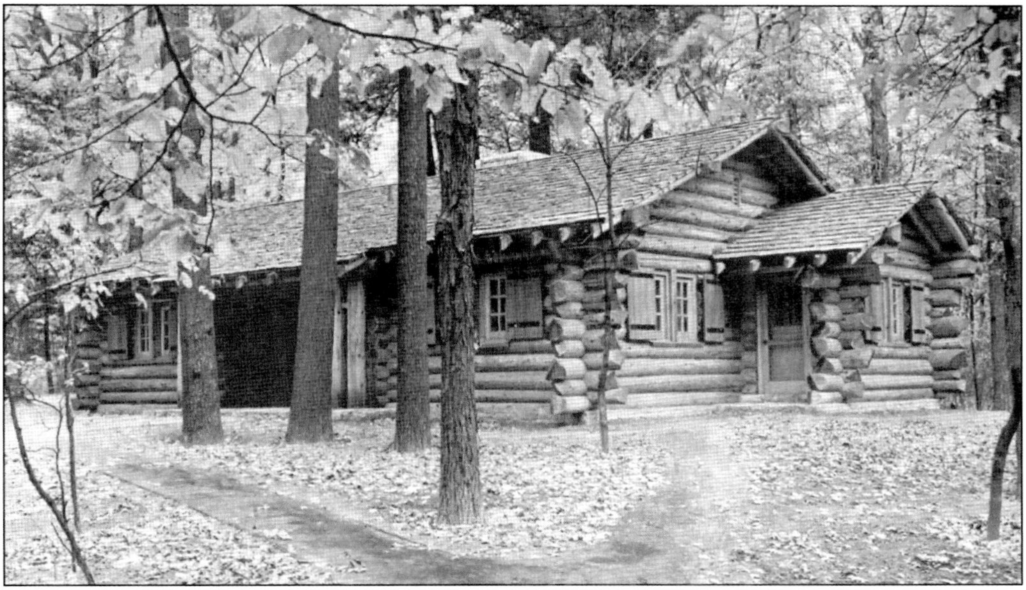

A White Pines "Super Cabin," a bit more lavish and spacious than the others shown on this postcard, c. 1950. Modern conveniences include air, heating, television, and phones, in addition to blankets and towels.

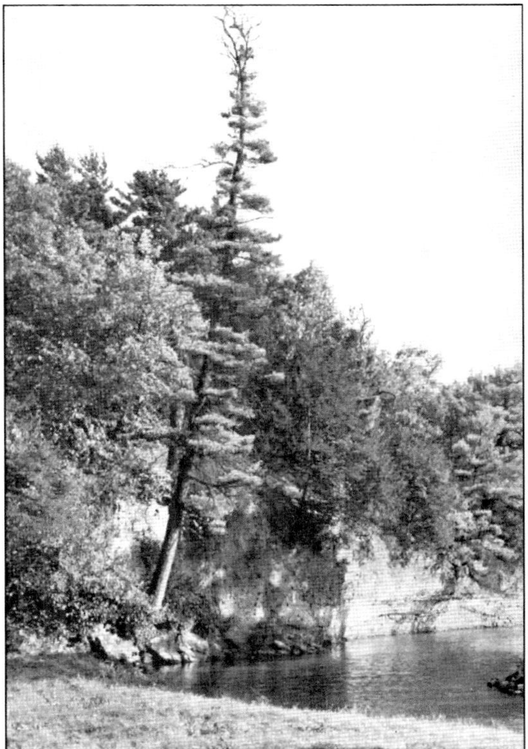

"The Sentinel" guarding Pine Creek is shown on this postcard, c. 1950.

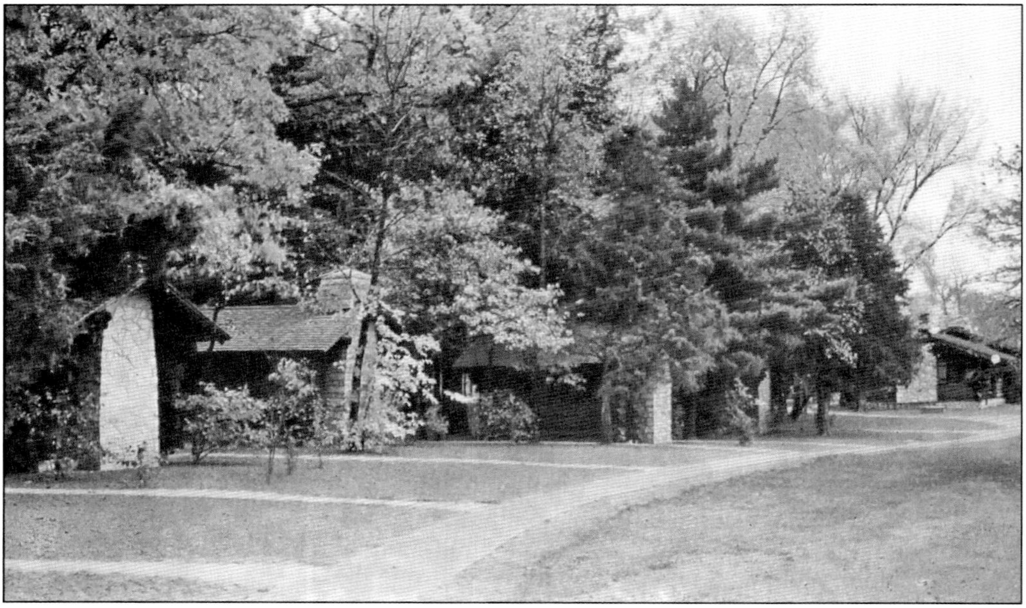

White Pines Pioneer Cabins, postcard *c.* 1960. The 25 one-room cabins now contain gas fireplaces, hardwood floors, a hand-hewn queen-size log bed and a private bath. "Sweetheart Cabins" offer champagne and a fully stocked refrigerator.

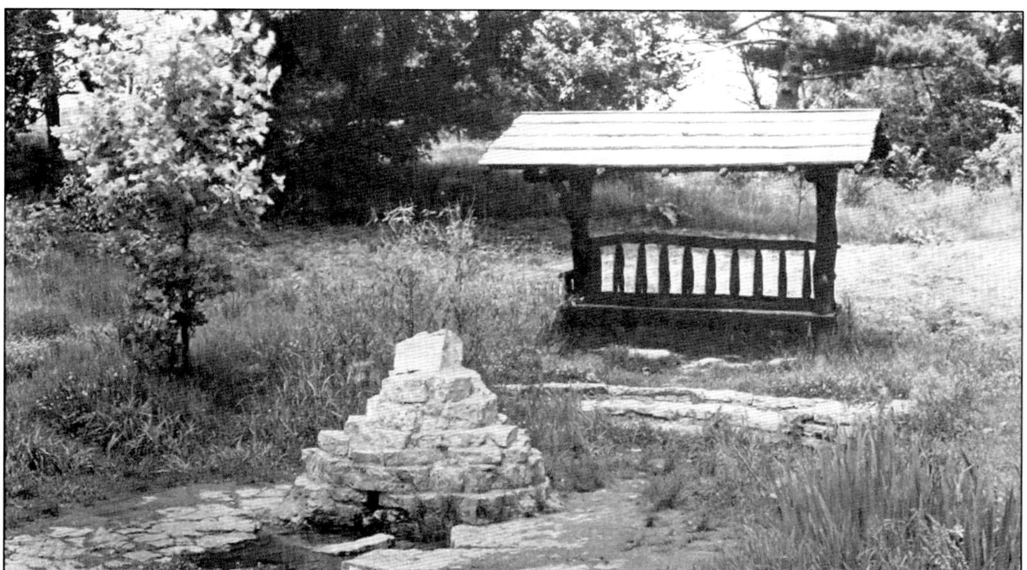

The Wishing Well is captured in a postcard *c.* 1950.

Seven

And the River Rolls On

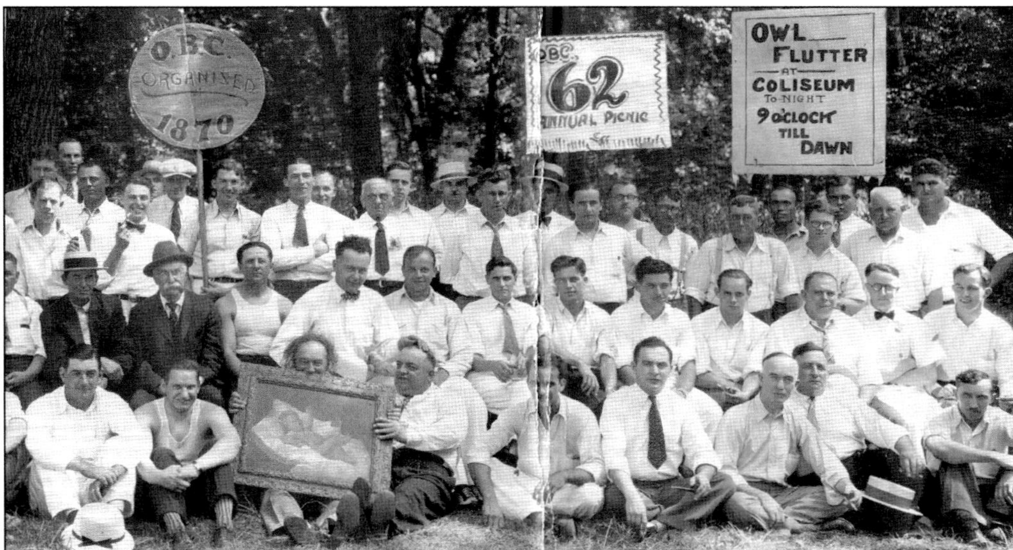

Of all the multitudinous clubs and societies congregating in the Sinnissippi valley, one of the most enduring—and certainly one of the weirdest—was the Oregon Owls (Oregon Bachelor Club), established in 1869 by Judge Cartwright, then a 27-year-old bachelor. Meetings to determine members were called with a six-foot horn, blown at sunset from the Opera House. The unsuspecting candidate was then abducted from his home and whisked by rowboat to Margaret Fuller Island where he was shown a red-hot poker, then blindfolded and paddled in the nude. The smell of burning hair (the poker pressed to fur) assaulted his nostrils. This was a warning.

After the bracing initiation, the club enjoyed a hearty all-day picnic consisting of fried chicken, catfish, corn, tomatoes, gravy, pies, melons, and lemonade. After lunch, they rowed, played poker, pitched horseshoes, and raced. At the end of day, a pipe and drum corp led the march into town, with the most likely prospect for marriage compelled to carry the portrait of a baby, "Little Dan," trudging along with two members, each wielding a long cane hooked around his neck, as onlookers cheered and jeered. Upon tying the matrimonial knot, the groom paid a $5 fine to the Club. The order's symbol was a sunflower. After a long and storied history, the Owls disbanded in 1935. (Courtesy of the *Oregon Republican-Reporter*.)

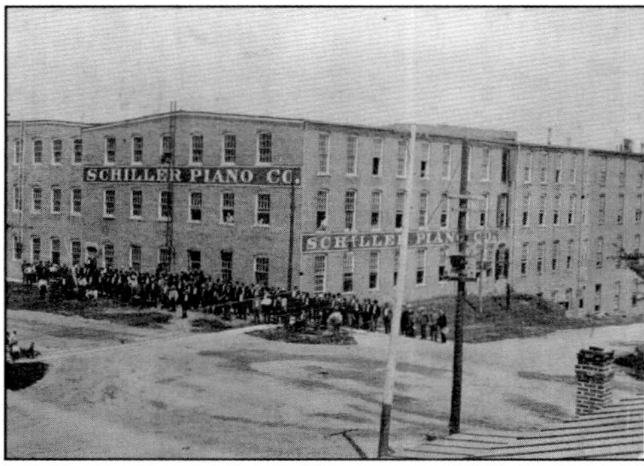

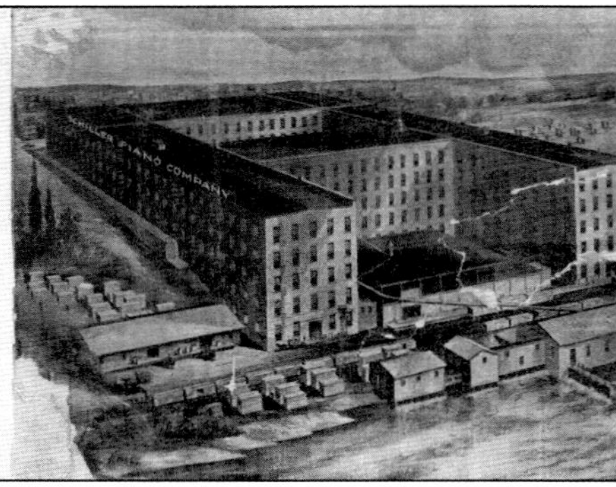

The 13,000 square foot Schiller Piano Factory at north 3rd and Franklin, manufacturers of Cable, Schiller, Conover, Kingsbury, and Wellington pianos. At its peak, Schiller assembled 30 pianos daily, employing up to 500 people. In 1945, the Schiller Cable Piano Co. beacome Conover-Cable Piano Co. The above right image shows the power plant that energized the company and much of Oregon. The Oregon operation closed in 1977, and its equipment was shipped to the main factory in Tennessee. The water tank is gone but the tower's legs remain. Situated on the Rock River, the building is now a mall, featuring several displays of Schiller's history.

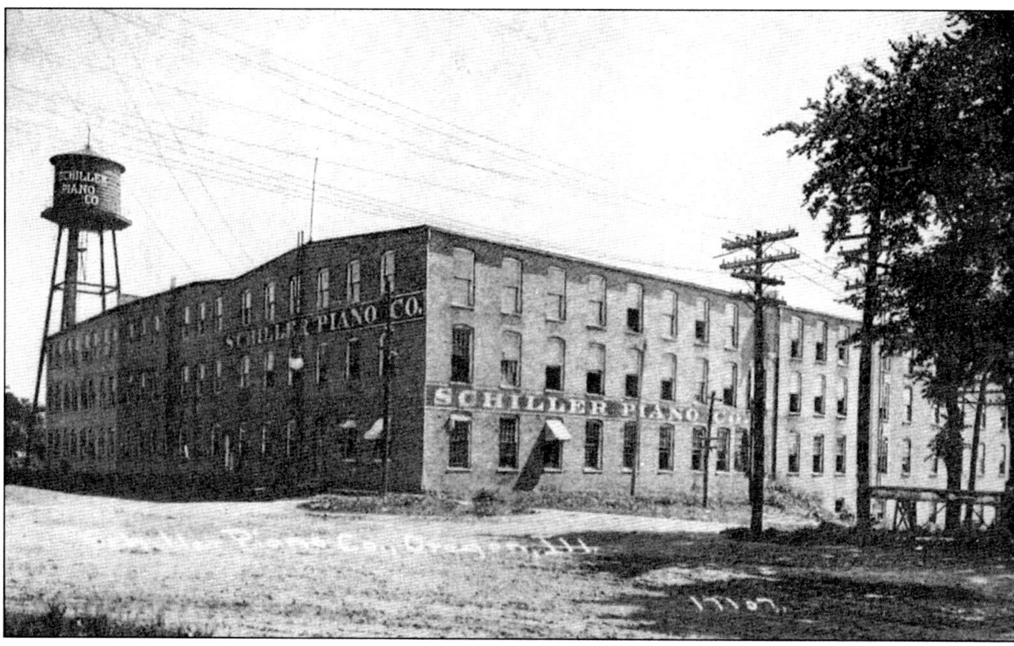

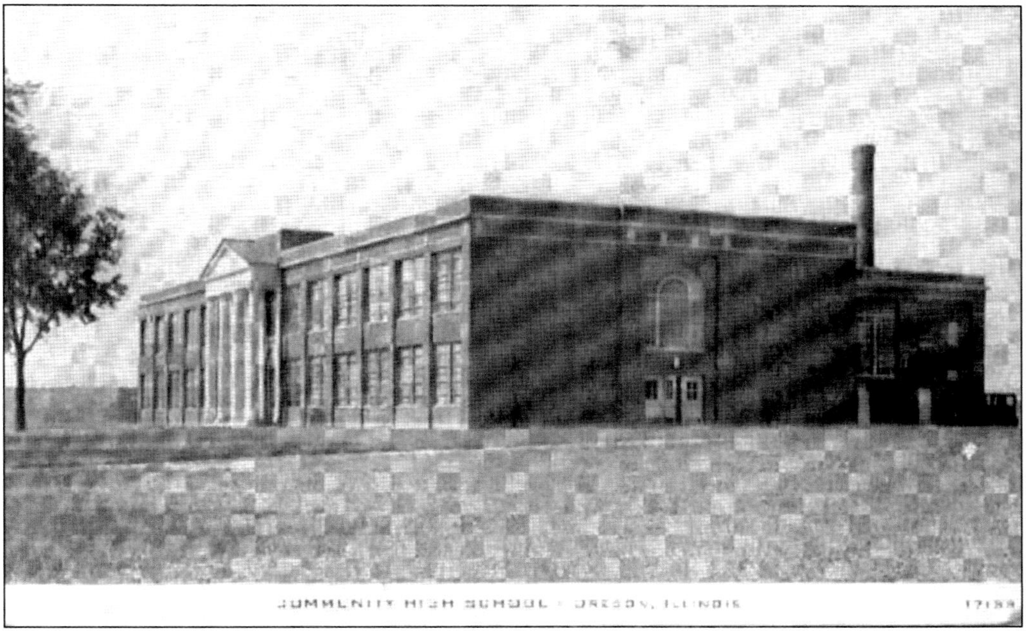

Oregon High School was constructed at 10th and Madison in 1936, replacing the Madison School, which served both grade and high schools. The new high school graduated its first class in 1938. A $750,000 addition was built in 1961, and in 1975, a Special Education Annex was added. (Courtesy of the Ogle County Historical Society.)

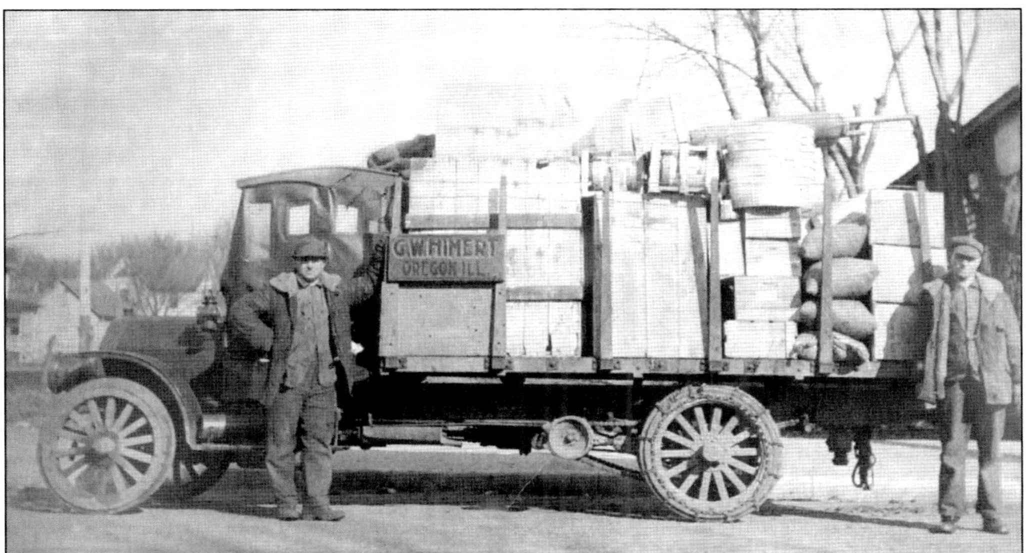

William G. Himert operated a delivery service between the 1890s and about 1930. Here Himert and a helper stand with the first truck in Oregon, loaded heavily with a variety of crates, boxes, bags, and sundries. As a younger man, Himert was a member of the Owls Club, Oregon's exclusive bachelor society. (Courtesy of Bob Rees.)

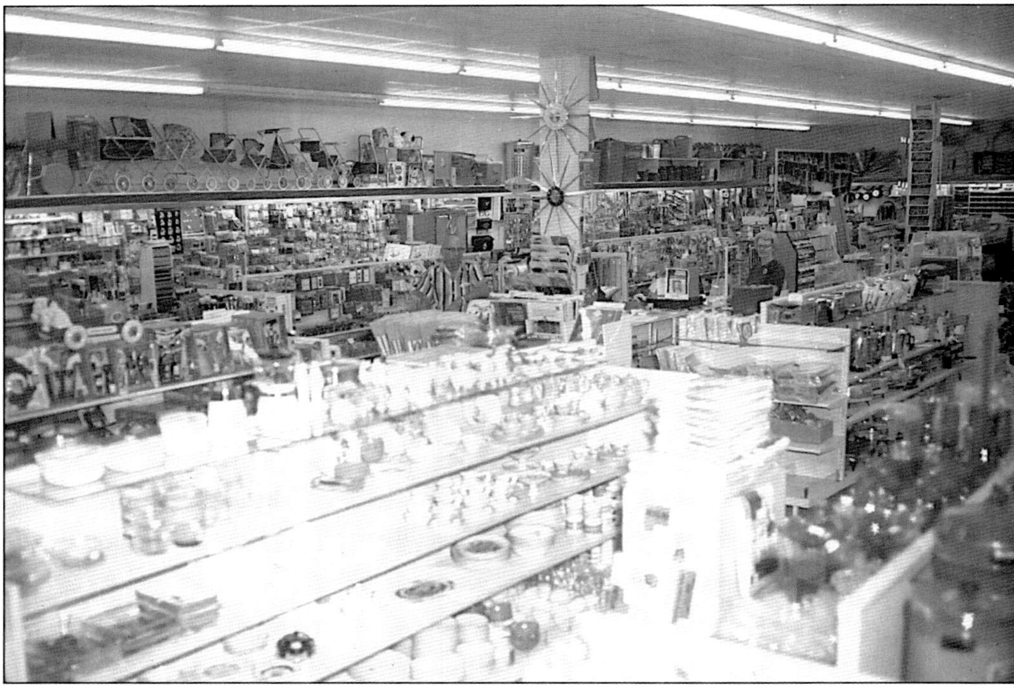

This is probably the Ben Franklin hardware store, *c.* 1965, well-lit and efficiently ordered. The shop suffered fire damage in the early 1970s. Firemen battled the blaze for 12 hours. Beneath was a bowling alley, where the fire is believed to have ignited, resulting from a pin stuck in the automatic pinsetter on the seventh alley. The motor overheated, bursting into flames. The store was rebuilt in 1974. (Courtesy of the *Oregon Republican-Reporter*.)

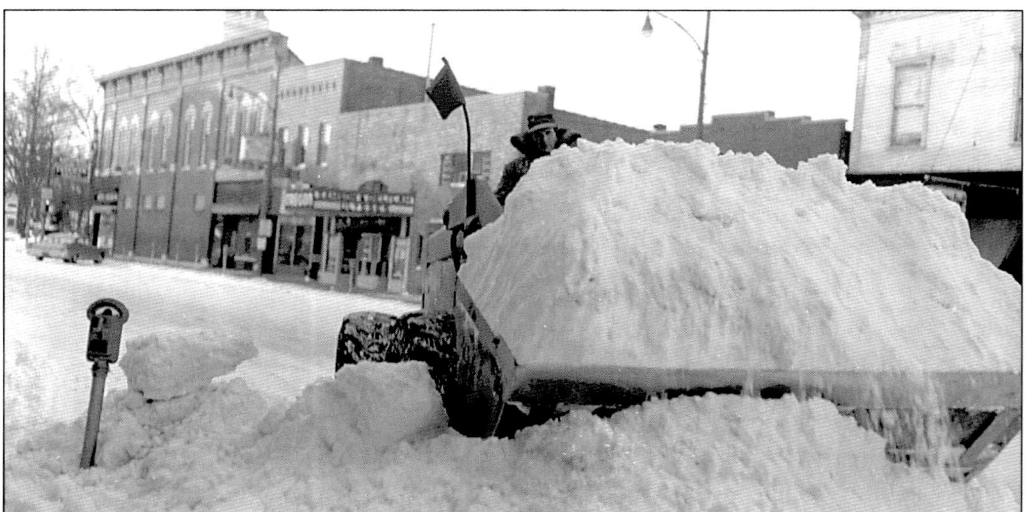

Oregon recovers after a particularly brutal blizzard in 1960. Like all Midwestern towns, a bit of white stuff does not disorient or terribly inconvenience its residents. As with mosquitoes and dandelions, the snow is simply factored in to the seasonal package. (Courtesy of the *Oregon Republican-Reporter*.)

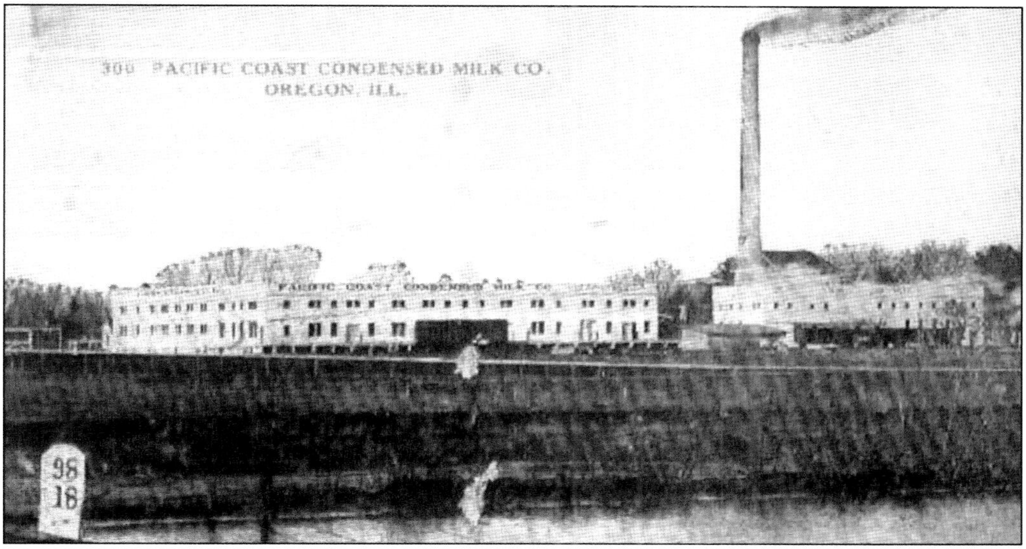

Pacific Coast Condensed Milk Company (later Carnation) stands on what was once an onion patch south of Oregon on the Rock River. Groundbreaking occurred on April 12, 1911. At one time, the plant produced 500,000 lbs. of fresh milk per day, as demand required, daily yielding 5,000 cases of evaporated milk. The building now functions as a storage facility for books and magazines. (Courtesy of the Ogle County Historical Society.)

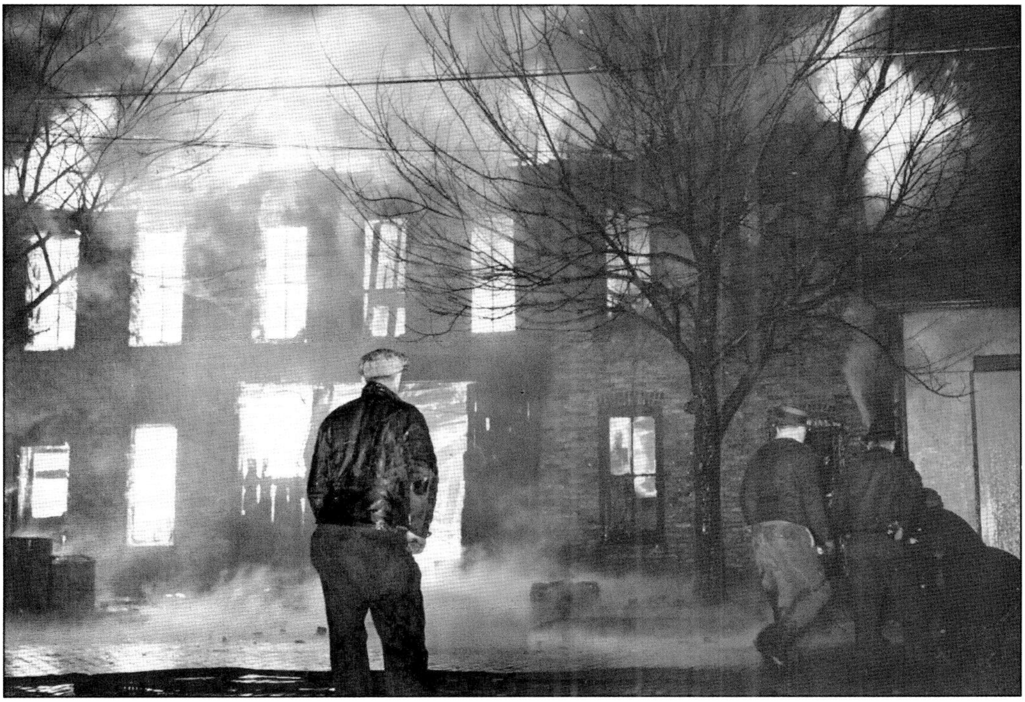

Abe Behr's Junk Yard, located at 126 N. 3rd Street, was totaled by conflagration. The unfortunate man watching the fire is Abe Behr. The grounds were formerly a livery and feed shed. This image is c. 1950. (Courtesy of the *Oregon Republican-Reporter*.)

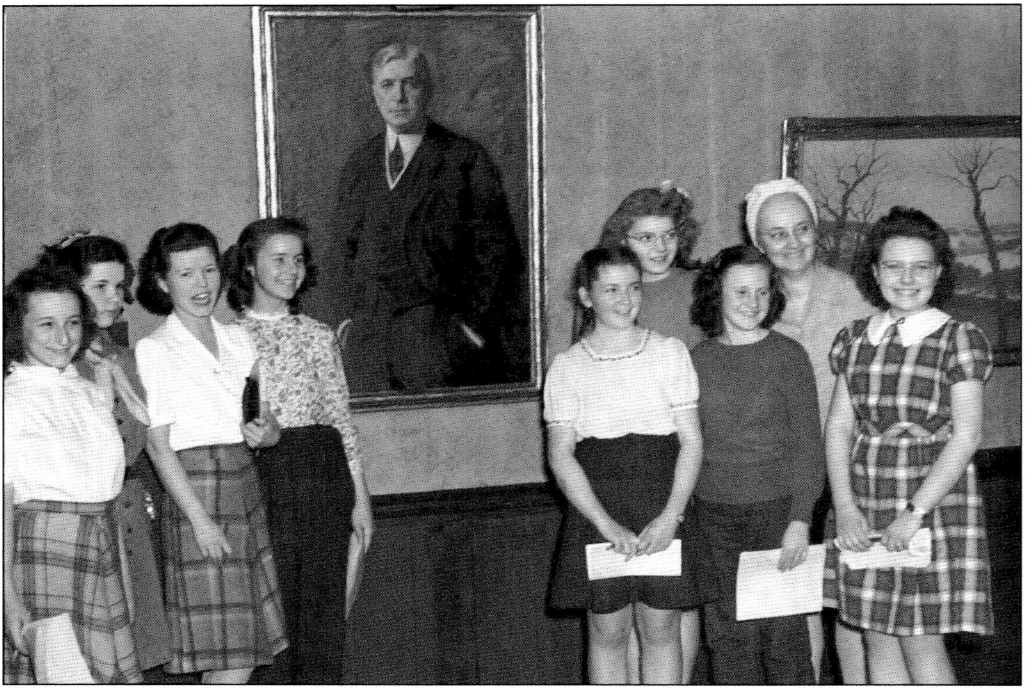

Unidentified grade school students visit the Oregon Public Library in 1950. Note the portrait of Frank Lowden by Ralph Clarkson, a gift from the Eagle's Nest Art Colony. It hangs in the upstairs gallery with many other paintings and sculptures. (Courtesy of the *Oregon Republican-Reporter*.)

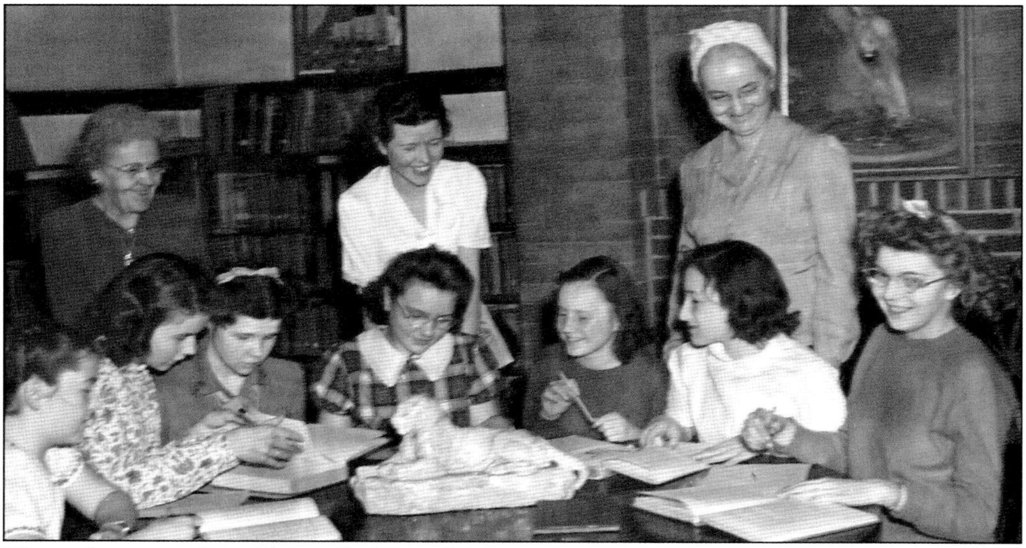

The sculpture on the table is called *Tiger*, by Antoine Louis Barye (1796–1875), a Parisian artist who displayed at the Universal Exhibition in Paris. The piece was probably acquired by Lorado Taft so that children might enjoy the opportunity of touching the forms and textures of sculpture. Eventually it was included with other Eagle's Nest artwork at the library. (Courtesy of the *Oregon Republican-Reporter*.)

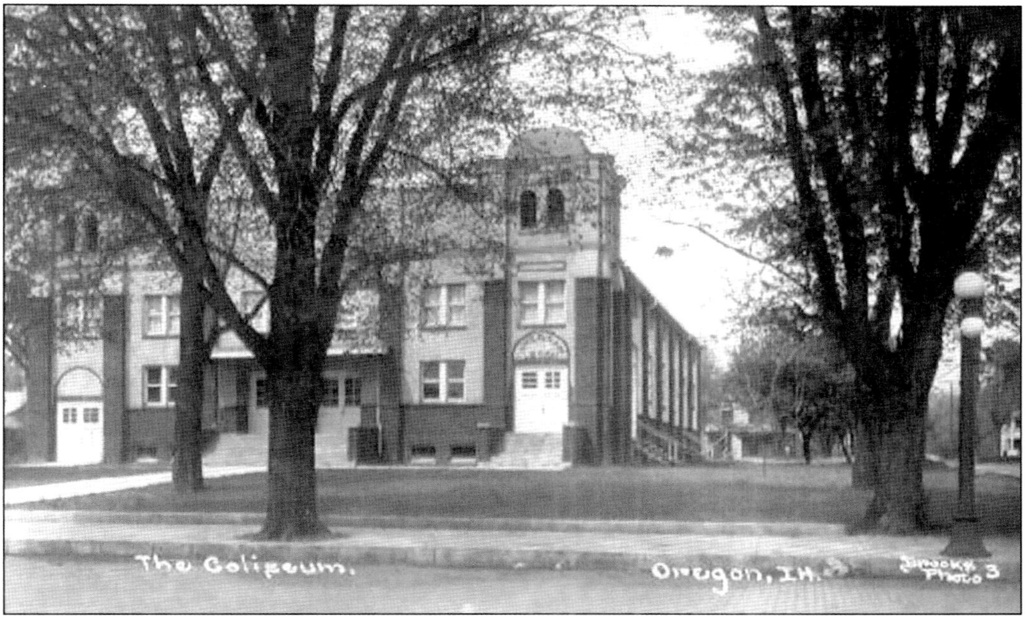

Answering Oregon's objection that ". . . there is nothing doing or no place to go," the city fathers built the Coliseum to provide an activity center in 1923 for $27,000. Through the years it has been used for suppers, basketball games, dances, plays, roller skating, flower shows, recitals, and many other civic events. The second floor housed offices for the local American Legion Post. (Courtesy of the Ogle County Historical Society.)

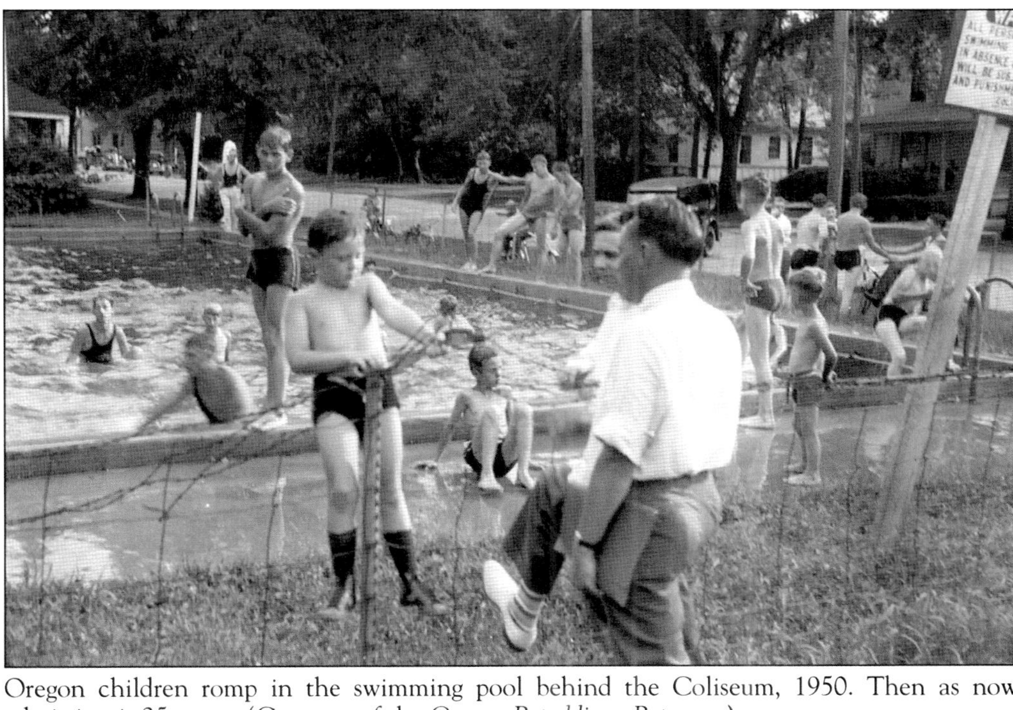

Oregon children romp in the swimming pool behind the Coliseum, 1950. Then as now, admission is 25 cents. (Courtesy of the *Oregon Republican-Reporter*.)

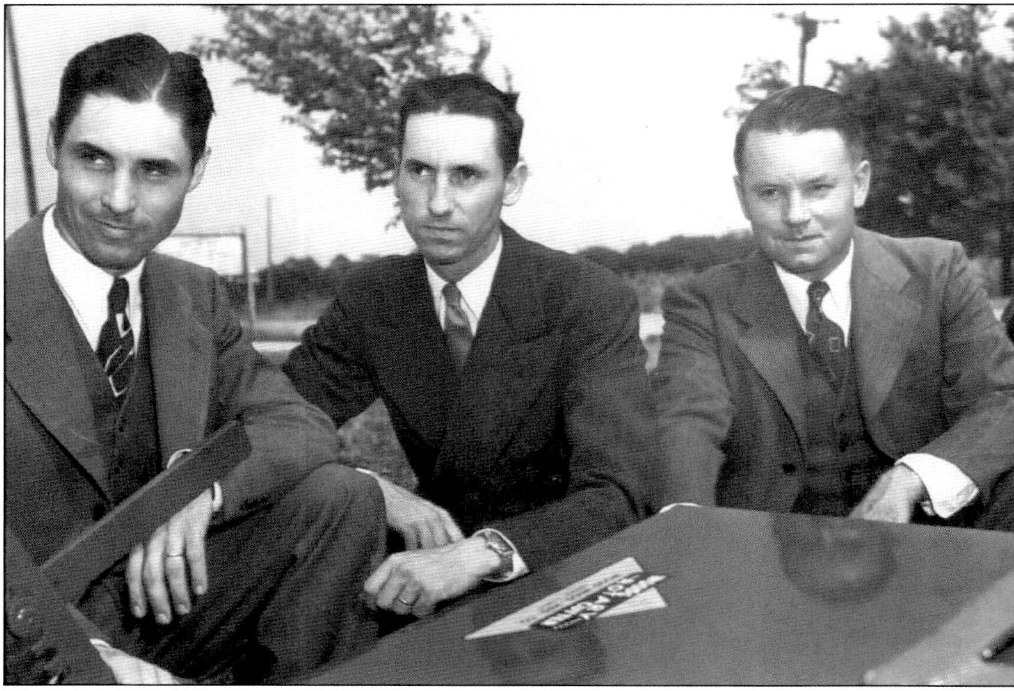

The Wood brothers are pictured here, from left to right: Keith, Merval, and Leonard. In 1946, the Woods arrived in Oregon to manufacture racks for curing fresh cement blocks. After the curing block market exhausted, the enterprising Woods bought a patent for rotating horizontal stalk shredders. Gradually shares increased, and Wood Bros. enjoyed tremendous success as a leader in the field of tractor-powered rotary mowing. (Courtesy of Vada Wood.)

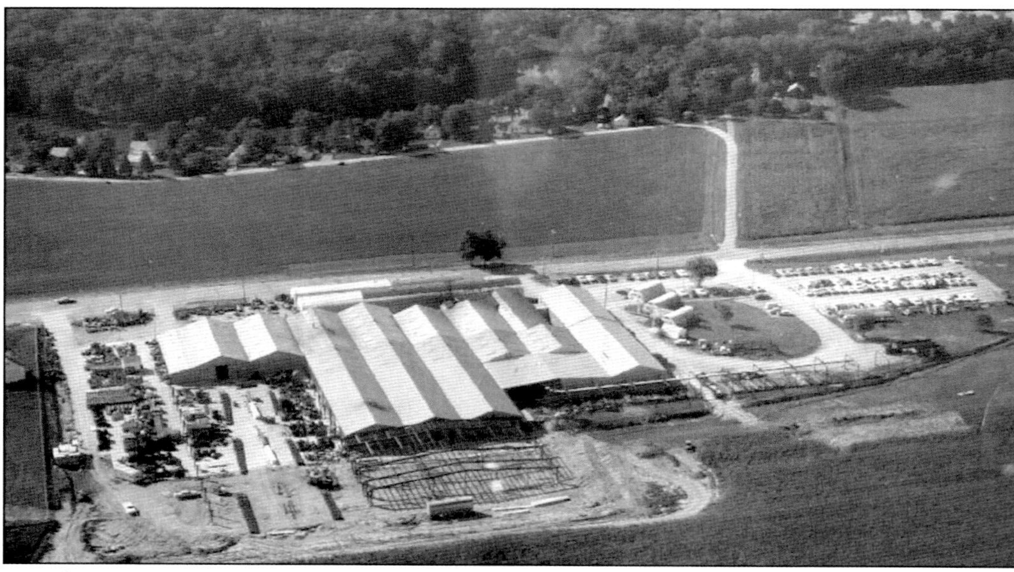

Wood Bros. Manufacturing is pictured as seen from the air, c. 1960. It is located on Rt. 2, south of Oregon. The company diversified as it grew, developing a specialized snow plow, overrunning clutches, quick-detachable blades, segmented solid-rubber tires, and a patented potato vine shredding equipment. (Courtesy of Vada Wood.)

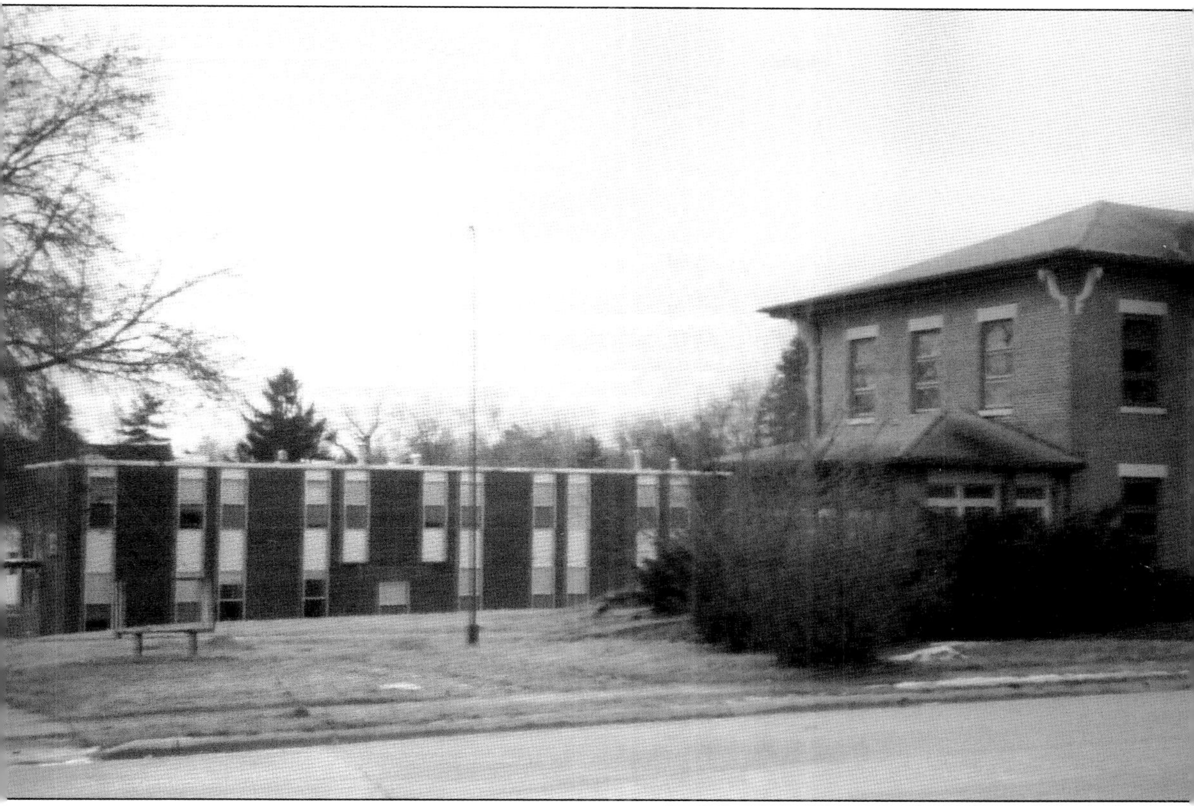

These buildings were once the Oregon Bible College, located at 110 N. 7th Street. In 1922, the Church of God bought the 1858 house, formerly used as the Union School. The Church refurbished it as a retirement community before remodeling the interior. It then functioned as the school's administrative offices and classrooms. Growth allowed for the construction of the dormitory. The Church of God General Conference (CGGC) moved to Atlanta, Georgia, and these buildings are now apartments.

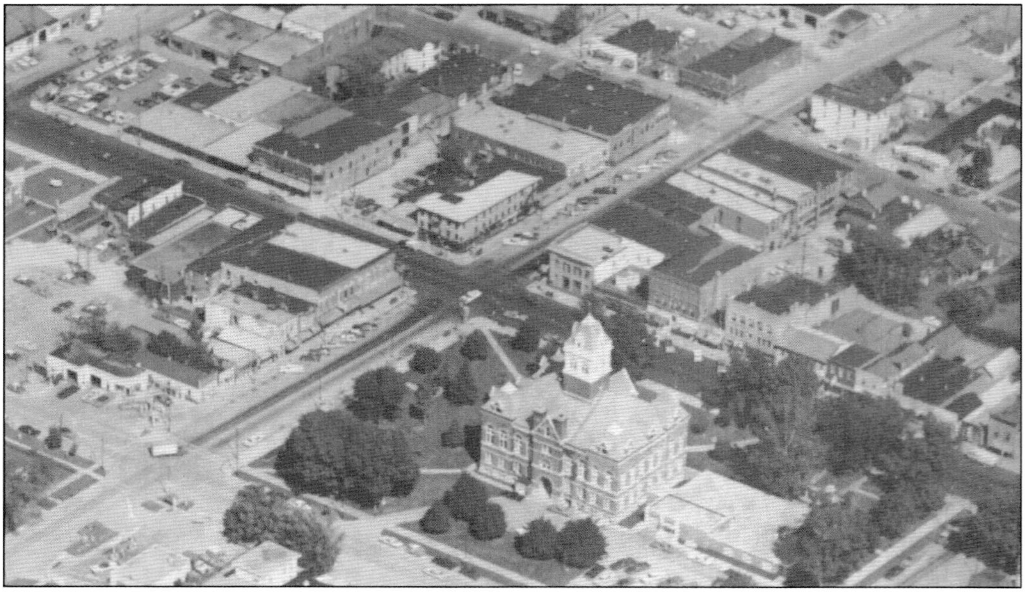

This aerial photo of Oregon displays the courthouse as the dominant structure, with Sinnissippi Hotel northwest on the corner of Washington and Fourth. The new jail is seen connected to the courthouse on the south lawn. At the top edge is Schiller Piano Factory, still operating when this photo was snapped, *c.* 1970.

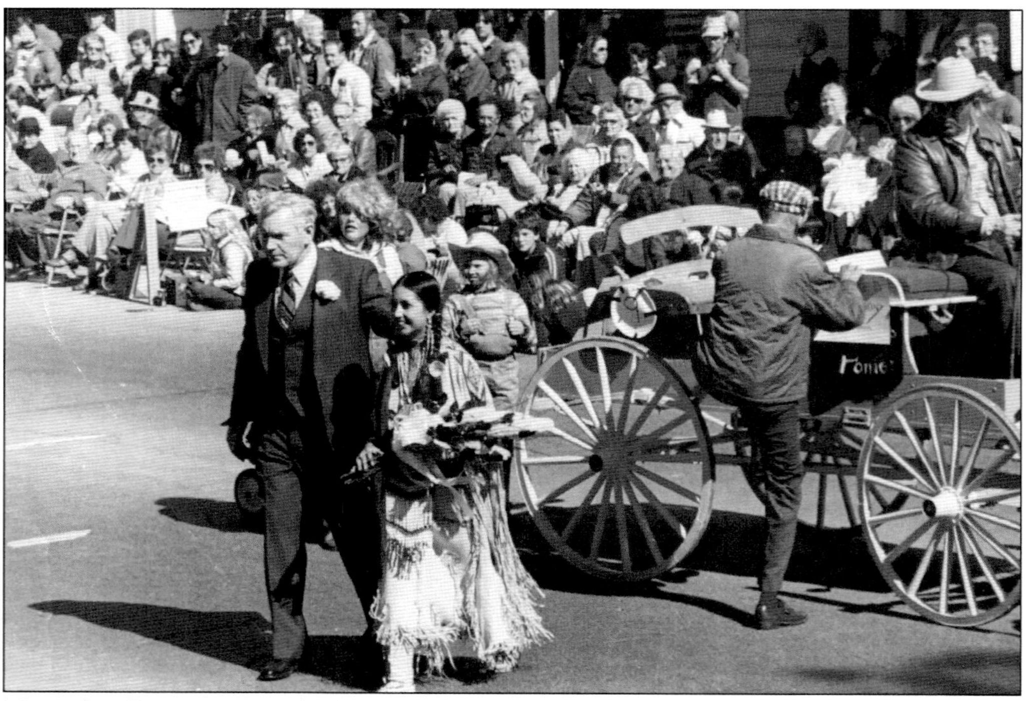

Mayor Jim Barnes escorts the lovely Jessica Paterson, Indian Princess and Chief Blackhawk's great granddaughter, to the reviewing stand. Princess Jessica's direct connection to Oregon's heroic past thrilled the watching crowd. (Courtesy of the Ogle County Historical Society.)

Taft is gone, but his ideals live on in sculptor Jeff Adams, whose foundry is located in Mt. Morris. His extraordinary bronze statue, *Paths of Conviction*, *Footsteps of Fate*, portrays Lincoln on one side, Blackhawk on the other. Their paths crossed briefly during the 1832 altercation, but no other connection is intended. Adams' purpose is to portray Lincoln's spirit, one hand offered generously, "with malice toward none," and the other firmly holding his homeland.

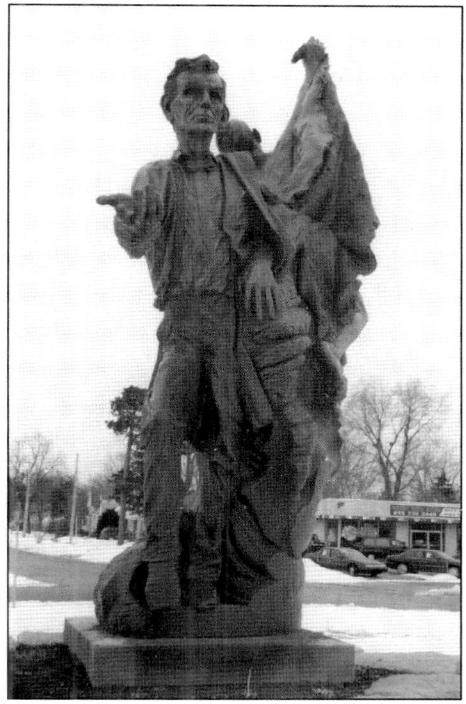

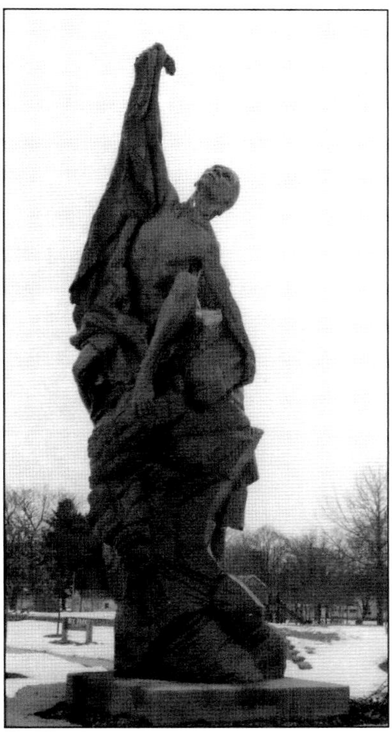

For his marvelous rendering of Blackhawk, Adams consulted historical portraits of the Sauk chief, realizing a more intense, sinewy form than Taft's reserved monolith. Here, Blackhawk sits upon a rock incline, ". . . symbolic of the precarious position of the Native Americans during the white settlement of the prairie," Adams comments. The chief's left hand clutches his homeland, his right hand holds a buffalo blanket, the only covering left him. The statue is located in Mix Park in Oregon, and was dedicated in 2002.

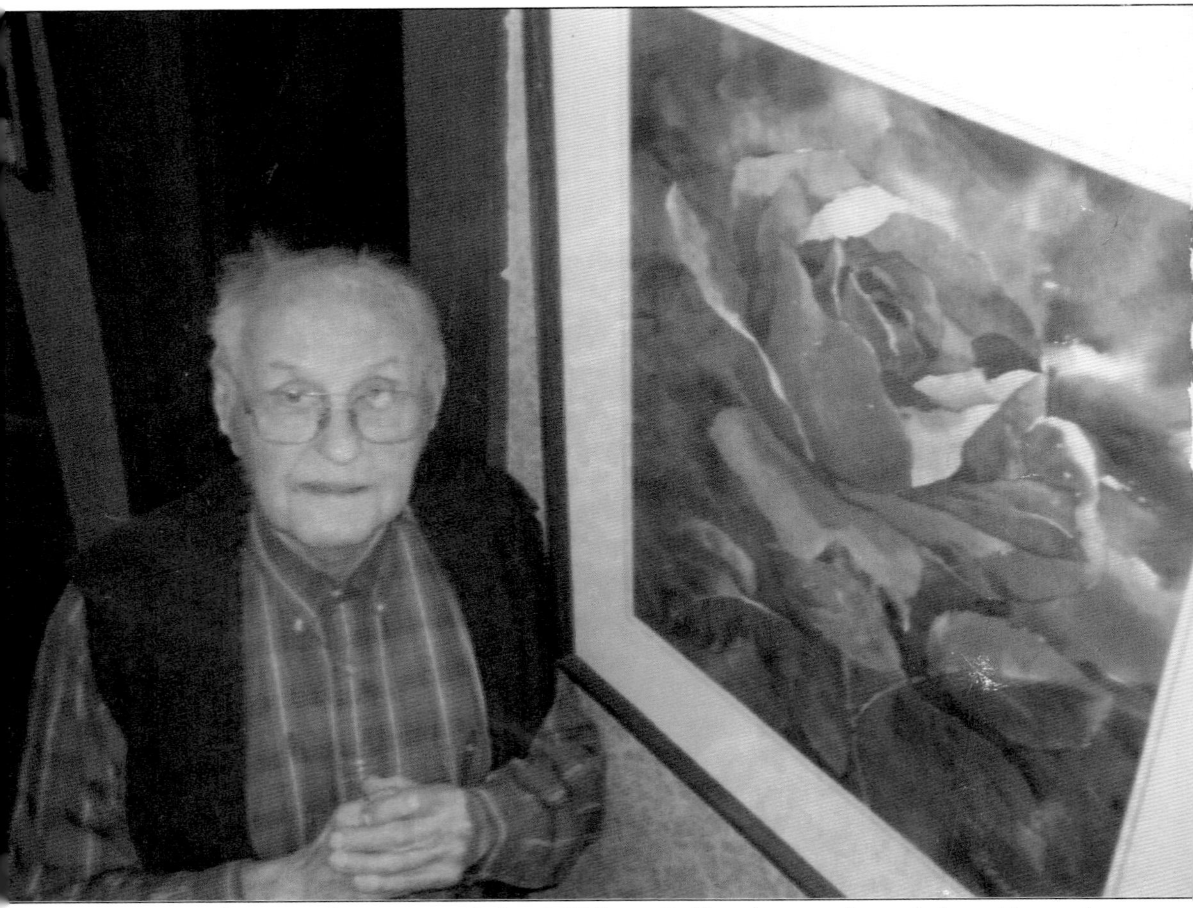

Our story began with a patriot, Colonel William S. Hamilton, and concludes with another, Harry Nurmet. Here, he poses in his Oregon home with his painting of a rose, a symbol of Christ. Born in 1909 in Tallinn, Estonia, Nurmet studied law at Tartu University, concurrently pursuing his passion for art. As a high school student, he modeled for a statue representing freedom, placed prominently in the Tallinn town square. When the Russians occupied Estonia in 1940, they duly removed it, rightly perceiving a conflict of interests. In 1991, Estonia declared independence from Russia, and requested that the statue be restored. Contacted in Oregon, Nurmet drew the figure from memory, and the reproduction was cast from his sketch. The statue was unveiled on February 23, 1992, the 75th anniversary of Estonia's first declaration of independence. A tribute to perseverance, the muscular figure stands solidly on the former site, with its image proudly imprinted on stationery and other material. Nurmet and his family settled in Oregon in 1950 through the auspices of a Lutheran placement agency. He worked first as a painter, then as an applied artist for Watt Publishing, in addition to freelance work. In 1957, he founded the Eagle's Nest Art Group, an unofficial continuation of the Eagle's Nest Art Colony. In 1976, he painted a huge, very visible mural on a downtown building, celebrating 200 years of American independence. In addition to his private work, Nurmet also designed the Oregon City flag, and in 1993 the city elected him the Grand Marshal of its annual Autumn on Parade Fall Festival. His esteemed works, executed in oils, watercolor, monotypes, and acrylics, are displayed in private collections and galleries the world over. A member of St. Paul's Lutheran Church, Nurmet is a gracious, humble, Christian gentleman, and is, undoubtedly, Oregon's most distinguished citizen.